THEODORE ROETHKE

Kennikat Press
National University Publications
Literary Criticism Series

LYNN ROSS-BRYANT

THEODORE ROETHKE

Poetry of the Earth . . .
Poet of the Spirit . . .

National University Publications
KENNIKAT PRESS // 1981
Port Washington, N.Y. // London

Manufactured in the United States of America

Published by
Kennikat Press Corp.
Port Washington, N.Y. / London

Library of Congress Cataloging in Publication Data

Ross-Bryant, Lynn.
Theodore Roethke, poetry of the earth, poet of the spirit.

(Literary criticism series) (National university publications)
Bibliography: p.
Includes index.
1. Roethke, Theodore, 1908–1963–Criticism and interpretation. I. Title.
PS3535.039Z8 811'.54 80-19271
ISBN 0-8046-9270-X

To my mother and father
and to the lands of Nevada and California,
where I first learned my love of the earth

ACKNOWLEDGMENTS

My first debt of gratitude is to the poet. Theodore Roethke's poetry has been and continues to be a great source of joy for me. As I have tried to dwell in the world of this poetry my own thinking has been invaluably enriched by the work of the increasing company of Roethke scholars. I am especially appreciative of the work of Ralph J. Mills, Jr. who was very important to me as I began my studies of Roethke and who still seems to me to have touched most deeply the roots of the poetry. I am also grateful to Nathan A. Scott, Jr. for his work on Roethke and for his insights into the relation of poetry and religion. Joseph Sittler, with his care for both poetry and the earth and his understanding of a theology that includes both, has been an inspiration to me throughout my explorations of the natural world and Roethke's poetry. Giles B. Gunn has been of immense importance in leading me to Roethke and enriching my understanding of American culture and religion. David Rasche provided both creative vision and support in the first stages of the work. Rui Sadamura contributed her fast and accurate typing of the manuscript. Finally, Elliott, my husband, has stood by me as consultant, especially regarding the thought of Martin Heidegger and Alfred North Whitehead; critic and editor; and patient and encouraging companion. I am grateful to all these people as well as many other friends, students, and colleagues, all of whom helped to make this work possible. In Roethke's words, "We never enter / Alone."

Grateful acknowledgment is also made of the kindness of publishers and authors who have granted permission to quote from their works.

The following poems by Theodore Roethke: "Epidermal Macabre," "The Premonition," "The Minimal," "Forcing House," "The Long Alley," "The Lost Son," "The Shape of Fire," "Cuttings (later)," "Transplanting,"

"Unfold, Unfold," "A Light Breather," "Elegy for Jane," "I Cry, Love! Love!," "Praise to the End," "The Visitant," "Where Knock is Open Wide," "Bring the Day!," "O Lull Me, Lull Me," "Sensibility! O La!," "Frau Bauman, Frau Schmidt and Frau Schwartze," "O, Thou Opening, O," "Old Lady's Winter Words," "The Siskin," "I Knew a Woman," "All the Earth, All the Air," "The Dream," "The Snake," "The Song," "Words for the Wind," "The Sententious Man," "The Pure Fury," "The Renewal," "The Swan," copyright © 1932, 1941, 1942, 1946, 1947, 1948, 1949, 1950, 1951, 1952, 1953, 1954, 1955, 1956, 1958 by Theodore Roethke.

In "Four for Sir John Davies," "The Dance," copyright 1952 by *The Atlantic Monthly Company;* "The Partner," "The Wraith," "The Vigil," copyright 1952, 1953 by Theodore Roethke.

In "Meditations of an Old Woman," "Her Becoming," copyright © 1958 by Botteghe Oscure; "First Meditation," "I'm Here," "What Can I Tell My Bones," and "Fourth Meditation," copyright © 1955, 1956, 1957, 1958 by Theodore Roethke.

"The Manifestation," "In a Dark Time," "The Motion," "The Restored," "The Lizard," "The Tree The Bird," "The Marrow," "Once More, The Round," "The Abyss," "The Geranium," "Infirmity," "The Moment," "The Right Thing," "Wish for a Young Wife," "Heard in a Violent Ward," copyright © 1959, 1960, 1961, 1962, 1963, 1964 by Beatrice Roethke as administratrix of the estate of Theodore Roethke. In "North American Sequence," "Meditations at Oyster River," "Journey to the Interior," "The Longing," "The Long Waters," "The Far Field," "The Rose," copyright © 1960, 1961, 1962, 1963 by Beatrice Roethke as administratrix of the estate of Theodore Roethke. "Carnations," "Flower Dump," "Moss Gathering," "Weed Puller," copyright 1946 by Editorial Publications, Inc.

In "The Dying Man," "His Words" and "They Sing, They Sing;" "Memory," copyright © 1956 by *The Atlantic Monthly Company*.

"The Cycle" copyright 1941 by The *Virginia Quarterly Review,* the University of Virginia; "River Incident" copyright 1943 by the F-R Publishing Corp.; "Root Celler" copyright 1943 by Modern Poetry Association; "Night Crow" copyright 1944 by *Saturday Review Assoc.;* "Old Florist," copyright 1946 by Hearst Magazines, Inc.; "Big Wind" copyright 1947 by the United Chapters of Phi Beta Kappa; "A Field of Light" copyright 1948 by The Tiger's Eye.

All poems from the book *The Collected Poems of Theodore Roethke.* Reprinted by permission of Doubleday & Company, Inc.

Excerpts from the unpublished notebooks of Theodore Roethke are reprinted by the kind permission of Beatrice Roethke Lushington.

Excerpts from *On the Poet and His Craft: Selected Prose of Theodore Roethke,* edited by Ralph J. Mills, Jr. are reprinted by permission of the University of Washington Press, copyright © 1965 by Beatrice Roethke as administratrix of the estate of Theodore Roethke.

John Berryman's "A Strut for Roethke" is reprinted from *77 Dream Songs* by permission of Farrar, Straus & Giroux, Inc., copyright © 1959, 1962, 1963, 1964 by John Berryman.

Excerpts from Howard Nemerov's "The Dependencies" and "Runes" are reprinted from *The Western Approaches* and *New and Selected Poems,* published by the University of Chicago Press, by permission of Howard Nemerov.

Excerpts from Richard Wilbur's "Seed Leaves," "Thyme Flowering among Rocks," and "Objects" are reprinted from his volumes *Walking to Sleep* and *The Beautiful Changes* by permission of Harcourt Brace Jovanovich, Inc., copyright © 1947, 1964, 1968, 1975 by Richard Wilbur.

CONTENTS

THEODORE ROETHKE

ABOUT THE AUTHOR

Dr. Lynn Ross-Bryant is an assistant professor of religion at the University of Southern California in Los Angeles and an active participant in the American Academy of Religion. She is the author of a study of literature and religion, as well as numerous articles and reviews in *The Drew Gateway*, *Journal of the American Academy of Religion*, *Religious Studies Review*, and *Christianity and Literature*.

INTRODUCTION

Theodore Roethke's poetry comes out of the slime, out of the primordial unity that human beings leave—with anticipation and regret—when they begin the struggle to become persons in the world. From these small beginnings Roethke develops a poetry that explores the furthest reaches of the spiritual dimension of human life. From first to last the poetry achieves moments of affirmation of shared life that are grounded in the given, immanent world. The intention of this study is to enter fully into this "poetry of the earth" in order to explore Roethke's vision of the rootedness of human beings in the natural world and the necessity of relationship for the life of the spirit.

The importance of rootedness in the earth and shared life are revealed in several ways. First and always, there is the present actuality of the things of the earth with which he acknowledges his kinship by paying loving attention to their particular manifestations, whether as person or plant or animal. In this sharing of life one both experiences and learns about the dimension of spirit because of the correspondence that exists between all living things. This respect and care for the earth are obviously important in a time when we are reexamining our relationship to and use of our threatened natural world.

The rootedness also involves a psychological dimension as it reveals the archetypal connectedness of human beings with primordial reality. Archetypal roots involve both the mutuality of human experience and the evolutionary continuity and recapitulation of all life. Thus, ancestors are important in Roethke's poetry: whether they be those from the mire or from the cultural tradition or from the personal family, they are part of who we are.

The affirmation one comes to in Roethke's poetic world through acknowledging and experiencing the shared life of the things of the earth is not without its times of darkness. In this respect his vision is once again of special relevance to the contemporary world. He neither denies nor attempts to escape from the darkness that is part of human experience and humans themselves. With insights we can trust both psychologically and theologically, Roethke reveals that from the darkness of the depths of experience we can learn to see. This is not a seeing that abolishes the depths; rather, it comes to know them as necessary to wholeness of life.

Roethke's poetry, then, offers us a vision of spirit that is firmly rooted in the earth and in the relatedness of life. I wish to explore this dimension of the poetry and the religious implications it has for our world as it offers a grounding for meaning and action based on the connectedness that is given in the nature of things. Wholeness of human life and meaningful action, then, depend on life lived in relation.

This affirmation of the earth is made in a poetry that moves through a number of different forms, beginning with the most basic and minute perceptions and from these moving outward, never forgetting its origins, to encompass increasingly greater ranges of human perception. What can be seen as a spiritual journey begins in the greenhouse with the search for the self; moves out to others; and, finally, explores the ultimate dimensions of human experience and fullness of the life of the spirit.

The poetry generally follows a chronological development both in terms of the order in which the poems were written and presented and in terms of the life of a person: the early poems are those of the child who must find his place in the world; the final poems are those of the old man who must face the inevitability of leaving this world. There is, however, an additional dimension to the poetry that is in opposition to the linearity of this chronological movement. There is a *circularity* in the life of the natural world with its cycles of decay and renewal and a *spiraling* in its recapitulating evolutionary movement. This pattern is reflected in the continuing movement from darkness to light and again to darkness and to light that is the controlling organization in many poems. Roethke describes the early poetry (in terms of both form and theme) as having a cyclical movement: "There is a perpetual slipping back, then a going-forward; but there is some 'progress.'"* The poetry as a whole seems to

*References are listed by page number in Notes chapter.

follow this spiraling development. It is also evident in the repetition of certain images that accumulate new dimensions of meaning each time they appear so they both are and are not the same images throughout the poems. This thematic and formal repetition and progress provide links that connect the stages of development as well as individual poems. Thus a whole world of meaning is gradually created. In this coherent world the early poems take on new meaning in light of the further stages of the journey. And the final poems are their richest when they are experienced as the final stage of the journey that began in the greenhouse.

The first volume of poems, *Open House,* will not be discussed here primarily because these poems are so overshadowed by the greenhouse poems that immediately follow. Also, with the poems of *The Lost Son* Roethke discovered the form and approach through which he would write his best poetry. *Open House* seems an experiment, a tentative expression. Although the concerns of this poetry–most basically the identity and assertion of the self–are important throughout Roethke's work, his means of expression in the early poems are traditional lyrical forms and his tendency is to explain, to tell, to convince. He seems at this point too unsure of himself as a poet and of his world as a viable subject to let the poetry reveal the world as it does in later poems. The sense of mystery and concreteness that emerge together when he is successful in creating an image that reveals the human and the natural worlds at once simply cannot be contained by this form. W. H. Auden, a friend and counselor to Roethke throughout his career, wrote in a review of *Open House:* "Both in life and art the human task is to create a necessary order out of an arbitrary chaos. . . . The order realized must . . . have been already latent in the chaos, so that successful creation is a process of discovery." He goes on to say that perhaps Roethke was "trusting too much to diction, to the poetic instrument itself, to create order out of chaos." Poetry is only an instrument; it cannot widen the area of experience with which it deals. It may be that this is the lesson Roethke learned following these first poems. Although he also seems to be trusting himself and his poetic instrument more in moving into new, yet unexplored areas, perhaps the crucial difference is trusting the world itself, trusting the chaos not to destroy. By accepting its existence and giving it its due, he discovers in it an order that is beyond his willing or understanding but which he can accept and affirm.

The real starting point and continuing renewal point for the poetry is the greenhouse world of the poet's childhood. The minute particulars of nature, observed with the wondering, open eyes of the child, form the beginnings and the foundation for the possibility of an affirmation of all life. It is through an acceptance of the natural world in all its mystery and fecundity that the poet is able to affirm himself in this world and to move to an affirmation of other individuals and, finally, of the sacred. With the greenhouse poems the formal rhyme scheme and the more intellectual attitude that accompanied it are gone. Roethke seems to have opened himself to that given, concrete world and apprehended directly its powerful life. The world has been considerably enlarged not only because of the freedom of form but also through a much richer, livelier vocabulary and a greater use of alliteration. He creates a world of which we are an integral part not only because there is a similarity between the growth of a plant and the growth of the spirit, although this is extremely important, but also because we are made to feel our kinship with Roethke's root cellar and his flower dump–that darker side of life. He is beginning here to call on the basic unity of all things on which the poems depend for their power and coherence. He trusts that this will work not only because of his poetic skills but also because this connectedness actually exists. William Meredith says of the *Lost Son* poems, "Instead of ordering experience, these poems attend on experience with the conviction that there is order in it. . . . This *revealed* order was the only one Roethke served from this time on."

The longer poems of *The Lost Son* and *Praise to the End!* in which Roethke attempts to create the return to the world of the child, also depend heavily on the assumption of the fundamental connection between the things of the earth. The poems of this period require a form that is extremely open and variable and a language that defies our normal patterns of speech in order to reflect both the chaotic world of the child and the mysterious logic that governs our first perceptions of the world. It is through the openness of the child–and of the poems–that this world becomes something to be affirmed.

The primary organizing device for these poems is the circular pattern that is repeated, with some movement forward in each poem and in the sequence as a whole. This pattern is based on Roethke's notion that "to go forward as a spiritual man it is necessary first to go back." The form, then, and the content are the same. There is an attempt to return to one's origins, to the time of childhood or before. Roethke tries to re-create this experience of the primordial for us so that we too will be able to experience the movement to light, the new creation of the self in the world. But in Roethke's world this light comes only after the very real experience of darkness. Roethke's fidelity to his vision and his technique are revealed here as he places himself before a great darkness in the *faith* that order will emerge. The light comes, if it does, through the objects of the natural world. Through "long looking" and acceptance of what is, he experiences the world in such a way that affirmation is the natural response—an affirmation both of the world with all its terrors and all its delights and of the self with its capacity for joy and despair, love and anger, life and death.

In the poems following *Praise to the End!* the apparently irrational and formless structures disappear. They were necessary to recapture the moment of chaos and the childhood conflicts, but through them a self was established that was able to face and come to terms with its past. In the poems that follow, then, there is generally a return to a more traditional form and language, though remnants from this past life recur throughout the poetry. They serve, as do many of the repeated images, to create a sense of an entire world in which the past is not forgotten but is a constant, creative force in the continually new present.

With their more traditional forms and Roethke's increased sense of personal and universal order, the poems of *The Waking* and *Words for the Wind* add to this growing poetic world Roethke's version of the social—his love poems. These two volumes contain the poetry of the mature adult who, having come to an affirmation of himself and his world, is able to reach out to another person and share the joys and sorrows of existence. But with the other also come the double dangers of the desire for total unification and the fear of loss of self to the other, both of which must be avoided if real relation is to occur. This adult consciousness also brings with it an awareness of death. The joys of the body, the natural world, and love are in the process of passing even as they are most fully experienced. Once again, it is only through an acceptance of the totality of life, which includes separation and death, that finite existence can be affirmed.

In the final volume of poetry, *The Far Field,* the poet builds on his concrete experiences of nature and other people to make explicit what has been present from the beginning—the dimension of spirit. Two quite different approaches are used. *North American Sequence* is in many ways similar in technique to the poems of the earlier volume, *Praise to the End!* Memories from childhood appear, the things of the natural world dominate, and each poem and the sequence as a whole develop from a time of darkness to a new sense of meaning and a rejoicing in the light. However, significant differences separate the earlier and later poems. The memories that are recaptured are no longer those from the primordial past. The self has been gained; the question is now one of spirit. There are also differences in technique. Although the poet still uses the device of creating a series of images that then settle into a unified vision, this has been significantly modified to suit the new dimension of human experience. Roethke has extended his idea of correspondences so that a whole catalogue of things or events from the natural world or the world of childhood experience is explored to reveal, through its likeness, the human spirit. In addition, both the natural and the human are brought to a fullness as together they compose a new spiritual center. He immerses himself in the sights and sounds and silences of America, and through the experience of their endless variety he comes to the vision of the unity of the "rose in the sea-wind" at the end.

In *Sequence Sometimes Metaphysical* he still attempts to preserve the tension, the variety, and yet to discover the unity. However, instead of the expansive, flowing verse of *North American Sequence,* we find the tightly compacted lines of "In a Dark Time." It is contraction that dominates here. Within a strict form and with end-stopped lines and bare, often monosyllabic language, Roethke tries to create, almost as a single image, a direct, intense experience. Despite the tremendous difference in form, however, the poems seek the same reality of the self in its fullest spiritual dimension within and through the natural world.

This is the goal of the striving, the exploring, begun in the greenhouse, which, while reaching far beyond the greenhouse, never leaves behind the close attention and openness to the mystery of the natural world in which all Roethke's poetry is firmly grounded. Through the experiences of the life that is presented in the poetry–from the seeking of the self, to the other, and, finally, to a more inclusive "Other"–the fullness of the life first found in the flowers and dirt of the greenhouse is realized and made a part of the man. Martin Buber describes three similar stages of life in *I and Thou:*

> The spheres in which the world of relation is built are three.
> First, our life with nature, in which the relation clings to the threshold of speech.
> Second, our life with men, in which the relation takes on the form of speech.
> Third, our life with spiritual beings, where the relation, being without speech, yet begets it.
> In every sphere in its own way, through each process of becoming that is present to us, we look out toward the fringe of the eternal *Thou;* in each we are aware of a breath from the eternal *Thou;* in each *Thou* we address the eternal *Thou.*

This study will be an exploration of this flowering of the spirit that has such deep roots in the earth and relies on the interrelatedness of all things.

I begin with the assumption that Roethke has created a world we can participate in—a world that is poetic, that is hypothetical, but that points beyond itself. Such a created world, Giles Gunn suggests, has at its center, as its organizing principle, "some deeply felt, if not fully or even partially conscious, assumption about what can, or just possibly does, constitute the ground of experience itself. This primal intuition then becomes the organizing principle for the hypothetical structure which the work turns out to be." Robert Langbaum says of the romantic and symbolist poets that "the poem exists not to imitate or describe life but to make it manifest." This organizing principle operates in a hypothetical creation in a way analogous to religious symbols in life. Every work of art has a consistent "point of view" that includes a world view—an understanding of the way things are—and following from that a set of values, a belief that certain actions are meaningful. Religion provides this same ordering function within a person's life. We are invited to enter this "as if" world of a work of art, to live as if this were the case. To uncover the organizing principle, the primal intuition, the life the work makes manifest, is, then, to explore the religious grounding of the work and to see how it points beyond itself, how it does or does not speak to the world in which we live. It will be my intention to explore this dimension in Theodore Roethke's poetry.

To this end it will be necessary to engage the poetry in a close analysis as well as to place it within a larger context of other writers who share Roethke's primal intuition of the world. The close analysis is necessary because one must work through and live in the poems themselves if one is to come to know the world Roethke has created. Thus, although it is necessary to see many poems as parts of sequences, I have chosen to work with certain poems in greater detail; this has necessarily meant neglecting others I might equally well have used (the sequences *Meditations of an Old Woman* and *North American Sequence* are the exceptions to this, and all the poems are dealt with in some detail).

Placing the poems in a larger context is also important for an understanding of Roethke's world as well as its relation to our own. Roethke describes a similar approach in his teaching of literature:

> The best teachers don't teach it as a "subject" at all (as body of information, as "culture," etc.) instead as experience (and not tippy-toe Gustonianism) but the complete assimilation, the mastery of complex texts: getting the whole of what appears on the page or on the canvas. This includes bringing to bear on the material the best thought of the past (in criticism, for instance, Aristotle,

> Coleridge, etc.) as well as modern insights (Freud, Groddeck, Marx, Richards, Burke, etc.). It includes questions of value (granted almost as dubious a word as culture) and taste (the area where the hacks and boobs are always weakest) Etc. etc.

Thus, as I explore the poetry, concentrating on those aspects that reveal the relatedness of the things of the earth, I shall refer to several areas that are not poetic in themselves but that touch on the poetic world Roethke has created. I do not presume that Roethke was familiar with these other writers–though in some cases he was–for it is not my contention that he turned ideas from theology, philosophy, or psychology into poems. The point is that such people as Martin Buber, Gabriel Marcel, Carl Jung, and Martin Heidegger are dealing with the same area of reality that concerns Roethke. Insofar as such investigations serve to open up the world of Roethke's poetry and to reveal an intuition about reality that makes an affirmation of the things of the earth possible within his poetry, our understanding of the poems will increase as will our knowledge of the relationship they bear to the reality of this other world in which we live.

CHAPTER ONE

ROETHKE'S SHARED WORLD

The poetic world Theodore Roethke has created depends on mutuality of life. The self comes to itself and the fullness of spirit is realized only in relation to others. This shared life is equally important in Roethke's creation of the poetry. Not only does he expressly call on his poetic ancestors frequently, he also carries on an extensive unacknowledged dialogue with other poets, as Jenijoy La Belle has so thoroughly demonstrated in *The Echoing Wood of Theodore Roethke.* In addition, as noted above, he shares a world with other thinkers, acknowledged or not; and the exploration of this dialogue can only add to our understanding of the poetry. Finally and because of these things, Roethke's is a shared world in terms of the poetic process and its relation to reality. "The human problem is to find out what one really *is:* whether one exists, whether existence is possible," Roethke says in "On 'Identity.'" This is no fictional or fanciful problem: it is the problem of how to live; and apparently it is Roethke's belief that in the creation of his poetry he can in some sense discover the answer as well as create an experience for others that might also help them to find the answer.

Communication, then, becomes important in all aspects of Roethke's poetry. The "I" must make contact with another if the message is to have meaning. This is true both within the world of the poems, as the protagonist communicates with the things and people around him, and in the poems as artistic creations, as they communicate with those who read the poetry. In "Voice as Summons for Belief" Walter Ong describes the process that takes place in human communication in general and in literature in particular. Communication, he says, cannot be compared to a sending and receiving system in which there is an emission center and a reception center, the one active, the other passive, and all the messages moving in one direction only. Communication depends, rather, on the presence of the individual consciousness, the "I," who is aware of him or herself and is at the same time aware of another individual consciousness, the "other," who is in some way part of oneself. It is the belief in that other and the presence of a kind of otherness in oneself that creates an interrelated network of messages in which the speaker also listens and the listener also speaks. In the use of language, then, the speaker necessarily takes on a persona to give expression to the other within. When this is accompanied by a belief in that persona by the other without, communication occurs. In literature this same strange combination of otherness and hiddenness, closeness and intimacy, creates the possibility for the communication that lies at the heart of the artistic process:

> "Poetic truth," which seems so difficult to bring to earth, to isolate, to state clearly, and which is also so strangely intimate, has its roots in a sense of communion with other persons, persons perceived through masks, yet somehow decidedly there, who have believed in us enough to invite us to this uncommonly intimate response and in whom we, in turn, are called on to believe.

Roethke's poetry calls for this response of belief, and this communication is also the process at work within many of the poems themselves. It is poetry both about belief and of belief. This communication is possible because Roethke's poetic world is an ordered, meaningful creation in which human beings have a place and are able to discover it. Further, this world is meaningful because it is composed of connections, interrelations, so that people have a place in the order of creation through and because of other living things. There is communication and communion because there is shared life. We enter into the substance of Roethke's poetic world as we see it as an expression of communication and belief, presence and otherness, and through these things an affirmation of the earth.

THE AMERICAN PRESENCE

The effect this view of reality and the imagination has on Roethke's work makes the American poetic tradition an important part of his shared world. With Emerson, who is in so many ways the paradigmatic voice of the tradition, he focuses on the concrete actualities of the world and finds there what he can affirm. Roethke is also close to Emerson in the *way* he looks at the world. He is generally concerned with the non-analytical and, in part of his poetry, with childlike perceptions of the world. This is, however, only a stage for Roethke. He must reexperience the world as a child, but he must go beyond this. "Here's for the plain old Adam, the simple genuine self against the whole world" could not serve as a motto for Roethke's poetry. Nor could "It is very unhappy, but too late to be helped, the discovery we have made that we exist. . . . That discovery is called the Fall of Man." He is not the American Adam, nor does he wish to be. His poetry struggles with and accepts the dark side of life in a way that Emerson's does not, but there is still a closeness of the two men in their final affirmation. "I count myself among the happy poets," Roethke says. "I proclaim, once more, a condition of joy!"

The joy grows out of the experience of relatedness to the particulars of the world, but this does not mean that Roethke (or Emerson) does nothing more than record the physical minutiae of the world. Tony Tanner says, "The lesson could be drawn from Emerson's thought that if the writer looks after the details the significances will look after themselves." Kenneth Burke says in "The Vegetal Radicalism of Theodore Roethke," "The poet need but be as accurate as he can, in describing the flowers objectively; and while aiming at this, he comes upon corresponding human situations, as it were by redundancy." Roethke's world is, in its own way, a world of correspondences in which the growth of a plant and the spiritual development of a human being are genuinely related. Because of this relatedness Roethke is able to say, "It is paradoxical that a very sharp sense of the being, the identity of some other being–and in some instances, even an inanimate thing–brings a corresponding heightening and awareness of one's own self, *and,* even more mysteriously, in some instances, a feeling of the oneness of the universe."

This view is not without its paradoxes, and the question must be raised of his poetry as of Emerson's whether it is possible to maintain both the unique particularity of the minimals and the unifying wholeness of the spiritual dimension of life. Although my suspicion is that Emerson finally "kicks over the pail" and chooses the "horizon," I accept the caution of Raymond Benoit (and many other Emerson scholars) that Emerson's "double vision" cannot be reduced to a single sight without doing him an injustice ("A believer in Unity, a seer of Unity, I yet behold two" [*Journals,* May 26, 1837]). Many Roethke scholars also see him as opting for the horizon, moving from the concrete particulars of the earth to a spiritualization of them. Karl Malkoff says, "By the alchemy of his poetry he transformed a gross and ugly material world into an image of the spirit; he created something graceful out of an awkward reality." John Ciardi, while using the enticing description of Roethke as medicine man and his poetry as incantation, goes on to explain that the healing occurs as the poetry "dances its way from madness (symbolized by the wet riot of vegetable roots and the grossness of the flesh) to a reflective calm." Ralph J. Mills, Jr., while generally emphasizing the poet's kinship with growing things, makes the disturbing statement that man emerges "with the stain of earth upon him, but is driven by the spirit's rage and desire to break free of servility to the flesh, to the animal within that lures him to destruction." Although I acknowledge that a tension exists in the poetry between the particulars of this world and their spiritual significance, it is a tension that seeks unity and does not discount the world in its search for the spirit.

This emphasis on the concrete realities of existence, as well as the tension between the particulars and their universal significance, is found throughout the American poetic tradition, with Walt Whitman following closely in Emerson's path with perhaps an even greater realization of the particulars. This same attempt to discover a unity between the spirit and the physical world can be found among modern poets such as Hart Crane, who in "General Aims and Theories" speaks of "certain spiritual illuminations, shining with a morality essentialized from experience directly, and not from previous precepts or preconceptions," or T. S. Eliot in the *Four Quartets*. Moderns who have come down strongly on the side of the particulars are Ezra Pound, who in "A Retrospect" calls for "Direct treatment of the 'thing,'" and William Carlos Williams, who affirms in Book 1 of *Paterson* "No ideas but in things." In contemporary poetry this emphasis continues, with a tendency that Roethke shares, to overcome the gap between things and their significances while paying close attention to both. This will be discussed at greater length in the conclusion, but examples of the attention to the concrete world and the tension between particulars and universals occur in the poetry of Richard Wilbur and Howard Nemerov. In "Seed Leaves" Wilbur, describing the emergence of a sprout from the soil, reveals the tension between particular form and boundless being. The poem ends:

This plant would like to grow
And yet be embryo;
Increase, and yet escape
The doom of taking shape;
. . . .
But something at the root
More urgent than that urge

Bids two true leaves emerge,
And now the plant, resigned
To being self-defined
Before it can commerce
With the great universe,
Takes aim at all the sky
And starts to ramify.

The importance of the concrete particulars is also evident when he says, "'A World Without Objects Is a Sensible Emptiness,'" but "auras, lustres,/ And all shinings need to be shaped and borne." He calls us to the things of the world in "Objects": "Guard and gild what's common, . . . have objects speak." Howard Nemerov continues this emphasis in "Vermeer," directing us to things: "Taking what is, and seeing it as it is,/ . . . the care for daily things." In "A Spell before Winter" he says, "There is a knowledge in the look of things,/ . . . A knowledge glimmers in the sleep of things." Finally, not only the thing and its significance come together but also the human and the natural in "The Dependencies":

Change is continuous on the seamless web,
Yet moments come like this one, when you feel
Upon your heart a signal to attend
The definite announcement of an end
Where one thing ceases and another starts;
When like the spider waiting on the web
You know the intricate dependencies
Spreading in secret through the fabric vast
Of heaven and earth, sending their messages
Ciphered in chemistry to all the kinds,
The whisper down the bloodstream: it is time.

Roethke also follows the Emersonian tradition of the poet as "Seer" and "Sayer" who discovers and reveals the truth for others through himself as representative voice. Burke's formula for Emerson—"I, Eye, Ay"—means for Roethke that the personal search through his attentiveness to nature leads to an affirmation he declares to all who will listen. His intention in presenting his poetry as the personal search of one man is to make the experience of the search for oneself more immediate and more "real." This creates a confessional or meditative poetry, which is also a dramatic poetry that draws the reader into a personal world. This "I" at the center of the poetry connects Roethke with many in the American tradition. Walt Whitman and Hart Crane stand out again as those who deliberately placed themselves before their readers in order to create the epic of the American people through themselves as representative men. William Carlos Williams also does this in *Paterson,* though in a more objective way. And in spite of Eliot's theoretical impersonalism we have the *Four Quartets.*

In contemporary poetry, as M. L. Rosenthal points out, we often find the poet at the center of the work, often as the victim who must salvage what he or she can of life through the meaning created in the poem. In contrast to many modern poets more recent writers generally present this "I" simply as a personal consciousness rather than in the role of artist. Although scholars such as La Belle and Blessing have understood Roethke's poetic voice to be very much that of the artist, I would place him closer to the group Rosenthal describes which presents a central consciousness distinctive in its "strongly confessional, literally self-exposing vulnerability." In such poets as Robert Lowell, Sylvia Plath, and John Berryman, we find some of the characteristics Rosenthal describes: "Sexual candor, frankness about family life, and confession of private humiliations of varying psychological kinds. . . . Failure and self-doubt . . . disturbance and confusion . . . are further instances." Many of these characteristics are found in Roethke's poetry as well. However, each of these poets opens her or himself to this subjective world in a different way, and to see them—or Roethke—as belonging to a school of "confessional poets" seems to deprive them of their uniqueness. What they do share in common with each other and with Emerson's poet is the view that poetry is a revealer or creator of truth and that through their poems they are creating or finding themselves. And because they are representative voices, they are also making this a possibility for others.

Roethke seems closer to Plath and Berryman than to Lowell in reaching into the depths of himself and facing the unconscious terrors he encounters there. Lowell seems to have the protection of a strong social tradition even in the most intimate of the *Life Studies.* But unlike Plath and Berryman, Roethke in his poems transforms the personal into the universal. He does explore the terrifying realities of his personal life, but his poetry is best when it is personal as it touches the deep roots of every human being. Once again, there is expressed here the implicit belief in the commonality of persons that makes communication possible. Because of this he comes to an affirmation that Plath and Berryman were unable to make either in poetry or in life. The attempt of the "I" to meet with another—with the several dimensions of the self and with the "other" outside the self—is the achievement of Roethke's poetic world.

For this reason the too frequent criticism of Roethke's poetry as lacking a social dimension is not justified. While it is true that the few poems he attempts about "society" are seldom very good and never his best, it is also true that the basis of societies is individual relationships, and in Roethke's poetry the "I" never remains isolated, as it does in much contemporary poetry. Through the experience of the self within the world, the separateness is overcome, and relationship is affirmed. Harold Bloom makes the interesting point that we remain very much within the romantic tradition as it is exemplified by the Solitary of Wordsworth's *The Excursion.* He sees the concern with self–or the search for the subject–as dominating contemporary poetry: "To embrace personality is as irrelevant for modern poetry as to flee it (in the pronouncements of Eliot and his school). Our poets were and are Romantic as poets used to be Christian, that is, whether they want to be or not." However, he differentiates between those who remain strictly within the personal mode (he cites Robert Lowell as representative of the "fashion for confessional verse") and those who write, as Wordsworth did, out of the "I" that speaks for us all (Wallace Stevens is his example). Roethke exemplifies the latter mode, and thus, though he writes as "I," he speaks beyond himself.

Roethke, then, shares much with the Emersonian tradition in American poetry. R. W. B. Lewis's "American Adam" and Tony Tanner's "Wondering Child" are very much a part of his poetry. However, as he is able to affirm both himself as an individual, creative being and the world itself, in its darkness and its light, in a living, creative relation to himself, he makes an important contribution to the "matter of Adam." He is appreciative of the modes of wonder and newness that are characteristic of the best of the American tradition, but he is also open to the spiritual potentialities that are possible only for the person who accepts, affirms, and enters into relationship with the ambiguous world outside the garden–the world in which we live.

THE MAGIC OF THINGS

Although Roethke's poetry is firmly rooted in the American tradition, many people outside this tradition, both poets and philosophical thinkers, share the vision of life that his poetry reveals. Some are acknowledged ancestors of his, some perhaps were unknown to him. But insofar as they move within a world that is similar to his, they serve to deepen our understanding of his poetry. Three poets with whom he declares his kinship are William Blake, John Clare, and W. B. Yeats. In the final poem of *The Far Field* he says, "And I dance with William Blake / For love, for Love's sake." Roethke has obvious affinities with the English romantic poets;

not the least of them is Wordsworth, to whom he refers indirectly many times. But it is perhaps Blake with whom he felt the greatest kinship. Blake's experiments with new forms and rhymes, as well as his visionary stance, were doubtless congenial to Roethke's poetics. In addition, his probing of the doubleness of things and of the darkness and light of experience—the tiger and the lamb—and of their necessary reunion in the "Marriage of Heaven and Hell" is in sympathy with Roethke's awareness of both the roots and the flowers as being necessary parts of life.

In "Heard in a Violent Ward" Roethke refers, in addition to Blake, to Christopher Smart and "that sweet man, John Clare." Clare's sweetness and his madness probably appealed equally to Roethke. Through his innocent vision, his clear recording of the things of nature, he presented with loving concern the small lives that Roethke also loved. Roethke's "The Meadow Mouse" may be his way of joining hands with Clare, whose "Mouse's Nest" inhabits the same region of careful, loving observation of what exists independently of humans yet can touch them and be touched by them. Clare's madness, on the other hand, also joins him to Roethke. Like Roethke's, it gave him a special way of seeing that was visionary; for despite the great anguish Roethke's mental illness caused him he often saw it as a source of poetic creation, as Seager points out in *The Glass House.*

A third member of Roethke's company is William Butler Yeats. Although more must be said about this important influence on Roethke's poetry, at this point he should be mentioned in connection with Clare and Blake in two ways: first is his vision, his way of looking at reality that transcends what we normally call reality; and second is his attempt to unite the ideal and the actual in much of his poetry. "Yes, I was dancing-mad and how / That came to be the bears and Yeats would know," Roethke says in "Four for Sir John Davies," celebrating Yeats's cosmic dance in which conflicts are reconciled and the dancer is one with the dance. As with Blake's mythology, Roethke was intrigued by Yeats's *Vision.* Although Roethke never created his own mythological structure, he seems to have been very attracted to the possibility. In a symposium he describes the creation of "In a Dark Time" in a way that parallels Yeats's moments of visionary, involuntary writing, and Allan Seager mentions in his biography of Roethke that, after visiting Mrs. Yeats, "he complained bitterly that Beatrice [Roethke's wife] could not do the kind of automatic writing Mrs. Yeats had done for Willie."

The difference between Roethke and each of these three poets is great and very important, as are their differences from each other. But one common bond unifying them reveals a quality basic to Roethke's poetry. In their separate ways these poets all touch on an experience of reality that can be described as magical. There is something in our experience of the world that is mysterious and nonrational. This element is pure, spontaneous being with a life of its own, which cannot be categorized but can only be engaged. There is a hint of madness in such a world because it defies our usual ways of ordering and controlling our experiences. In Roethke's poetry this side of the world is always subtly present. It is an indication of vitality and possibility when the protagonist is open to this powerful, uncontrollable side of life. When the individual is strong, it is experienced as awe-full and can be affirmed. In weakness or hesitation, however, it takes on the face of the demonic and the terrifying and must be repressed or deliberately rejected.

This aspect of Roethke's poetry connects him, among more recent poets, with D. H. Lawrence, James Dickey, and Gary Snyder. Snyder's world especially shows a number of similarities to Roethke's. He writes in his introduction to *Myths and Texts,* "As poet I hold the most archaic values on earth. They go back to the upper Palaeolithic: the fertility of the soil, the magic of animals, the power-vision in solitude, the terrifying initiation and rebirth, the love and ecstasy of the dance, the common work of the tribe." Richard Wilbur also shares this sense of magic, closing the poem "Objects" in this way:

> Oh maculate, cracked, askew,
> Gay-pocked and potsherd world
> I voyage, where in every tangible tree
> I see afloat among the leaves, all calm and curled,
> The Cheshire smile which sets me fearfully free.

This openness to the mysterious center of our everyday lives is at the heart of Roethke's affirmation of the earth. What he stands before is not something he has created or something he can control. He can only enter into the mystery of its being, which is sometimes terrifying, sometimes tender, but always vitally alive and present to the person who will be open to its givenness. He characterizes life in this world in this way in his notebooks:

> The feeling that one is on the edge of many things: that there are many worlds from which we are separated by only a film; that a flick of the wrist, a turn of the body another way will bring us to a new world. It is more than a perpetual expectation. Yet sometimes the sense of richness is haunting: It is richness and yet denial. In living a half a step, as it were, from what one should be.

In the mysterious presence of created reality he discovers that magic, that promise of the more, that makes affirmation of himself and his world possible.

There are many other poets, both those whom Roethke mentions as colleagues of his in this special world and those who seem quite naturally to be present there, but there are also a number of philosophers and theologians who seem to be a part of Roethke's "visionary company," again whether acknowledged or not. Martin Buber, whom Roethke does mention in his prose, expresses the presentness of the world in terms of I-Thou relationships. When we cease to see a person or even a thing as an object to be utilized, we come into an alliance with that "Thou" in which a mutual relation is created through our standing in relation to a common living center. It is neither the "I" nor the "Thou" but that to which they are equally related that makes the relationship possible. When speaking of the I-Thou relationship that is possible between human beings and the things of nature, Buber says it is possible to see a tree either as an object, having certain specifications and useful for certain purposes, or as a Thou, as a whole that stands in relation to me. In such a case, Buber says, "The tree is no impression, no play of my imagination, no value depending on my mood; but it is bodied over against me and has to do with me, as I with it—only in a different way." This seems to point to the same uniqueness and independence of being that animates Roethke's poetic world. And when Buber speaks of the "magic of life," he seems again to be a comrade of Roethke's in a world that cannot be analyzed without remainder. There is a mystery of being to which human beings can only point and with which they can perhaps enter into relationship as a Thou: "Believe in the simple magic of life, in service in the universe, and the meaning of that waiting, that alertness, that "craning of the neck" in creatures will dawn upon you. Every word would falsify; but look! round about you beings live their life, and to whatever point you turn you come upon being."

Sam Keen offers a different entry into a similar world. The title of his book, *Apology for Wonder,* announces his theme. He attempts to recall people to something they seem to have lost—an awareness of the wonder of the things of creation that lie around them. He describes the qualities that evoke wonder as being contingency, mystery, and presence. By contingency he means that "the object we apprehend in wonder comes to us without bearing its own explanation." It dwells in mystery—that is, in that realm where the distinction between subject and object breaks down. Keen quotes Gabriel Marcel to clarify this point: "A mystery is something in which I am myself involved, and it can therefore only be thought of as a sphere where the distinction between what is in me and what is before me loses its meaning and its initial validity." Finally, "presence" indicates the "Thou" nature of the object as it is encountered without analysis in a mutual interaction. Keen emphasizes that the meaning and knowledge that emerge from the experience can only be understood as a gift.

Marcel also differentiates "presence" from an object. He uses the terms "inclining towards" and "gathering to oneself" or "welcoming" to describe the response to a presence and "grasping at" and "seizing" to describe the response to an object. A presence can only be invoked or evoked, and this, he says, is fundamentally magical. In this association of presence, mystery, and magic may be a clue to the magic in Roethke's poetry. The meaning of life is found in the presence of the other with the self, in the I and Thou of relationship, in the mystery of being.

THE HOLINESS OF THINGS

The fact that Roethke seems to share in the world of these religious thinkers from the Jewish and Christian traditions raises the question of whether this means that he is a "religious" poet and the further question whether his poetry shares in the Judeo-Christian understanding of the world. There seems to be no question that, according to these traditions, the creation is basically good because it was created by God. However, the instructions given by God to humans in Genesis to "fill the earth and subdue it" and to have "dominion" over the things of the earth have often been interpreted in such a way that nature is indeed made a slave to or an enemy of human beings that must be controlled and made to serve their purposes. In addition, the emphasis on the historical in these religions has often led to a neglect of nature. Perhaps this was because the Hebrews repudiated local fertility religions, which were associated with nature. In Hellenistic Christianity it may have been because of the fear of pantheism and the emphasis on Christ as the revelation of God.

In spite of this tendency either to neglect or to disparage the natural world, however, there is within the Judeo-Christian heritage a continuing thread that emphasizes the goodness of the creation and its value in itself. It is difficult even to talk about the view of nature in Tenakh (Old Testament) because our notions of what the word means are so different from those of the early Hebrews. In fact, there is no equivalent in Hebrew for our word "nature." In Tenakh "nature is not an entity or a process set alongside God and having its own autonomy. . . . It is, rather, continuous with the reality of God as Creator." This difference in understanding also appears in the fact that the Hebrews make no separation between the material and the spiritual aspects of existence. As Conrad Bonifazi says, "For them, soul and body are *not* united; body *is* soul in its outwardness, and soul *is* body in its inwardness." Both body (and all that is of the physical world) and spirit are animated by the life-force, or *nephesh,* and thus all living things, from what we call the human spirit to the life of a tree, are capable of making manifest the glory of God. Finally, the Old Testament apocalyptic strain envisions a transformation of the world rather than a movement beyond it. The world of nature is not rejected nor is it ever questioned as the natural dwelling place of human beings.

In discussing the place of nature within the New Testament, Joseph Sittler emphasizes the thread found in both the Gospels and the Pauline Letters that stresses the cosmic dimension of Christ. The Fourth Gospel begins by placing the Son at the point of creation and so brings together "the redemptive grace which is the burden of its new message with the uncovenanted and covenanted grace of God in creation and in Israel's history." The early Christians began with the Hebrew understanding of nature as coming from God and as being capable of bearing his glory; and so naturally redemption would come not only to humans but to all God's creation: "For the realm of redemption cannot be conceived as having a lesser magnitude than the realm of creation." But in the New Testament this was no longer only a hope, for with the Incarnation of Christ the new age had actually begun. As Sittler quotes Galloway: "Already in the Anointed One the things of heaven and the things of earth were joined together." The early Christians saw nature as well as human beings participating in the redemption brought by God through Jesus Christ. Sittler points out that this idea of a "cosmic Christ" has never been stressed or developed as thoroughly as its potentialities warrant, but the basis for it is nonetheless present in the Epistles.

Conrad Bonifazi makes the point that the very doctrine of Incarnation affirms man's "roots in matter." The emphasis is always put on Christ's entering into the historical life of human beings, but of course of equal importance is his entry into the physical life of men and women and so of the world. That Christians have chosen to celebrate this event through reenactment by means of bread and wine, physical objects of the earth, is a way of speaking of matter as holy. Nathan Scott stresses the breakdown of the boundaries between the sacred and the secular as these elements of common life become the elements of the Eucharist. He then draws out the implication of this "essential congruence between the Liturgy and the common life":

> For bread and wine could not be set apart for consecration unless ours were in some basic sense a sacramental universe. . . . And thus one of the most searching questions posed by the sacramental principle concerns what general perspective on reality it may be under which the world, in its every aspect, can be found to be itself something essentially sacramental.

Pierre Teilhard de Chardin speaks in a similar vein in his "Mass on the World":

> Since once again, Lord—though this time not in the forests of the Aisne but in the steppes of Asia—I have neither bread, nor wine, nor altar, I will raise myself beyond these symbols, up to the pure majesty of the real itself; I, your priest, will make the whole earth my altar and on it will offer you all the labours and sufferings of the world. . . . Through your own incarnation, my God, all matter is henceforth incarnate.

The attitude that modern theology has taken toward the natural world will be discussed at greater length in the conclusion, but it is clear that we do find a current running throughout the Judeo-Christian heritage that shares Roethke's love and respect for the created world. This is not to say that Roethke is part of this tradition, but the understanding he has of the world and the meaning he finds in it through relationship with created things share a great deal in common with many religious thinkers. His assumptions "about what can, or just possibly does, constitute the ground of experience itself," his "primal intuition" about the nature of reality, seem close to those of such theologians of our time as Buber and Marcel and Sittler.

There is another sense in which Roethke's poetry may be said to have a religious dimension. Martin Heidegger says that in our "dark time" of the absence of the gods it is our poets who may bring us back into the presence of Being. In "What Are Poets For?" he says, "To be a poet in a destitute time means: to attend, singing, to the trace of the fugitive gods." The poet is willing to venture into the region of the unknown, to stand before the mystery, with an attitude of releasement toward things or letting be *(Gelassenheit)*. He does not assert his will on the world but attends closely to what is given because, as Scott says, "his literary craftsmanship is wholly dedicated to the disclosure of the things and creatures of this world in their sheer specificity, 'in the starkness and strangeness of their being what they are.'" By taking away our "forgetfulness of Being" and teaching us to "pay heed" to the things of the world and to stand in their presence, the poet brings us into the neighborhood of Being and "teaches us how to 'hail' Being–which is to say that he takes us into the dimension of the Holy, or, as Heidegger likes to put it, he 'names the Holy.'"

Such a description of the act of poetry is very congenial to a poet like Roethke both because of the fullness of the particulars of the world in his poetry and because he says, with William Blake, "Everything that lives is holy!" As we explore the poetry, beginning with the greenhouse poems and moving toward his final, universal dance of joy, we will see this affirmation of the holiness of the things of the created world, which depends for Roethke on his understanding of existence as an I-Thou experience of shared life.

CHAPTER TWO

THE ROOTS OF THE POETRY

In *The Lost Son* and *Praise to the End!* Roethke establishes the concerns and methods that are crucial to all his poetry. The importance of the natural world, both as an indicator of analogous human concerns and as something to be rejoiced in for itself, is revealed in the greenhouse poems as well as the longer poems of these volumes. Especially in these latter poems nature appears in some sort of positive relation to human beings. The things of the earth are sometimes called upon to serve as a guide to the poet: "Snail, snail, glister me forward, / Bird, soft-sigh me home" ("The Lost Son"). They sometimes seem to participate in his joy: "The weeds believed me, and the nesting birds" ("A Field of Light"). And very often the poet finds a cause for rejoicing through participation in nature's fullness, in the sun glittering on small rapids ("A Field of Light"); "The glad hen on the hill; and the trellis humming" ("The Shape of the Fire"); and through recognition of the very existence of things, their tenacity in clinging to life: "Nothing would give up life: / Even the dirt kept breathing a small breath" ("Root Cellar").

One of the methods used in the poetry, along with one of the central motifs, is established in his prose piece "Open Letter": "I believe that to go forward as a spiritual man it is necessary first to go back." "Going back" seems to have a twofold meaning. There is one sense in which the return to the origins is a return to the source of life, the primeval seat of power. As the poet is able to return to his childhood and preanalytic perceptions generally, he is able to renew himself through his participation in this power, a power that derives from the basic unity and indestructibility of the livingness of creation. But the return to childhood has a second meaning as well. It is necessary for the man to go back in order to relive his childhood perceptions as an adult. To re-see the world through a child's eyes is the only way he can come to terms with the conflicts and the guilt, as well as the joy and feeling of unity, that were a part of his earlier life. As he is able to relive and understand these feelings in a conscious way, he acquires another sort of power. He is able to understand the conflicts and learn to incorporate the childhood feelings of joy and unity into his adult perceptions of the world.

A final point must be made concerning the idea of the power of the origins. The primordial beginnings of life are shared in by human beings; along with all life, we too come out of this undifferentiated vitality. Insofar as we are able to acknowledge this and participate in it, it can be a source of power. However, this primordial slime also poses a danger for human beings: it is a death urge as well as a life source. It is stasis and inactivity as well as vitality and creativity. To return to the unity of nondifferentiation is a temptation that we, faced with the multifariousness and separateness of life, must resist. The return to origins is not our final destiny. We must break the unity; we must rejoice in seeing the "separateness of all things" ("A Field of Light") so that we may enter into relation with them as individuals, aware of ourselves as persons, as spiritual beings.

The significance of the idea of "going back" for Roethke's method is that the process is never completed, the moment of grace is never final. Each poem must repeat the cycle of returning, must encounter the darkness and grow out of it into a moment of light and awareness of the self in relation to the things of the world; then must follow another period of return, with, as Roethke says, a little progress being made each time. It is interesting to note the similarities between this spiraling movement in Roethke and the spiral in the romantic pattern as M. H. Abrams describes it in *Natural Supernaturalism:*

> In the most representative Romantic version of emanation and return, when the process reverts to its beginning the recovered unity is not . . . the simple, undifferentiated unity of its origin, but a unity which is higher, because it incorporates the intervening differentiations. . . . The self-moving circle . . . fuses the idea of the circular return with the idea of linear progress, to describe a distinctive figure of Romantic thought and imagination—the ascending circle, or spiral.

He further describes this romantic "plot" as

> the painful education through ever expanding knowledge of the conscious subject as it strives—without distinctly knowing what it is that it wants until it achieves it—to win its way back to a higher mode of the original unity with itself from which, by its primal act of consciousness, it has inescapably divided itself off. . . . [This process is] a circuitous journey back home.

In the circuitous journey of the poems of *The Lost Son* and *Praise to the End!* we see both a method and a concern. Both, it seems to me, are directed toward one primary end: the development of the individual self who can affirm and participate in creation.

THE GREENHOUSE WORLD

The concern with nature and the method of "going back" are both present in the greenhouse poems as Roethke explores nature and its relation to human beings. In these poems Roethke establishes the primary world of his poetry. Even though his later poems move beyond the greenhouse, the response to growing things which he establishes here remains fundamental to all his poetry. The poems are also significant in that they announce his break with the more traditional forms he used in his earlier poetry and lead into the more radical forms that follow in the long poems of *The Lost Son.* Even though he has shown the importance of the natural world in his first volume of poetry, *Open House,* his poetic approach to his subject changes significantly with the greenhouse poems. For example, in "The Heron" and "The Premonition" there is a formality that restricts the force of his feeling. "The Premonition" presents the remembrance of an experience, but it is not a living experience as in the following volume of poetry. Although the rhyme scheme is not restrictive, the poem relies on a rather forced interjection ("Oh that was long ago!") to take us into the past and on a form close to a metaphysical conceit ("Hair on a narrow wrist bone") to bring out the meaning of the past. "The Heron" is given in the present, but it lacks the feeling for the heron because of a rigid, elaborate stanzaic form. With the greenhouse poems all this has changed. Roethke is no longer simply an accomplished technician. He has found the mode in which he can create most brilliantly. This is a personal mode both in content, which grows out of his childhood experience of the greenhouse, and in aesthetics, as he loosens his form and opens it more to the mysterious ambiguity that he finds in growing things.

Theodore Roethke's grandfather, Wilhelm, began a greenhouse in Saginaw, Michigan, which was continued by Roethke's father, Otto. Roethke says of his father and the greenhouses:

> My father's chief interest was the growing of the flowers. When the firm was at its height, it took up twenty-five acres within the city of Saginaw with a quarter of a million feet under glass. . . . Its advertising created the slogan, "The largest and most complete floral establishment in Michigan" and undoubtedly it was, for it had its own icehouse, a small game preserve, and the last stand of virgin timber in the Saginaw Valley (mostly walnut and oak–not pine). . . . As a child I heard Europeans, Dutchmen and Belgians, say repeatedly that it was the most beautiful greenhouse in America. My father specialized in roses and orchids particularly.

Thus, one essential part of Roethke's childhood was living among the growing things of the greenhouses, which were his father's world. Roethke describes the greenhouse as "my symbol for the whole of life, a womb, a heaven-on-earth." It is significant that his heaven on earth is filled with the fullness of life as we know it. The process of growth and decay, the struggle for survival, the plentitude of life and the grasping for it and clinging to it–these are the elements that make up his heaven on earth.

The greenhouse itself is well suited to Roethke's understanding: it is made by humans and depends to some extent on them for its functioning, yet it is not in human hands alone. It takes people and plants and something beyond both to have a greenhouse. The greenhouse poems record how these living things work together in their struggle for growth. They are poems of the earth, of the givenness of life and the natural striving to realize and preserve it. The greenhouse poems are concerned, then, primarily with two things: the abundance of life and the way in which the human and the plant life work together to realize it. The driving force in both cases is mysterious and compelling. It has about it a sense of the magical or the mad. This life force is revealed in the irrational tangle of roots and the symmetry of the flower. It is growth that is uncontrollable and majestic, that is ever regenerative and ever terminal. It elicits both our faith and our fear as through it we touch the vital givenness of life.

What is striking about the greenhouse poems is that, even though Roethke speaks of the greenhouse as the symbol for all of life, these poems are not symbolic in the sense that the plants are significant only as they stand for something in the life of human beings. Of course, his concern is with life as apprehended by humans; but part of that life is the life of the plants. The plants, then, do not serve simply as analogies for human life. They are significant in and of themselves. Both plants and people are part of the life of the greenhouse that is apprehended and given expression by the poet. It is not necessary for the poet to describe this world analogically both because of his interest in the plants themselves and because of the natural relation that exists between the plants and human beings. In addition, in both there is a mystery here that is not presumed to be understood. Although the power of the growing things and the kinship of humans to that power are felt, it remains mysterious, something to be wondered at. The vision is not, then, of the outsider who understands the principles of the growth of people and of plants and then uses the one to explain the other, but rather of the man in the greenhouse, surrounded by and filled with the wonder of life, who attempts to experience this wonder through the tools that are uniquely his as a human being–through poetry–and so to share in the process of growth. It is to the things themselves that he turns, to the actualities of life in the greenhouse, and it is these actualities that he is able to affirm through his poetry.

"Cuttings (later)" is one of the first of the greenhouse poems and presents as one model for the growth of life a cutting that has been severed from the parent stalk and its lifegiving roots and must thus reestablish itself as an independent plant. This image of the cutting struggling to begin life again, life that is new but somehow a continuation of the old, is one important way in which Roethke understands growth. As a way of giving greater force to the cutting itself, he compares this process to the life of the saint who is born again. Of course, this comparison also emphasizes the life of the saint, the human counterpart of the plant's struggle; but it is significant that in this case it is the plant that is central, and the human analogy is given to make the plant growth more real. The microscopic view of the plant as it struggles for new life in the second stanza again contains an implicit comparison to human life, but the primary effect of the poem is to make us aware of the life of the plant and finally to make the struggle of the plant and of a human being seem one and the same:

> I can hear, underground, that sucking and sobbing,
> In my veins, in my bones I feel it,–
> The small waters seeping upward,
> The tight grains parting at last.
> When sprouts break out,
> Slippery as fish,
> I quail, lean to beginnings, sheath-wet.

The mystery of growth that is presented is painful, difficult, and triumphant. It is this awesome struggle for life, and joy at its coming into being, that is the subject of the poem. We participate in it, we become as the plant, we know that it is our struggle and our joy. It is this struggle and triumph that, wherever they happen, whenever they happen, are the reason for the affirmation that pervades the poem.

"Root Cellar" follows this poem in the collected works and is indeed another aspect of the principle of fecundity. Whereas the first poem was presented in the present tense so that we might feel the immediacy of the struggle, "Root Cellar" is presented from the point of view of the past. It is slightly distant from us. It is that side of life we cannot look at too closely. The lines are longer and there is less emphasis on rhythm, with the result that the tone is more conversational. It is the dirty, down-to-earth world of the root cellar that is described, a world that is notable for its ceaseless activity and its smells. It is "dank" and "rank"; there is mildew and mold. But out of this very common, mostly disagreeable place come two important things. The first is that the apparently objective view of the life in the root cellar takes on a sense of mystery that is at least as great as, perhaps greater than, the delicate mystery of growth in the previous poem. The shoots were "Lolling obscenely"; they "Hung down long yellow evil necks, like tropical snakes." The struggle for life is going on as surely, as mysteriously as—if more frighteningly than—in the gentler cuttings.

The second aspect of the poem that adds to our feeling for this life comes from the structure. The description of the cellar in the poem is surrounded and cut in the middle by three comments that all relate to the fecundity there. The poem begins, "Nothing would sleep in that cellar"; the middle line is "And what a congress of stinks!" and the final two lines are "Nothing would give up life: / Even the dirt kept breathing a small breath." What breaks through each of these exclamations is a feeling of exuberance, of admiration for the power of the life that is here discovered. Although this underground vitality may be more difficult for us to appreciate and identify with than the life force found in the beauty of the cuttings, it is as surely an indication of the persistence of life, and it is a side of life of which we too are a part.

As a dark, underside view of life is given in "Root Cellar," so is it in "Weed Puller," where the young boy is found working under the flower benches, below the flowers—"Whole fields lovely and inviolate"—among the "perverse life" of the "lewd monkey-tails" of roots, the "fetor of weeds." "The indignity of it!" he says and describes himself as "Alive, in a slippery grave." But it is undeniably a part of life, inextricably connected to the gorgeous blooms above him. To have the one without the other is unthinkable. The boy's denial of the one at this stage points to the rediscovery of himself and nature with which he must later come to terms.

A third model for growth is presented in those poems that deal with some kind of interaction between the human and plant worlds. The poet approaches the relationship in which they exist from various angles, trying to get at the whole, to understand the nature of this alliance he experiences between the life of a person and the life of a flower. In "Forcing House" he brings together the delicate cuttings and the raucous weeds, the flower and the roots, in a world that is made by humans. Both the "mildews" and the "delicate cyclamen tips . . . pulse with the knocking pipes." And we are given the power of the machine that brings nourishment and warmth to the plants with the pulsing of the pipes that "drip and sweat,/Sweat and drip." The poem opens from these short, mesmeric lines into the swelling, the upwelling of life, the machine-produced heat and fertilizer both bringing growth to the plants and being alive themselves:

> Swelling the roots with steam and stench,
> Shooting up lime and dung and ground bones,–
> Fifty summers in motion at once,
> As the live heat billows from pipes and pots.

In this strong, pulsating rhythm of growth we feel the surging power of life that is shared in and transmitted by the live heat pulsing its life-giving power into the live plants.

"Big Wind" also recounts this sharing of the power of life within the world of the greenhouse. To the elements of the greenhouse machinery and the plants whose lives are strengthened by it are added the additional characters of humans and the world of nature outside the greenhouse. The greenhouse is compared to a ship, struggling against the wind-waves for its survival. When the machinery fails because of the high wind, the men join the greenhouses in their struggle to preserve themselves and their flowers against other forces of nature. The poem opens with a question:

> Where were the greenhouses going,
> Lunging into the lashing
> Wind driving water
> So far down the river
> All the faucets stopped?

The syntax, alliteration, and diction all set a tone that is in the mood of

Hopkins, and the greenhouses are in this way endowed with a certain nobility and treated with a kind of respect and affection that is reminiscent of Hopkins's attitude of adoration toward created things. In the next part of the poem, however, the tone changes. The role of the men engaged in the practical necessity of saving the greenhouses is now described, and this straightforward activity is reflected in the tone of the poetry. However, their practicality is tempered by the caring that was revealed in the first part of the poem. The reason for their work is clearly loving concern for the flowers. Another aspect of the men's activity becomes clear in the final part, where the old rose house is compared to a ship weathering a storm, which begins, "But she rode it out." We see people caring and so struggling to preserve the greenhouses and their flowers, but it is not human activity alone. They join in the struggle, they do what they can; but it is finally the old rose house who "hove into the teeth of it" and finally, triumphantly, "sailed until the calm morning, / Carrying her full cargo of roses." In this final section the word choice again reflects a nobility on the part of the greenhouses and a respect, almost adoration, on the part of the human beings. Working together they, who are parts of nature, have survived the onslaught of another part of nature, but the victory is really with the greenhouses.

In "Old Florist" and "Transplanting" the interaction between humans and plants is continued. The first poem centers on the man. He is caring for plants, so they are part of the dialogue, but his dedication is the center of concern: he can "fan life into wilted sweet-peas with his hat" and stand "all night watering roses, his feet blue in rubber boots." "Transplanting" begins in much the same way. The first stanza describes, with a great deal of admiration, the skilful hands of the florist as he works with the young plants. The second stanza, however, moves from its focus on the florist to the plants themselves, once they have left his skilful hands behind. He has done his part; now it is for the sun and the loam to aid the plants as they continue their growth. The process of growth described in this stanza is similar to that of "Cuttings (later)," with the flower seeming to take on human characteristics as it unfolds itself:

> The young horns winding and unwinding,
> Creaking their thin spines,
> The underleaves, the smallest buds
> Breaking into nakedness,
> The blossoms extending
> Out into the sweet air,
> The whole flower extending outward,
> Stretching and reaching.

One final thing must be noted about the poem as a whole. The work of the man in the first stanza and of the flower in the second are integrally related by the form of the poem. This is accomplished first by the point of view. The first word in the poem is "watching." The boy watching, not the florist transplanting or the plants growing, is the center of the poem. Through his eyes the two processes become one. This sense of the unity of the two stanzas is further emphasized by the fact that the poem is composed of a single sentence. Thus there is no break between the two stanzas; both are part of a single thought. It is the boy watching

> hands transplanting,
> . . . .
> The sun warming
> . . . .
> The whole flower extending outward,
> Stretching and reaching

that forms the single image of the poem. In this single image we see Roethke's third model for growth in its fullest form: the work of the man and the work of the plant, resulting in a flowering that is understood and participated in by the child in the greenhouse, in whose consciousness this process becomes a single, unified expression of shared life.

Although this does not exhaust the richness or variety of the greenhouse poems, it is clear from the poems I have discussed that the greenhouse is a place of mysterious and compelling growth. One further aspect of this struggle for life must be noted, however. This is the fact of death, which is also present as a part of life. It is present by implication because the natural process in which flowers are involved inevitably involves death as well and because the very fact of the struggle for life, the stubborn unwillingness to give up life, implies that which must be struggled against. This is shown explicitly in "Flower Dump"—a graveyard, of course, for the dead flowers—with

> Everything limp
> But one tulip on top,
> One swaggering head
> Over the dying, the newly dead.

The victory is splendid, but tragic in its necessary briefness. Death is present also in the downward pull of the roots, the underside of life that was mentioned previously and emphasized in "Weed Puller" by the reference to the "slippery grave." In both instances death seems not in conflict with nature but an integral part of the cycle of birth, growth, and decay that one must feel and understand to live with the nature of things.

There is another aspect to death, however, that does not seem to be in keeping with the natural process. This is found in "Moss-Gathering." The first half of the poem describes in great detail the process of moss gathering and the appearance of the moss. Described as "the kind for lining cemetery baskets," it connects the human use of moss with death. The second half of the poem, however, clarifies the significance of the human act:

> But something always went out of me when I dug loose
> those carpets
> Of green, or plunged to my elbows in the spongy yellowish
> moss of the marshes:
> And afterwards I always felt mean, jogging back over the
> logging road,
> As if I had broken the natural order of things in
> that swampland;
> Disturbed some rhythm, old and of vast importance,
> By pulling off flesh from the living planet;
> As if I had committed, against the whole scheme of life, a
> desecration.

There is a human order and use, then, that is in conflict with the given order of nature. There is no shared life in this poem, no affirmation of the process of growth, but rather a mutual destruction and death as both the boy and the moss lose something in this act of desecration, which is contrasted sharply to the acts of celebration that are affirmed in most of the greenhouse poems. What this poem does affirm is a "rhythm, old and of vast importance." Nature participates in this rhythm; yet it is deeper, more mysterious than the natural world, and humans must also align themselves with it if they are to live in harmony with the order of things. This would seem to be a prescription for poetry as well as for living. The poet is to take his rhythms from the rhythm of nature, and a poet may re-create in his poems the order of nature. Such poetry will be an affirmation of life and an expression of the unity shared in by human beings and nature that is discovered in the experiencing of this natural bond.

Thus, we find in the greenhouse poems the whole process of life, including growth and death. There is, however, a third experience, which takes account of these two aspects of life yet moves beyond them to bring them together in a coherent, continuing significance. This is done in two quite different ways in "Frau Bauman, Frau Schmidt, and Frau Schwartze" and "Carnations." In the first poem the process of memory performs this function. The time of the greenhouse is past: "Gone the three ancient ladies" who were keepers of the growing things. They are given mythical qualities in the way they work and in the fruit of their work as

> Quicker than birds, they dipped
> Up and sifted the dirt;
> . . . .
> Like witches they flew along rows
> Keeping creation at ease;
> . . . .
> They trellised the sun; they plotted for more than themselves.

The ritualistic nature of their actions is applied in the second stanza to the person who is remembering them. As a young boy he too was struggling through the process of growth and needed their care:

> I remember how they picked me up, a spindly kid,
> Pinching and poking my thin ribs
> Till I lay in their laps, laughing,
> Weak as a whiffet.

The time now changes to the present. The boy is gone, along with the old women. But they are all still present in the man's memory:

> These ancient leathery crones,
> With their bandannas stiffened with sweat,
> And their thorn-bitten wrists,
> And their snuff-laden breath blowing lightly over me in my first
> sleep.

The women are described once more as they minister to the boy—now a man—not primarily in terms of their life-giving powers, as when he was young, but in terms of themselves. They are present in his memory both with their magical powers and with their unidealized actuality. The past is brought into the present and made effective there in a way that is both realistic and magical—just as they were to the boy in the greenhouse. The force of memory is able to accomplish this, to create in the present a moment that encompasses the past and makes possible a meaningful equilibrium between them.

"Carnations" also presents a moment of wholeness, of meaning, but this time through the natural image of a carnation:

> Pale blossoms, each balanced on a single jointed stem,
> The leaves curled back in elaborate Corinthian scrolls;
> And the air cool.

Clarifying the image of the flower is a reference to the "Corinthian scrolls," a human area of meaning. The rest of the poem is an attempt through metaphor to describe that "cool air" in terms of both human and natural meaning:

> And the air cool, as if drifting down from wet hemlocks,
> Or rising out of ferns not far from water,
> A crisp hyacinthine coolness,
> Like that clear autumnal weather of eternity,
> The windless perpetual morning above a September cloud.

The moment of "eternity" that I have been discussing in this and the previous poem is achieved in the first through human memory; here it is found in nature itself. The cool air around the stately carnation is the focal image, and the metaphors following make this image more concrete. The carnation is not used as a metaphor for something else, and eternity is found not as an abstract philosophical idea but in a scene from nature. This is eternity: "The windless perpetual morning above a September cloud." Given eternity as a subject, we might expect Roethke to move from the carnation to a philosophical abstraction. But he does not. He remains steadfastly tied to the concrete images of his "symbol for the whole of life . . . a heaven-on-earth"--the greenhouse.

An understanding of life, then, as consisting of growth, death, and a moment of eternity is revealed in the greenhouse poems. The mystery of each is continually present, as is the concreteness of each. There is also always a sense of shared life. These things together make possible the affirmation that is found in and through the things of the earth.

"THE RETURN"

In the second and third sections of *The Lost Son*, several poems anticipate the themes and structure of the title poem, basically through their notion of "return." In the poem by that name, for example, the return is connected with a period of mental illness in which the protagonist sees himself as returning to an animal-like state as he loses his sense of meaning and connectedness with the world. He is returning in one sense to an earlier form of existence and thus, it would seem, escaping from the particularly human problems of existence. But if the return is to an earlier stage of development from which he must begin again, it is also the beginning of a return to the world he came from. He is beginning from this point to move back to a state of human wholeness. We see this pattern in "The Lost Son" and the long poems of *Praise to the End!* To become what he would be, he must return to an earlier phase of being.

In the third section of *The Lost Son,* other forms of the return a person must make in order to come to her or himself are given. And, again, they are precursors to the longer poems that record the struggle of the individual from the beginnings of life to a sense of separate identity. Both "Night Crow" and "River Incident" explore the deep roots of human life, the ties it has with a past that is older than time and yet eternally present within each person. Through this dimension of life one is connected with all living things through all time. In "Night Crow" we see that this connection creates the possibility of correspondences, of perceiving a living connection between the things of the mind (often the unconscious mind) and the things of the external world:

> When I saw that clumsy crow
> Flap from a wasted tree,
> A shape in the mind rose up:
> Over the gulfs of dream
> Flew a tremendous bird
> Further and further away
> Into a moonless black,
> Deep in the brain, far back.

The poet is able to move from an object in the external world to an image deep within the brain because of the shared life of all things and specifically because of the fact that he has shared in such a life. It is part of his "collective unconscious," in the language of Carl Jung. Such an understanding is important to this poetry in two ways. First, it reveals an aspect of being human that we can expect to see amplified in the rest of the poetry; and second, it is an indication of what Roethke thinks about the poetic act itself. We have seen the correspondences between human beings and the flowers of the greenhouse. It seems that such a movement between the things of nature and the life of humans is possible in the poetry because this connection between them actually exists. Thus, Roethke does not use the things of the earth in simply a metaphorical way. His are, rather, "radical metaphors" in that there is in fact a living connection between natural and human life.

In "River Incident" the roots of human beings are revealed in a different way. This is the first reference in the poetry to a kind of reincarnation. This theme never develops explicitly, but such poems as "Snake" and "The Far Field" hint at life recurring in different forms. In "Snake" we find the possibility of a new form in the future, but in "River Incident" is the certain realization of a form that was lived in the past. In this poem the recognition of previous experience can be explained by the collective unconscious. Since we all share in all of life and have deep within us the memory of primordial existence, when we are able to touch on that collective unconscious we will be aware of this past life.

The poem begins, as did "Night Crow," with an experience in the external world in the present moment:

A shell arched under my toes,
Stirred up a whirl of silt
That riffled around my knees.

From this moment of standing in the river, connected to the sea from which all life comes, the person experiences something beyond human existence and beyond all time:

Whatever I owed to time
Slowed in my human form;
Sea water stood in my veins,
The elements I kept warm
Crumbled and flowed away,
And I knew I had been there before,
In that cold, granitic slime,
In the dark, in the rolling water.

In this moment of knowledge beside the primordial sea, he has returned to his roots, to the all-encompassing unity from which individual life springs. As we will see in the following longer poems, only through such a return to the slime, to the rolling water, can the person emerge as a unique spiritual being.

In "The Minimal" this same consciousness of connection with life in other than its human form is presented on a different level. The poet describes how he studies "the lives on a leaf," the tiny, scarcely noticed world that exists alongside the human world but which we seldom acknowledge. The life that is shared by all things in all times is found too in

> the little
> Sleepers, numb nudgers in cold dimensions,
> Beetles in caves, newts, stone-deaf fishes,
> Lice tethered to long limp subterranean weeds,
> Squirmers in bogs.

He moves from those things that we can see if we will take the time to look, to the forms of life that completely elude the human eye. They are all a part of that shared life in which the poet participates as well. They all participate in the life force that reaches to the roots of things and is without beginning or ending. "River Incident" describes these minimals that are not visible and of which he is aware only on the level on which he was in touch with them in his previous existence; this poem reveals the nature of this life:

> And bacterial creepers
> Wriggling through wounds
> Like elvers in ponds,
> Their wan mouths kissing the warm sutures,
> Cleaning and caressing,
> Creeping and healing.

Not only is there a connectedness between all living things, but the connection is basically life giving. It is, as Nathan Scott says, a "sacramental universe." This understanding of the world is affirmed throughout the poetry. What is significant here is that the poet discovers this through close looking at the "minimals." This intimate observation occurs both through the use of the senses, through being intensely aware of what exists in the external world, and through the imagination, by which one participates in life that lies beyond the possibility of experience through the senses. What is discovered in both cases is a realization of the I-Thou relationship within the life of the world.

"The Cycle" leads directly into "The Lost Son" in that the cyclical motion described in this poem, in which water participates as it moves from beneath the ground, into the open air, and back to the ground, is similar to the cycle Roethke uses as an organizing and thematic technique in the longer poems in this section. There too we find a continuing, repetitive movement from darkness into light. Here this cycle of human spiritual life is described as it is found in the world of nature. Once again, there is an actual correspondence between the life of a human being and the life of the world. The poem describes the

> Dark water, underground,
> Beneath the rock and clay,
> Beneath the roots of trees

that moves into "common day." The moisture becomes a mist that forms a cloud that lies

> Far from that colder source
> Where elements cohere
> Dense in the central stone.

The stone is the center of the poem and the center of the world. The water moves from beneath the stone to rest in the air above the stone; and

> The full rain fell straight down,
> . . . .
> Under even the rock-shut ground,
> Under a river's source,
> Under primeval stone.

It has completed its cycle and returned to its resting place. But the cycle will recur. The water will again move to the surface, into the air. And in this movement, always with the stone as its center, is its meaning. So, we find in later poems, it is with the human spirit. Through cyclical movement the lost son comes to know who he is; and, knowing who he is, he moves through times of darkness and light to discover his spiritual being. But always at his roots is the "primeval stone," giving meaning and stability to his journey.

THE JUNGIAN PRESENCE

The mythological nature of Carl Jung's world is very congenial to the aspect of Roethke's world we have been discussing, with its emphasis on a return that involves both depths and darkness. It is not clear how much Roethke actually knew about Jung, Freud, and the whole field of depth psychology. In response to a letter from a graduate student asking how much he had been influenced by Freud, he responded that he had read very little Freud, though he had some friends who were analysts; and he had read part of Jung's *Modern Man in Search of a Soul.* But this slight acquaintance with both occurred "a good deal after the writing of the poems that you would probably consider 'Freudian.'" It would appear that this disclaimer might be a slight exaggeration; in any case, it is clear that he was familiar with Jungian Maud Bodkin's *Archetypal Patterns in Poetry.* Roy Harvey Pearce adds the following note on Freud, quoting Carolyn Kizer: "After all his long poems exploring a child's history of consciousness had appeared, he was discovered in a Morris chair by a friend, with a copy of Freud's *Basic Writings* on one arm, his book *Praise to the End!* on the other, and his notebook in his lap, checking references, and chortling to himself, 'I was right! I was right!'" Pearce adds, "One can only suppose that the friend mistook Winterset Rothberg for Theodore Roethke." (Winterset Rothberg was a pseudonym under which Roethke occasionally published.)

Whatever the self-conscious parallels, the pattern Jung discerns in the process of coming to selfhood seems to have connections with Roethke's "going back" as a way of moving forward. The images of the primordial world would be described by Jung in terms of the collective unconscious. Thus, Roethke's reliving of a childhood world and a vital association with the things of nature would be for Jung a dramatization of the struggle that takes place in the mind during the process of individuation or coming to selfhood. Jung's collective unconscious is a psychic entity that is identical in all people and contains archetypes that are "not only the residues of archaic, specifically human modes of functioning, but also the residues of functions from man's animal ancestry." Thus, in Jungian terms Roethke's affinity with the animal forms, with the beginnings of life, is due in part to his unconscious kinship with them. And, as he imagines himself feeling the slime of a wet nest or being a fish or a dog, he is reenacting the original and continual process of evolution from the unconscious to consciousness.

This event is literally enacted as a child acquires a separate ego, but it lasts through a person's life with continuing assimilation of the unconscious into the ego until selfhood is acquired. Jung calls this enterprise the process of individuation. For the archaic person the greatest threat is being overcome by the unconscious, because the conscious mind is far less developed. For the civilized person the threat is generally from the other side: "The more differentiated consciousness becomes, the greater the danger of severance from the root-condition" (although an excess in this direction can also lead to one's being overtaken by the unconscious). These two aspects of the person must work in conjunction if the self is to emerge. Individuation would then mean "becoming one's own self."

The process of individuation involves a meeting of conscious and unconscious contents, which is mediated for consciousness through archetypal images. An archetype "represents or personifies certain instinctive data of the dark, primitive psyche, the real but invisible roots of consciousness." As this side of a person is revealed, the threat of being overcome by this darkness is very real to the ego. It is a time of regression and introversion, of laying aside the protective covering and of facing a real risk. Maud Bodkin says, "It may be felt by the sufferer as a state of compulsion without hope or aim, as though he were enclosed in the mother's womb, or in a grave–and if the condition continues it means degeneration and death." In Roethke's poetry a parallel event seems to occur in the long poems of *Praise to the End!* where images of death or the womb precede the moment of enlightenment. The way out is through the archetypal images, which, because they are able to bring together the opposites of the conscious and unconscious, have a transcendent or numinous quality.

One of the archetypes most commonly found in this evolution is that of the child. The child is able to bring into conjunction usually opposing qualities (the child hero, e.g.); the threat of the darkness is made that much greater by the entry of a child into it, and thus also is the victory greater when the child is able to conquer it. The child is, of course, the one who must literally emerge from the womb and develop a consciousness of his or her own. Independence can be achieved only by detaching oneself from one's origins, by gaining a sense of otherness. Finally, Jung says that the child is a natural archetype for this process because "it represents the strongest, the most ineluctable urge in every being, namely the urge to realize itself."

The parallels that exist between the process of individuation, with its regression and progression as it moves toward its goal of selfhood, and the struggles of the lost son are important because Jung's understanding of the progress of the soul presents a useful psychological framework for comparison with the "effort to be born, and later, to become something more" that occurs in "The Lost Son" and other long poems in *Praise to the End!* The parallels between this struggle and the process of individuation are evident, but there is also a basic difference that should be pointed out. Jung's theory may be said to involve a kind of affirmation in that one must accept one's origins (the unconscious) while at the same time rejecting them–in order, of course, to take them up again in a new way (that is, to bring them to consciousness so that they become a source of strength for the individuated person rather than an unconscious dependency). And there is also a sense of immanence in that all of one's past, both personal and suprapersonal, has its meaning in the present moment.

In both respects Roethke's poetic world is in touch with Jung's psychoanalytic one. However, the difference arises in the way the process occurs. The one element that is strikingly absent from Jung's theory is the external world, either animal or human. Although we see the personal importance of the natural world for Jung in his autobiographical *Memories, Dreams, Reflections,* the process is described primarily as a reflexive one; the moment of numinosity is created by the powers of the psyche. In this sense there is a transcendence of this world and the things and people of this world. For Roethke this is death of the self rather than a rebirth. In his poetry it is not only through archetypal images (though his plants and animals and women may have this same sort of power as well), but also through the things of the earth that a person can come to some kind of integration of the self within the world.

The role of the unconscious in the process of self-development involves several things for Jung. At the level of the *personal unconscious* there is the necessity of coming to terms with certain personal matters, perhaps the death of the father and sexual guilt in *Praise to the End!* although these personal matters have a more universal, archetypal meaning as well and must be faced on that level also. The contents of the *collective unconscious* are important to development in that they are part of humankind; they are its roots, and humans cannot cut themselves off from this source of power without destroying themselves. In addition, through the child archetype we see that reenacting the overcoming of the darkness has a renewing power. This seems close to the description Mircea Eliade gives of the "return to origins" and the "rites of renewal" of archaic people. If validity resides in the very first occurrence of a thing, the child's coming to consciousness is the original act. This is symbolized through the conquest of darkness by the child who is at least a hero, sometimes a god. By reliving this through the archetype a person presumably is able to "overcome time," to begin again as a child, having participated in the power of the original moment of creation (of consciousness), the overcoming of chaos (the unconscious).

It seems that both functions of the unconscious are at work in the longer poems of *Praise to the End!* The moment of vision that is realized in each poem seems to result from two things: from touching a power in the primordial unity, which is a way of reestablishing roots; and from reenacting the primary movement from participation in an undifferentiated unity to separation, an awareness of self (the time of creation out of chaos, the movement from the unconscious to consciousness). This raises an additional point that is of great importance to Roethke's affirmation of the immanent. In facing the darkness, the chaos, he is taking a risk that he will be overcome by it. There is implicit in this a faith that order will indeed come out of chaos, that humans do not have to and should not attempt to impose their own order on it. By re-creating through the poetry the experience of chaos, Roethke attempts to do away with the old, imposed perceptions of order and to let the order, if order in fact exists, reveal itself. Finally, Roethke's going back to the darkness seems to imply that one must choose life over death. The mire, the womb, is often enticing; the undifferentiated unity is at least unity. Freud describes this as "the most universal endeavour of all living substance—namely to return to the quiescence of the inorganic world." It takes courage to resist the attraction of its downward pull. Insofar as persons are able to do this, they are giving an affirmation to the life of this world, a life of ambiguity and struggle and ever-repeated conquests of the dark.

Jung's description of the process of individuation is one way of understanding the struggle at work in the long poems of *Praise to the End!* The struggle is more than psychological, however. "To go forward as a spiritual man," Roethke says, "it is necessary first to go back." "Spiritual" cannot be equated with "mature" or "psychologically stable." What is being enacted here cannot be so categorized. It is the mystery of being and of how man grows to participate in this process to the fullest, how he turns from what means death and alienation and chaos to the life sources that bring communion and an order that cannot be systematized but can only be lived. However, because there is a psychological dimension to this search, Jung is useful as a beginning point in understanding the poetry. He is also close to Roethke's understanding of the world as a place of mystery. In Jung there is a sense of presences, which he describes as archetypes, that remain mysterious and that cannot be fully brought into control through rational processes. Like Roethke's, his journey is, finally, a spiritual quest.

This sense of the mysterious may be augmented by the understanding of Gabriel Marcel. The "mystery of being" he evokes involves an understanding of reality that moves beyond what he calls "primary reflection," or problem solving, to "secondary reflection," in which the unity of experience is restored through entering into the mystery rather than seeking to objectify and analyze it. Within this world "going back," or what Marcel calls recollection or "ingathering," is very important. Marcel describes this turning inward as having the

> character of being a *return*—only a return in which what is given *after* the return is not identical with what was given *before*. . . . I am weighing the actual life I have been leading in the balance of the

> of the potential life I carry within me, the life that I aspire to lead, the life that I would have to lead if I wanted to become fully myself.

Although this description of returning in order to actualize the potential that is already present is similar to Jung's description of the process of individuation, Marcel stresses a quality of grace and wonder before the mystery that is important in Roethke's world as well.

As we see the shared world of Jung and Marcel and Roethke, we ought, of course, to remember the simple fact that poetry remains poetry and cannot be explained by depth psychology or theology. Gaston Bachelard explains this by saying that the poetic image creates a reverberation in us that makes the image become "a new being in our language, expressing us by making us what it expresses; in other words, it is at once a becoming of expression, and a becoming of our being. Here expression creates being." Because of this "a poetic image eludes causality." Something new and without antecedents is created in a poem; and, in addition, it creates something in the reader that cannot be causally accounted for either psychologically or theologically. The poetic creation must be fully entered into in its own newness and its own mystery. The purpose of bringing other disciplines to bear upon an analysis of Roethke's poetry is simply to reveal the mysterious richness of worlds that are related to the poetry and thus to increase our openness to the mystery of that world.

As we return to Roethke's poetic world, we find that in it Marcel's secondary reflection is at work. Sometimes he uses the child as a symbol of preanalytic thinking, and part of the process of the poem is actually coming to terms with childhood and moving to a kind of secondary reflection. More often, however, the poems work by association in an attempt to create an apprehension of the world that is based on intersubjectivity and a nonanalytic, wondering response to the things of the world. "Going back" has to do here with re-creating this kind of response to the world, going back to the time before one has imposed one's "system" on the world and ordered it to suit one's fancy on the basis of primary reflection. Thus, the world found in most of the longer poems begins as a very chaotic one; without our established order we find no way of living in connection with the world or ourselves. The truth underlying the poetry seems to be that there is an order, a presence, in the world that, if we will let it, will reveal itself to our attending selves. This is similar to what Heidegger calls *"releasement toward things"* and *"openness to the mystery."* Nathan Scott relates this way of being in the world to Roethke's poetry by saying that the "determining framework of Roethke's vision" is

> the sense of the human situation as, most fundamentally, one of our simply standing (as Heidegger would say) in-the-neighborhood-of-Being, in the outright *presence* of that-which-is. The gesture which his poetry performs is a gesture of *Gelassenheit* [releasement], of abandonment, of surrender to the sheer presence of Being in the things and creatures of earth.

He calls this in Roethke a sign of the "sacramental imagination."

"THE LOST SON"

As we return to the poems themselves, we can see this understanding of the world revealed as the poet begins his search for himself and his world in the longer poems of *Praise to the End!* I will begin with a rather detailed analysis of "The Lost Son" and then describe how the other poems in this sequence adapt the pattern that is established here. The title of this poem has a double meaning. It refers to the child who is wandering in a strange, bewildering world as he begins to leave behind his original relationship with nature and his parents and attempts to discover himself. At the same time, however, the lost son is that part of the adult that has been lost and must in some way be recovered and transformed if the adult is to move forward on his spiritual journey. Both levels are at work in "The Flight" as the poem begins. The first section opens in a place of death: "At Woodlawn I heard the dead cry." This time of psychological and spiritual lifelessness is presented concretely through images of activity in the world around the poet, but the activity seems either negative or purposeless. It should be noted as well that the actions are presented in such a way as to create a feeling of unreality, of separation from the world we know: the dead crying, "Toads brooding wells" (simply by leaving out the "in" he creates a wholly different order of causality), the leaves sticking out their tongues (by our usual metaphorical associations we might say the leaves *are* tongues). The feeling of disintegration in the poet is present: "I shook the softening chalk of my bones." But this is a turning point: we are given both the image of death in the softening bones and the renewal as he rouses himself to activity. This leads him to the first of many invocations in the poem; this one is to the small things of nature—the snail, the bird, the worm. Alliteration creates a gentle rocking motion, the barest of movement, and each plea is directly suited to the nature of the living thing he calls on:

Snail, snail, glister me forward,
Bird, soft-sigh me home,
Worm, be with me.
This is my hard time.

Yet in the next two stanzas he has turned back upon himself. The gentle motion has ceased. The lines are short, usually three-beat, and harsher. The poet tries self-pity, which he presents through a combination of feeling and natural states:

Fished in an old wound,
The soft pond of repose.

But this does not work. The old ways of retreating from the hard times are not adequate here. He imagines himself in an empty house, a place of aloneness and inner emptiness, peopled only by shadows made by a fly. There is an attempt to forget the quest for self; but as these old ways fail he reaches beyond himself again with the second invocation, this time to a "Voice." "Come out of the silence," he says; he asks for the presence of life, even in the form of a spider or a moth. He asks for direction:

Which is the way I take;
Out of what door do I go,
Where and to whom?

And the reply does come; he is no longer left alone and in silence. But the words are the cryptic speech of nature:

Dark hollows said, lee to the wind,
The moon said, back of an eel,
The salt said, look by the sea.

The replies of the voice are not the most life-giving for this person seeking himself in this world, but they are, at least, there. And they do give him guidance by criticizing his person and his place and thus set him in motion, seeking something else.

He begins "Running lightly over spongy ground," and the images become at the same time more realistic and more charged with life. Stones and trees, which are often present in Roethke's poetry at moments of joy and participation with nature, begin to appear. The "quick-water, wrinkling and rippling," toward which he is running, is also a sign and a place of new life. As Mircea Eliade points out in *Patterns in Comparative Religion,* these forms are often manifestations of the holy insofar as they embody something other than themselves. Regarding sacred stones, Eliade says, "The hardness, ruggedness, and permanence of matter was in itself a heirophany in the religious consciousness of the primitive. . . . Above all, stone *is.* It always remains itself, and exists of itself." The tree has numerous mythical patterns associated with it. In Roethke's poetry it seems at least to represent "the *living cosmos,* endlessly renewing itself." The tree is firmly rooted in the earth and is enduring, as a stone is, yet, unlike a stone, it is able to undergo changes, to participate in the cycles of life, and yet to endure. Finally, of water symbolism he says, "Principle of what is formless and potential, basis of every cosmic manifestation, container of all seeds, water symbolizes the primal substance from which all forms come and to which they will return. . . . It will always exist, though never alone, for water is always germinative, containing the potentiality of all forms in their unbroken unity."

But the water he reaches is the water of the slime. He is

> Hunting along the river,
> Down among the rubbish, the bug-riddled foliage,
> By the muddy pond-edge, by the bog-holes,
> By the shrunken lake, hunting, in the heat of summer.

The lines stretch out and slow down, becoming difficult to maneuver. He must begin with the extremities of things, whether we think of them as the beginnings or the endings of life.

The final part of the first section is a series of questions and answers that reveal the nature of the reality he is involved in. They resemble nonsense verse but have a sense of desperation about them that takes them out of this realm. The lines are short, two-beat, and irregularly rhyming *abab.* Thus, they are more regularly structured and have more of a constant rhythm than most of the poem. Yet they create a sense of the irrational or, better, the prerational. Like a nursery rhyme they have a lilt to them, yet they are filled with an ominous feeling. The result is almost like an incantation to hold off the powers of darkness:

> The shape of a rat?
> It's bigger than that.
> It's less than a leg
> And more than a nose,

Just under the water
It usually goes.

. . . .

It's sleek as an otter
With wide webby toes
Just under the water
It usually goes.

The poet asks the shape, the feeling, the functions–of what, he does not know. And the answers seem to shed no light on the mystery. What they do show, perhaps, is that the way to discover both what he is seeking and where to find it is through a form of perception associated with the child or the preconscious. It is something that must be lived with, not rationally explained. Rosemary Sullivan, citing Jung, suggests that "The Lost Son" "is patterned on the immemorial night journey: 'We must surely go the way of the waters, which always go downward, if we would salvage the treasure, the precious legacy of the father.' . . . To recover the soul-treasure at the bottom of the river, we must become 'fishers who catch with hook and net what floats in the water.'" She goes on to say, "Jung actually identifies the otter as a fantasy image of the self as night-fisher." In "The Abyss" Roethke uses the image "A night-fishing otter"; here the implications seem similar as we move with the otter below the water. Only as he is able to enter this mode of perception, to enter the mystery, will he begin to get answers to his questions.

At this point, however, the questions are useless. The second and third sections record his downward journey, the increase of darkness, of chaos. This is where the questions lead him, perhaps even pull him. As the first section ends,

Just under the water
It usually goes,

the second section begins, "Where do the roots go?" This section, "The Pit," again uses the question-answer approach, this time with a catechetical rather than a nonsense rhyme quality. It is much darker. The mystery of the unknown has increased:

Where do the roots go?
    Look down under the leaves.
Who put the moss there?
    These stones have been here too long.
Who stunned the dirt into noise?
    Ask the mole, he knows.

underside of things is present here. The roots, the stones under the s, the mole—they are all reaching underground, backward in time, p into the unconscious. He is asking about the origins of life—his gins. The first question and answer are the most rational. The second answer only obliquely refers to the question. The third response does not even try to answer the question, which itself seems power-filled with the irrational, but points beyond itself to an equally strange source. Here he is at the point of origins, in the womb of nature: "I feel the slime of a wet nest." But this is not a place of safety and security, because it may mean death to the person who is attempting to find himself. He must beware of "Mother Mildew." It is a risk to have let himself be drawn into the pit both because he may not be able to crawl out and also because he may be so numbed by the anesthetic of this womb that he will cease trying. Thus, the final line, "Nibble again, fish nerves," is a plea to keep going. The fish often seems to symbolize for Roethke the earliest animal evolutionary stage and the preconscious side of man; thus, although only a few steps above the wet nest, it is a movement forward out of the pit.

The third section, "The Gibber," is a continuation of this time of darkness. Harry Williams points out that one meaning of "gibber" is the "bulb or swelling at the bottom of the calyx, corolla, and the like," and in this respect the poem continues the womblike surroundings of "The Pit." But because the poet has moved from the questions to his own recognition of his predicament, "The Gibber" goes further. It begins:

> At the wood's mouth,
> By the cave's door,
> I listened to something
> I had heard before.

The terms indicate a reliving, which is seen as a dangerous time. The child is engaged in his struggle with the darkness, but there is no assurance that he will conquer it. The images show him about to be swallowed by the woods, by the cave. "Dogs of the groin" indicate sexual and predatory instincts that cannot be controlled; his own nature is rising up against him. All nature joins in rejecting him; he is being shut out of his previous state of unity, left alone in the darkness. This section, with its short, two-beat lines, moves into a verse of lengthened lines, smoothed out. But if there was a kind of deathlike incantation in the previous rhyme,

The weeds whined,
The snakes cried,
The cows and briars
Said to me: Die,

the more dreamlike tone of the next section is equally devoid of vital life. Only the most minimal existence is present: "a small song . . . slow clouds . . . dark water." It is a time of beginnings. The poet asks, "Hath the rain a father?" This is a quotation from the section of Job in which the all-powerful God asks Job what right he has to question anything the Almighty has done, for he is the originator, the Father of all life. As Karl Malkoff has pointed out, the previous section, "The Pit," is also concerned with the origins of life and so may be associated with Job and with alienation from the Almighty Father. The father whom the poet finds here is "Father Fear." This is also a time of contraction, of drawing in on the self. Having been rejected by the things of nature, he tries, in an image that captures the powerful longing of the lonely child, to return to the security of father and mother ("I'm cold, I'm cold all over. Rub me in father and mother"). Thus the father of all life and the father of his life are combined as he seeks comfort. But all he finds is that

Fear was my father, Father Fear.
His look drained the stones.

Short, usually off-rhyming *(aabb)* lines reappear, but the movement is more gentle. They present the visions of sleep: a "gliding shape," a "substance flowing," a pouring out of the self, but into no container. The self wakes alone, isolated:

Like a slither of eels
That watery cheek
As my own tongue kissed
My lips awake.

With again lengthening lines and a continuation of the cryptic questions, the poet asks, "Is this the storm's heart?" The forces of nature are formless, the body is formless; order is not perceptible. Roethke describes this section as a "'rant,' almost in the manner of the Elizabethans." There is a flurry of frantic, contradictory images ("Let the kisses resound . . . / Let the gestures freeze") that generally express a feeling of losing the self, or at least the old patterns by which the self has lived ("Is the seed leaving the old bed?"). He cries out for the past with all its potential, which seems no longer to exist:

> What's left of my life?
> I want the old rage, the lash of primordial milk!

The old stones must be left behind, the old ways in which moments of joy and meaning were perceived. The old orders–history, time, childhood–are disappearing. There is an intense recognition of the breaking of bonds, of the isolation, of that which has separated him from the creative aspect of nature and from himself. All these outpourings come to a climax of alienation, symbolized in the poet's abandonment to the artificiality of the world:

> I have married my hands to perpetual agitation,
> I run, I run to the whistle of money.

This recognition flings the poet to the other side:

> Money money money
> Water water water.

The sources of life are touched on, though not understood, not fully participated in. They have been sensed without explanation, without analysis, without argument. They are simply there.

The final part of this third section is a continuation of the childlike questions and answers. Accompanying the feeling of desperation here, however, is an increased sense of the solidity, the reality, of the world the seeker confronts. The short, end-stopped lines and lighter rhythm heighten this feeling. The poet is able to observe something outside himself: "How cool the grass is. . . . The stalk still sways." He moves out in an instinctual way to wonder,

> Has the worm a shadow?
> What do the clouds say?

Although he is reaching out, he is still desperate for the answers, and there is a definite sense of his being caught up in the questions. The lines lengthen, the questions turn to exclamations:

These sweeps of light undo me.
Look, look, the ditch is running white!
I've more veins than a tree!
Kiss me, ashes, I'm falling through a dark swirl.

Still helpless, he is being carried away by something beyond his power, and the self is fighting not to be swallowed up. But the presentness of the things of this world yet enables the poet to call upon the darkness for help: "Kiss me, ashes." He is able to face this death, saying yes to it and risking the possibility that it will undo him entirely.

Here a word should be said about the title of section 3 and about the use that is made of language in the first three sections generally. The language in this section often does become almost gibber. "Gibber" is defined as rapid, inarticulate, and often foolish speech. It is the breakdown of the powers of language in Roethke's poetry. This is the nonsense rhyme or preconscious quality mentioned before. Language is our way of ordering our world. The disintegration of the organizing power of language as the poet struggles backward to his roots in the unconscious, in the darkness of the prerational, is what creates for the reader the sense of this backward journey. It is like a primitive or mythical world in that the immediate experience is predominant. As Cassirer says, "External reality is not merely viewed and contemplated, but overcomes a man in sheer immediacy." The normal ways of perceiving and organizing the world are broken down. Distinctions between subject and object disappear as do our categories of present, past, and future. There is no way to analyze or put in order because there is no sense of a separate self that can sort out the experiences. This part of the poem is a record of the process of separation; thus, there is not only no self to deal with the experiences (both of the external world of nature and the inner world of the unconscious), but the original solidarity with the world has been disrupted. This is the moment of hanging between separation and solidarity, consciousness and unconsciousness. In "A Field of Light" the moment of emergence from this precarious moment to a consciousness of self and a recovery of the powers of language is revealed in this way:

I could watch! I could watch!
I saw the separateness of all things!

This may be said to be similar to the world of the primitive, but of course it is the very careful work of the artist, using the most sophisticated potentialities of language to re-create for us the original struggle of the human race and of each child to come to consciousness. In addition, it is an attempt to objectify and so bring to conscious awareness the continual struggle that a person must go through to come to a real awareness of herself or himself and the world. Thus, the second reason Roethke uses language in this way is to break down our normal perceptions and so make it possible for us to see the world in a new way. This poetry can be seen as an example of Kenneth Burke's dramatistic view of language in *Language as Symbolic Action*—that language is best understood as a mode of action rather than as a means of conveying ideas. It is the action of the language, often conveyed through the sound of words and their rhythm, that brings us into this strangely living world and, if Roethke is successful, enables us to experience again the entry into the world of consciousness, the coming of the self. As we turn again to the poem, we are at that moment of emergence from the "dark swirl." If the previous analysis has validity for Roethke's poetry, we should see the language change, and along with this change we should discover a new ordering of time and space.

The fourth section is entitled "The Return," and it takes place in the greenhouse, a place that would provide a sense of security and safety for the child. In addition, it is a particular place. The time is also important: this is a memory from childhood. It is perceived and revealed as having occurred in the past; the poet is no longer caught up in sheer immediacy. The language has lost its frantic quality and reveals a fuller state of consciousness. The section begins with the darkness with which the previous section left off:

> The way to the boiler was dark,
> Dark all the way,
> Over slippery cinders
> Through the long greenhouse.

The boiler is the life-giving power of the greenhouse, as is the papa, and both these forces are analogous to the power of growth in creation, the God who is the giver and preserver of life; he is no longer "Father Fear." The roses are the flowers he focuses on here—roses which in his poetry are a symbol for the fulfillment of nature, as well as being important in themselves. They keep breathing even in the dark, even through the night. And the poet now seems to be participating more directly in nature and with the processes of nature:

> My knees made little winds underneath
> Where the weeds slept.

There is a greater sense of reciprocity, of a shared world.

To describe the return from the chaos of nature, Roethke has chosen an experience of the child that is not wholly introspective or wholly involved with nature since the greenhouse, though dealing with the natural, is yet made and to some extent controlled by humans. This chaos obviously includes the chaos of the psyche as well as of the external world. Roethke has chosen the experience of a child partly because of the emphasis he places on childhood as a time of unity and joy—things the adult has lost and can restore, transformed, only through the struggle in which the poet is engaged in this poem (although, as we have seen in this poem, childhood is not a time free from tensions or darkness). Also, at this stage of his understanding and growth as a person, the poet has nowhere to turn *but* to childhood, has no way of imagining God *but* as the father on earth. (In one of the late poems, "The Rose," he says, "What need for heaven, *then,* / With that man, and those roses?" [emphasis added].) Through experiences such as this one he will later be able to find another way of turning, even of returning, without relying exclusively on his childhood perceptions of order.

What is presented in this experience from childhood is a night spent in the greenhouse with a single light by the firepit, and the coming, slowly, of the morning. He is very much aware of the details of the external world—

> The light in the morning came slowly over the white
> Snow.
> There were many kinds of cool
> Air—

and he is able to attend to them. Extremely varied in length, the lines arrest our attention on particular details. Then the steam comes, flooding the greenhouse with its warmth; and with it comes "papa." These two powers are again closely associated. "Pipe-knock" brings them together, Roethke says in "Open Letter," as the image calls up both the knocking of the pipes once the steam begins to stream through them and the papa's knocking his pipe on the benches as he comes into the greenhouse. And with the steam and the father order comes to the greenhouse:

Scurry of warm over small plants.
Ordnung! ordnung!
Papa is coming!

He describes the flowers turning toward the light, even the weeds moving in a slow upsway. Another day is safely created out of the darkness.

The final section is entitled "'It was beginning winter,'" and it is an "in-between time." It is a time of waiting, of preparation, of potential. The field is frozen, which suggests inactivity and death, but survivors—the dry seed crowns, the bones of weeds—speak of life in spite of the presence of death. Thus, this death, this time of waiting, can be affirmed. The movement of the first two stanzas is gentle, restrained. It speaks of the potential present in the particulars of nature and in the poet's ability to observe them so closely. Both the presence of the things of the earth and the poet's ability to wait attending them in this in-between time create a moment of stillness, of gathering together, of opening to fullness:

Light traveled over the wide field;
Stayed.
The weeds stopped swinging.
The mind moved, not alone,
Through the clear air, in the silence.

In this moment the self is able to be at ease with itself and the other life around it. There is separation now, and yet there is solidarity. There is a sense of harmony, of tranquility, not beyond the world and the things of the world but with them, through them. Growing out of this moment come questions once more. But they are no longer desperate, no longer hovering frantically between life and death; there is acceptance:

Was it light?
Was it light within?
Was it light within light?
Stillness becoming alive,
Yet still?

The light, the light within, the light within light create a reflexive sort of action and perception, a mutual, reciprocal sharing contained within a moment of becoming and stillness. The poem closes on a note of expectation and tranquility: expectation because the moment has passed and the darkness will come again, as will the light, and tranquility because the lost son has found and been found and exists within the world to face both the darkness and the light. The lines narrow down almost to nothing, but it is a nothing that is not an emptiness but a fullness, a waiting that is not a despairing but an attending:

> A lively understandable spirit
> Once entertained you.
> It will come again.
> Be still.
> Wait.

What happens in this moment of light happens in the poem and through the poem. However, the fact that experiences of joy seem to occur when the poet becomes aware of the life that exists outside himself and is able to enter into some kind of relationship with it indicates that Martin Buber's I-Thou understanding of the world may help to open up this moment. He presents the view that it is only in I-Thou relations that meaning enters the world, that is, only as persons take their stand in relation. He describes three spheres in which this occurs: in our life with nature, in our life with human beings, and in our life with spiritual beings. It is with the sphere of nature that we will be most concerned when thinking of the first section of Roethke's poetry. Buber holds that from the first–with archaic human beings or the child–a person shares in an I-Thou relationship with the world. This natural relationship occurs before the I has been distinguished from the primal, undivided world out of which it comes. But gradually the separation from this unity begins, and a new relationship must be established through the separate I: "He has stepped out of the glowing darkness of chaos into the cool light of creation. But he does not possess it yet; he must first draw it truly out, he must make it into a reality for himself, he must find for himself his own world by seeing and hearing and touching and shaping it."

By entering into such relations the I emerges and is then able to enter into relations in consciousness of itself. With this, however, comes the possibility (and inevitability) of saying "It" to the world. With this tension, this twofold nature, human beings must live. Do we look back with longing, then, to that time of natural unity that had no tension? A person does have a longing, but it is

> not as though his yearning meant a longing to return, as those suppose who see in the spirit–confusing it with their intellect–a parasite of nature, when it is rather (though exposed to diverse illnesses) nature's best flower. But the yearning is for the cosmic

> connexion, with its true *Thou,* of this life that has burst forth into spirit.

Thus, although persons lose their natural connection with the world, individuation provides the possibility for real relationships and thus for the development of the spirit.

But how does the moment of I-Thou come about? It is not an "experience," for an experience must be *of* something, that is, of an object, an It. It comes in silent patience, and it is the sharing of a reality, the standing in a presence. It is spirit, and that spirit is not found in the I nor in the Thou but between them. It is not made manifest, it simply *is.* In this moment of relation our perceptions of the world will be changed. There is no subject-object split; there is only I-Thou. There is no past or future; "the *I* is aware with a single awareness of its solidarity of connexion and of its separation."

The similarities between Buber's understanding of the development and meaning of the self and Roethke's may help to bring a greater understanding of the last section of "The Lost Son." We have seen that there is a moment in which the self and the world seem to exist in a serene yet dynamic harmony. It seems to me that this is very much like the moment described by Buber as "standing in relation." In Roethke's poetry moments of joy and new life come when he can reach out to something beyond the self; in "The Lost Son" this would be some form of nature. The development of the I out of a primordial unity is also similar in these two men. Using Buber's understanding of what happens once the self has been separated from the unity, we can say one further thing about the last two sections. I noted above that in the fourth section time and place are restored. Through the coming of consciousness order is perceived; the laws of causality and space and time with which we normally live are established. But these disappear again in the final section, and Buber's thought helps to make this clear. Established here is a new kind of unity—a spiritual relation, Buber would call it—as the self is able to enter into relation and share in the presence of spirit, in a wholeness, without losing itself. Thus, the poem is cyclical or perhaps spiral because a new wholeness is established, a wholeness that includes nature but also includes the self, the individual: a spiritual wholeness. A final quotation by Buber seems to describe the journey of the lost son well: "It is a finding without seeking, a discovering of the primal, of origin. His sense of *Thou,* which cannot be satiated till he finds the endless *Thou,* had the *Thou* present to it from the beginning; the presence had only to become wholly real to him in the reality of the hallowed life of the world."

"TO HAVE THE WHOLE AIR"

The other long poems of *The Lost Son*—"The Long Alley," "A Field of Light," and "The Shape of the Fire"—make a similar search and follow a similar pattern, though it is not always made so explicit and though there is adaptation as the poet proceeds in his journey forward. "The Long Alley" begins with a river. But it is polluted water, running slowly and carrying dead fish. "A Field of Light" begins with a similar image of water that is not life-giving:

> Came to lakes; came to dead water,
> Ponds with moss and leaves floating,
> Planks sunk in the sand.

Chaos is also present in this dark time:

> Reached for a grape
> And the leaves changed;
> A stone's shape
> Became a clam.

Similar images are given in "The Shape of the Fire":

> Water recedes to the crying of spiders.
> An old scow bumps over black rocks.
> A cracked pod calls.
> Mother me out of here. What more will the bones
> allow?
> Will the sea give the wind suck? A toad folds
> into a stone.
> These flowers are all fangs. Comfort me, fury.
> Wake me, witch, we'll do the dance of rotten
> sticks.

Thus, we begin in a time of darkness and stagnation, of loss of identity and the necessity of facing the irrational and chaotic. As is generally true in Roethke's poetry, in such a time the protagonist is isolated and narcissistic as he says, "Return the gaze of a pond" ("The Long Alley") and "My meat eats me" ("The Shape of the Fire").

One of the reasons for this isolation and for the chaos is the fire of his awakening sexuality, which is alternately guilt ridden, repulsive, and riotously life-filled. For example, in section 3 of "The Long Alley" the question comes, "If we detach / The head of a match" what will the response of the animals be? Will we escape them? Or "Will the goat's mouth / Have the last laugh?" The last line of the poem is "I'll take the fire." Detaching the head of the match would eliminate the possibility of this fire, which connects him to his fleshy animal roots. The fire of the passions is a common enough association for us to make here. But, significantly, fire is also associated with the spirit. Destroying it to escape his fiery roots may also quench the flaming of the spirit.

As he comes to the acceptance of his own identity as both body and spirit, he also overcomes the isolation and is able to reach out beyond himself. "Shall I call the flowers?" he asks, and the invocation that follows is filled with a love and tenderness for the flowers that come from both a faith in their power to help and a reverence and joy for what they are in themselves. The stanza begins with a plea for communion:

> Come littlest, come tenderest,
> Come whispering over the small waters,
> Reach me rose, sweet one, still moist in the loam,
> Come, come out of the shade, the cool ways,
> The long alleys of string and stem.

"Bend down . . . Lean," he continues, calling on "small breathers, creepers and winders . . . Cyclamen dripping and lilies." He creates a feeling of the movement, growth, livingness of all about him and of the felicitous nature of the earth. This movement to the other is given beautifully in "A Field of Light":

> I could watch! I could watch!
> I saw the separateness of all things!
> My heart lifted up with the great grasses;
> The weeds believed me, and the nesting birds.
>
> . . . .
>
> And I walked, I walked through the light air;
> I moved with the morning.

Although no explanation can be given for how these grace-full moments are come to, they always involve the reaching out to another, and they follow or contain reflections on the past. In "The Shape of the Fire," for example, section 4 presents a return through memory to earlier times. The previous section has provided the image of the rose, and it ends, "The redeemer comes a dark way." These images provide the assurance that calls forth memories no longer of chaos but of gladness and unity. He describes the beauty and serenity of his childhood world and also his unity with it:

> Morning-fair, follow me further back
> Into that minnowy world of weeds and ditches,
>
> . . . .
>
> When the sun for me glinted the sides of a sand grain,
> And my intent stretched over the buds at their first trembling.
>
> . . . .
>
> Death was not. I lived in a simple drowse:
>
> . . . .
>
> And love, love sang toward.

It is the time before the redeemer and his dark way, a time of potential: he will awaken from his watery drowse to an active participation in the life of flowers and of human beings. Marcel's term "ingathering" describes well the process of realizing a potential that was then present but can now be brought to life. He seeks to reestablish the earlier time not as an escape from identity or a step toward the return to undifferentiated chaos but as a positive state that is to be affirmed and developed. The man must move the dark way of the redeemer, but he can draw on the potential contained in the "simple drowse" as he proceeds on his journey.

Section 5 describes the end of the journey, or at least a step on the way. As with "The Lost Son," it is a moment of light, of gathering together, of fullness. And again as with "The Lost Son," it is similar in many ways to the preceding section. The difference between the two sections in "The Shape of the Fire" is that the dark way has been traveled. What is discovered is not the original joy of the child but the received joy of the adult who has traveled through memory and experience to the present reality; that reality is filled with light and with communion and can be affirmed in its present moment because of the knowledge of the darkness that is also part of reality. The affirmation of the earth does not deny the darkness, the terror of reality, but it finds in that reality that which brings joy and unity. As would be expected in Roethke's poetry, the affirmation that comes at the end of this poem is filled with the things of the natural world and with human perceptions of and participation with them. The moment that is created and affirmed through these images is, as in "The Lost Son," a moment of stillness and of fullness in which life is shared in all its abundance. It is life that has about it a wholeness:

> To have the whole air!–
> The light, the full sun
> Coming down on the flowerheads,
> . . . .
> To see cyclamen veins become clearer in early sunlight,
> . . . .
> To stare into the after-light, the glitter left on the lake's surface,
> When the sun has fallen behind a wooded island;
> To follow the drops sliding from a lifted oar,
> Held up, while the rower breathes, and the small boat drifts quietly
> shoreward.

It is life that has about it a sense of grace:

> To know that light falls and fills, often without our knowing,
> As an opaque vase fills to the brim from a quick pouring,
> Fills and trembles at the edge yet does not flow over,
> Still holding and feeding the stem of the contained flower.

Roethke said that the journey would involve a "perpetual slipping-back, then a going-forward; but there is some 'progress.'" We see here the same struggle as in "The Lost Son" and a similar moment of affirmation. But where the potential for life and for the grace of the "lively spirit" was emphasized in "The Lost Son," we find that in "The Shape of the Fire" the emphasis is on the moment of fullness. But this is not final either. This is the last poem in the collection *The Lost Son* and so stands as an ending in that work. But the sequence continues in *Praise to the End!* and the periods of darkness and light, sorrow and joy, continue as well.

"HELLO, THINGY SPIRIT"

With the publication of *The Waking* these long poems from *The Lost Son* appeared as part of a longer sequence in which the poems of *Praise to the End!* part 1, precede the long poems of *The Lost Son*, which are followed by the poems of *Praise to the End!* part 2, beginning with "Praise to the End!" The sequence ends with "O, Thou Opening, O," which is a new poem in *The Waking*. Although this placement makes sense in terms of progression–the poems of *Praise to the End!* part 1, depicting a childhood understanding that precedes that of "The Lost Son"–the tone and style of the new poems in *Praise to the End!* are clearly different from those of *The Lost Son* and are closely related to each other despite the great difference in the progression between "Where Knock Is Open Wide" and "I Cry, Love! Love!" I will discuss the poems in the order in which they were written rather than as two parts of *Praise to the End!* even though such a reading is useful to see Roethke's progression.

The six poems in the first part of *Praise to the End!* are unified, representing the growth of the child from infancy to adolescence. The father and mother and both child and adolescent sexuality are important elements in the poems. They record the difficulty and attendant guilt of separating from the parents as well as the later problems and joys of sexuality. The poems do not follow the pattern set up in *The Lost Son* poems too closely. There are the same periods of confusion and darkness as well as times of rejoicing, but they do not correspond to the sections of each poem. It is rather the sequence as a whole that moves toward the beginnings of identity that come with adolescence. Roethke begins the sequence with "Where Knock Is Open Wide," a phrase from Christopher Smart's poem "A Song to David":

> Where ask is have, where seek is find,
> Where knock is open wide.

Roethke says that he takes several of the titles for the poems of this volume from "ancestors" he admired. Other ancestors he refers to are Wordsworth, from whose *The Prelude* he takes the title "Praise to the End!" Blake, from whose "Visions of the Daughters of Albion" he takes "I Cry Love! Love!" Vaughan, from whose "The Revival" he takes "Unfold! Unfold!" and William Strode, from whose poem beginning, "O lull me, lull me, charming air!" he takes the title "O Lull Me, Lull Me."

"Where Knock Is Open Wide" seems to refer both to the actual birth of the child and the state of childhood generally when the whole world is still open. The language and rhythms work to create this open world. We are placed in the mind of the child and asked to see the world once more as it was before we established our habitual cause-and-effect ways of organizing it. In that early time "A kitten can / Bite with his feet" and "His ears haven't time" accurately described the way the world was; this is not non-sense but the sense that comes without categories that tell us how to think. If we are able to experience this infant world in all its newness as a second birth, presumably we will be able to experience a rebirth, a spiritual birth, with the poet as he moves into adolescence.

This is an additional meaning of the title of the poem—the openness of the world to the spiritually childlike.

"Where Knock Is Open Wide" begins with the creation of the world of the small child. The question raised by evolutionary theory of our relation to other living things occurs to the small child in this way:

> What's the time, papa-seed?
> Everything has been twice.
> My father is a fish.

The meanings of these three lines seem multiple, as associative thinking often is. It seems he was present at the time of his conception because everything has been twice. And his father the fish could refer to the sperm cell that was to be him. But in terms of evolution his father was also a fish, and then "everything has been twice" would refer to a prehuman existence he led. In either case we have the sense of a continuum of living things in which this individual engages fully. Evolution is more than a theory. Roethke continues this theme through these poems, including in the boy's living ancestry the trees as well as animal forms. In the second part of *Praise to the End!* he develops the theme of active evolution quite extensively. His purpose is to create a sense of vital connection between living things. The participation and communion that are described in both *The Lost Son* poems and the later *Praise to the End!* poems are seen here to be more than chance or choice. There is an undeniable rootedness connecting the living things of the earth and binding them together in a way that humans can deny only at the cost of losing their complete identity. These connections are pointed to in various ways throughout the poems in this section, as in "Bring the Day!" where the convergence of certain living things is described:

> The herrings are awake.
> What's all the singing between?—
> Is it with whispers and kissing?—
> I've listened into the least waves.
> The grass says what the wind says:
> Begin with the rock;
> End with water.
>
> When I stand, I'm almost a tree.
> Leaves, do you like me any?
> A swan needs a pond.
> The worm and the rose
> Both love
> Rain.

The victory that is achieved in these poems comes through active participation with the whole realm of nature and through a response on the part of nature.

Additional themes involve the death of the father and his subsequent presence as a ghost, in these poems mainly a reproving and deadening force: "the ghost of some great howl / Dead in a wall" ("Give Way, Ye Gates"). In "Where Knock Is Open Wide" the death is preceded by a memory similar to the one in the greenhouse in section 4 of "The Lost Son." It begins with the memory of a fishing trip in which

> I was sad for a fish.
> Don't hit him on the boat, I said.
> Look at him puff. He's trying to talk.
> Papa threw him back.

The father is again seen to have the power of life and death, as in the greenhouse, and this memory brings up the greenhouse in this poem as well:

> He watered the roses.
> His thumb had a rainbow.
> The stems said, Thank you.
> Dark came early.
>
> That was before. I fell! I fell!

The fall, presumably, is from that childhood Eden into the world of separation and guilt (portrayed in these poems largely as involving conscious sexuality). From this point must come the knowledge of the world that will allow him to rejoice in his separateness, in his identity. But for now, at the point of beginning his journey, he knows only the anguish of separation: "Maybe God has a house. / But not here." "Love helps the sun. / But not enough" ("I Need, I Need").

But the sense of possibility is also present in these poems, promising the coming of the individual who can rejoice in his separateness in a world that is interconnected: "It's time to begin! / To begin!" ("Bring the Day!")

> We'll be at the business of what might be
> Looking toward what we are.
>
> . . . .
>
> The deep stream remembers:
> Once I was a pond.
> What slides away
> Provides. ("Give Way, Ye Gates")

I insist!
I am. ("Sensibility! Oh La!")

I'm more than when I was born;
I could say hello to things;
I could talk to a snail;
I see what sings!
What sings! ("O Lull Me, Lull Me")

The new poems of the second part of *Praise to the End!* are both a continuation of the concerns and style of the poems of the first part and also the completion of the sequence that begins with "The Lost Son." Phrases from the opening of the first poem ("Praise to the End!") and the closing of the last poem of the sequence ("O, Thou Opening, O" from *The Waking*) connect them and give an indication of the emphasis of this section of the poetry. "Praise to the End!" begins:

It's dark in this wood, soft mocker.
For whom have I swelled like a seed?
What a bone-ache I have.
Father of tensions, I'm down to my skin at last.

And "O, Thou Opening, O" ends:

I keep dreaming of bees.
This flesh has airy bones.
Going is knowing.
I see; I seek;
I'm near.
Be true,
Skin.

The importance of "skin" is worked out in several ways in the poems. One has to do with the conflict between the spirit and the body. "I hate my epidermal dress," Roethke says in an early poem, "Epidermal Macabre," and this struggle goes on throughout the poetry. The problem is inherent in Roethke's understanding of the world. It is clear that he delights in the physicalness of the world, in things–flowers, birds, dirt; in other people–when they do enter his poetry their physical description is important; and in his own body as he frolics with his love or with the bears ("Words for the Wind," "Four for Sir John Davies").

It is this world he loves and it is here he finds what he affirms. But the feeling is not unambiguous both because he has a longing for a union that can never be complete as long as he is an individual–and his individual body is the clearest sign of this–and also because his body grows old. It is well to rejoice in the cycles of nature that promise new birth with each death, but what happens when it is your own death that is seen as part of the cycle? This question appears throughout the poetry, and tentative, groping answers gradually come.

The skin, then, raises the question of the preeminence of the body or the spirit and the question of death. In addition, skin is what dead men do not have, and in this sense it is a symbol for life. The dead and ghosts, both as being in opposition to living and as being the conveyors of the past with its guilt and its joy, are part of the poems of this section as well. "Praise to the End!" begins with images of ghosts and death that speak of isolation and guilt. There is a movement toward acceptance of the past and through this a new power, which the poet expresses near the end of the poem in "Ghost, come closer" and "My ghosts are all gay." "Unfold! Unfold!" reveals a similar pattern in the movement from "The dead speak noise" to

> In their harsh thickets
> The dead thrash.
> They help.

Finally, on the other side of life, skin raises the associated questions of evolution, of the time before skin. Again the feelings are ambiguous. We find the poet both praising the present state of his evolution, his existence as a human being, and at other times resisting the inner forces that compel him forward out of the mire into individuality. These poems are written from the point of view of the adult, but there is a going back not only to childhood and adolescence but also through his entire evolutionary history. He longs to come to his spiritual identity, but how is he to do it? By returning to his origins, going back to the mire, and touching once more the roots of his life? By going forward to the realm of the spirit and touching the unity of the life force? Neither alternative is satisfactory:

> By snails, by leaps of frog, I came here, spirit.
> Tell me, body without skin, does a fish sweat?
> I can't crawl back through those veins,
> I ache for another choice.
> The cliffs! The cliffs! They fling me back.
> Eternity howls in the last crags.

But through the struggle he is able to accept both his evolutionary roots in the earth and his newly developing spiritual nature:

> I'm awake all over:
> I've crawled from the mire, alert as a saint or a dog.
> ("Praise to the End!")

And in "I Cry, Love! Love!" the threat of the return has given way to a joy in his beginnings and a solid sense of his present identity:

> I care for a cat's cry and the hugs, live as water.
> I've traced these words in sand with a vestigial tail;
> Now the gills are beginning to cry.
> Such a sweet noise: I can't sleep for it.
> Bless me and the maze I'm in!
> Hello, thingy spirit.

This seems to be what Roethke has come to by the end of this first stage of his poetry. A "thingy spirit" brings together those aspects of himself with and against which he has been struggling. If only for the moment, we have here that delicate balance in which wholeness is experienced, a wholeness that comes out of the darkness and makes possible a moment of light. In the final section of "Unfold! Unfold!" Roethke says,

> A house for wisdom; a field for revelation.
> Speak to the stones, and the stars answer.
> At first the visible obscures:
> Go where light is.
> . . . .
> What grace I have is enough.

Thus, Roethke comes in these poems to a sense of life that is filled with reverence for the fullness of life, which he calls grace. He comes to this through the things of the earth and through the recognition of himself as a thing of the earth that is also to be revered. The sense of I-Thou fills the moment and gives meaning to both its participants. And it has come about in these poems through a going back, an ingathering in which the poet has drawn on the full potential that he has as a living being. Having reached this point, it is possible for him to move into a realm that contains not only flowers and earth (although these are never left behind in the poetry) but also human relationships–that reaching out to another person that presents the same questions of individuality and unity that occurred in this "first world." It will be the exploration of this second realm of meaning that will be the subject of many of the new poems of *The Waking.*

CHAPTER THREE

TO BE FULLY HUMAN

The new poems of *The Waking* and *Words for the Wind* are a continuation of the movement toward a greater realization of spirit. The pattern of moving forward and then back remains but is less pronounced. The self has made that backward journey and has come to know itself, and though those original roots are never left behind they cease to play the dominant role in the struggle forward. The element that becomes more important in these poems is "the other" in the form of the human lover. This is not to say that the natural world is no longer important in the poetry. Nature as a source of life and communion remains part of Roethke's poetry to the end. But intermixed with images of the natural, there are now relationships that are specifically human. And if the primary struggle of the earlier poems was coming to the self, the flowering of the spirit is now central.

One of the first poems in *The Waking,* "A Light Breather," presents this new emphasis as well as the continuity with the earlier poems. The poem is about the spirit and its workings in the world: "The spirit moves,/ Yet stays," the poem begins. It goes on to describe this movement and stasis in terms of natural life—a blossom, a minnow, a snail. The images and analogies resemble those in the greenhouse poems, but now it is the soul as the growing thing that is the center of attention, and natural images work to exemplify this life. As in the earlier poems, what is being described is more than an analogy. As the flowers and fish and insects are an integral part of their environment and are involved in the process of nature, being indeed part of that process, so the spirit takes its life from—its life is *in*—the surrounding world. The process is described in terms of the things of nature as a movement outward, an opening, that is in part caused by the world and that relates to the world:

Stirs as a blossom stirs,
Still wet from its bud-sheath,
Slowly unfolding,
Turning in the light with its tendrils.

The spirit is also fully involved in the process of life around it, held to it yet moving of its own will as well:

Plays as a minnow plays,
Tethered to a limp weed, swinging,
Tail around, nosing in and out of the current,
Its shadows loose, a watery finger.

And, finally, it is an inward movement, a turning to the self that yet does not leave behind the world of which it is a part:

Moves, like the snail,
Still inward,
Taking and embracing its surroundings.

The connection between the world of nature and the spirit is thus made through the images Roethke uses to embody the spirit and through the structuring of the poem. The final lines continue the description of the snail, which has become as well a description of the spirit:

Never wishing itself away,
Unafraid of what it is,
A music in a hood,
A small thing,
Singing.

In this moment there is a balance between the world of the spirit and the world of nature; they are, in fact, part of one world. However, the question of body and spirit is never finally resolved. As it appeared in the earlier poems, it recurs through the poems of this section. This question is raised by the love poems through the tension between physical and spiritual love, which is temporarily resolved in such poems as "Four for Sir John Davies" and "Words for the Wind" but which, again, is never finally settled. The more mystical side of love appears in such poems as "The Dream" and "The Visitant," and the sensual is dominant in "I Knew a Woman" and "The Sensualists." The tension between body and spirit is also encountered in these poems through the realization of the coming of old age, the deterioration of the body, the approach of death. This is a theme that occurs in the earlier poems as well, but it takes on greater importance in such poems as "The Sententious Man," "A Walk in Late Summer," and the longer sequences *The Dying Man* and *Meditations of an Old Woman.*

The love poems raise the additional question of the nature of human relationships in general. What does it mean to reach out to another person, and how is it done? What are the differences and similarities between the reaching out to a person that occurs in these poems and the reaching out to the lives of the natural world that provided the I-Thou relationship in the earlier poems? It seems that there is something peculiar to human relationships, though this is not necessarily more significant than the relationships of the poet with the particulars of the natural world. But this is the area of life in which, according to Buber's understanding, the person takes on his or her most fully human nature and in which the life of dialogue is most fully developed. Communication through the I-Thou relationship is before words with the things of the world and beyond words with the things of the spirit. It is in this in-between ground that the uniqueness of human speech becomes important. This is, of course, the realm of all Roethke's poetry. It is through dialogue in language that we have his poems. Thus, it is through human relationships that we know by analogy the I-Thou of the earlier poems, where objects of the natural world join in the relationship, and the I-Thou of the last poems, where it is the "eternal Thou" who is met in relationship.

Gabriel Marcel adds to this understanding of dialogue and human relationships. He asserts that there is a quality of magic, of mystery, to all true meetings:

> The very act by which we incline ourselves towards a presence is essentially different from that through which we grasp at an object. . . . Between the two notions of gathering to oneself, or welcoming and seizing, there is a fundamental underlying difference. . . . A presence can, in the last analysis, only be invoked or evoked, the evocation being fundamentally and essentially magical.

The terms Marcel uses to describe this meeting of two people are descriptive of what occurs in many of the love poems of this section. Although they may also describe the earlier poems as well, what is distinctive about the relationships here is the possibility for human speech; Marcel says that words themselves may be essentially magical. They may evoke a presence not only in poetry, which would again be true of all of Roethke's poems, but also within the sphere of the meeting of two people. Thus, this section of the poetry possesses uniqueness in that it deals with the relationship between two persons, and it is central to all of the poetry in that through the language of human relationships we understand the earlier and later poetry as well.

The poems of *The Waking* and *Words for the Wind* are not built around the obvious structure of descent and ascent found in many of the long poems of *Praise to the End!* but there is a forward and backward movement from one poem to the other, so that the placement of the poems results in their commenting on each other and presenting various facets of experience. This suits Roethke's way of seeing the world as a series of differing, often contradictory experiences that only occasionally resolve themselves into a vision of unity—which is again broken into its contrasting elements. The primary tensions that arise are concerned with the specifically human aspect of existence as they are seen in the love of one person for another and in the conscious apprehension of the movement toward death. In both cases the struggle of body and spirit is central. These questions of human existence are embodied in relationships between the self and the self; the self and the other; and, as in the earlier poems, the self and the natural world. As before, whatever the poet's final affirmation, it is both achieved and presented through the life that comes from participation in the things and persons of the world in which he lives.

"THE WAKING"

The new poems of *The Waking* move us into this world, and with "A Light Breather" there is a waking to a new relationship between the spirit and the natural world. "The Visitant" also reveals this new sense of the spirit as well as providing another bridge between the two sections, as it begins with many images that are familiar to the world of the Lost Son. There are images of nature that are usually indicative of the coming of new life: clouds, wind, water, trees. And there are images of that primeval world of "slip-ooze" and slime that dominated in the earlier poems. The tone of the poem also contributes to the feeling of that world of the collective unconscious and archetypal images. After a time of preparation and waiting during which there is participation with the things of nature in a moment of stillness, the second section gives what the first has been waiting for:

Slow, slow as a fish she came,
Slow as a fish coming forward,
Swaying in a long wave;
Her skirts not touching a leaf,
Her white arms reaching towards me.

"She" is presented as being in total accord with nature, a part of the natural process, yet something distinct—a "visitant." In a complementary manner she is so described through alliteration and repetition that her presence is intermingled with the sounds and the activity of the natural world; yet she, the other, still enters as a distinct person. Because of the primordial, dreamlike nature of the poem and the connections with the world of the lost son, on one level the visitant can be compared to the Jungian concept of the anima. The poet is dealing with hidden aspects of himself that take form generally in the world of nature and now specifically in the woman. As in the earlier poems such explorations were a way of moving out to the things of the world, so "The Visitant" seems a prelude to the movement to persons in the world.

Jung describes the anima as "the *a priori* element in [men's] moods, reactions, impulses, and whatever else is spontaneous in psychic life. It is something that lives of itself, that makes us live; it is a life behind consciousness that cannot be completely integrated with it, but from which, on the contrary, consciousness arises." It is the feminine side of men, which "gives relationship and relatedness to a man's consciousness." The visitant in this poem, then, has several meanings. She is the coming of the feminine in the self and in the world; that is, there is a connectedness between man and woman in the nature of things just as there is a connectedness between the human and nonhuman elements of life. Also, the feminine is a symbol for the relatedness of all things and the ability to reach out to another in the world, which are central to the poetry. This, coupled with the appellation given to the woman—"the visitant"—makes her coming a movement of grace, a conveyance of spirit that yet comes through the body of nature (both through the participation of nature in her coming and in the visitant herself, who, though she has archetypal power, is also a woman). Although we are not presented here with an individual woman whose flesh and blood we can experience, as we are in later love poems, this is part of the reality both of the self and the woman on the one hand and of a human relationship on the other, and it is clearly through the forms of nature that she comes.

"Elegy for Jane" and "Old Lady's Winter Words" present two other sides of the woman. Both poems are concerned with particular individuals, as opposed to the more universal portrayal of the visitant. And both are concerned with the coming of death, as opposed to the renewal of life in "The Visitant." But there are extreme differences between these two poems as well. The one is about a young girl who is dead, and it is presented through the voice of one who loved her; the other is about an old woman who is dying and is presented in her own voice. "Elegy for Jane" presents the feeling of loss suffered by the poet at the death of a young girl who loved life fully and exulted in the things of the world. She is described in terms of flowers and birds, and both her joy and sadness are revealed through the things of the earth.

They also reveal the speaker's sadness at the time of her death. Both her lost presence and his sorrow receive expression through the concrete world:

> My sparrow, you are not here,
> Waiting like a fern, making a spiny shadow.
> The sides of wet stones cannot console me,
> Nor the moss, wound with the last light.

In the final stanza the girl is again addressed in terms of nonhuman endearment as "My maimed darling, my skittery pigeon," but the loss is finally expressed in terms of a uniquely human relationship:

> Over this damp grave I speak the words of my love:
> I, with no rights in this matter,
> Neither father nor lover.

This poem is one of the best of the few poems in which Roethke tried to capture an individual person, a specific character. He succeeds in creating for us Jane and, as the focal point of the poem, his feelings for her and his sense of loss at her death. This is done very simply and subtly through her association with nature and through the final statement of his love.

The "old lady" in the following poem presents quite a different picture of life and death. As one who is experiencing age, she raises the questions of the increasing decrepitude of the body and the increasing awareness of the imminence of death. Through her Roethke presents a reality with which he struggles in many later poems. How are we to rejoice in the body and the pleasures of the senses and believe in the inextricable unity and concordance of body and spirit, when old age says we shall forget the joys of the senses and death says our bodies shall die? I was a young girl once, the old lady says. I rejoiced in myself and the world. But now that the times of dryness, of winter, have come on me, in what is there to rejoice? The poem moves between the present and the past, the images from the past possessing life and vitality, those from the present, loneliness and discontentment.

The greatest hope in the poem comes near the beginning. The ending is an expression of the despair of the spirit as it loses its ties with the world. There is no resolution in the poem, though some possible hope is suggested through her plea for

> some minstrel of what's to be,
> A bird singing into the beyond,
> The marrow of God, talking.

But she cannot return to the past to find joy, and she cannot yet hear that bird singing into the beyond and find hope for joy in the future. All she can affirm is the necessity of facing life squarely–in despair if that is what she feels–and by this she makes an affirmation of life in spite of despair. Nonetheless, she has become separated from the joys of the earth, and, alone in the old silences, "The spirit / Hardens." The poem narrows down to the one word, and we are left without hope. The loss of life here is significantly different from the loss in "Elegy for Jane." In "Elegy for Jane" the loss is of one who loved life and participated in it fully, and the loss comes to one who loved Jane. With the old lady the loss is more bitter, more devastating, because it is seen to be part of life. The old lady's despair does not seem to be an accident, as Jane's death does, but the awful possibility is suggested that this is in the nature of things. This is only one possible understanding of life, and not the one with which Roethke ends, but the old lady's determination to look at reality unflinchingly reveals Roethke's desire to do the same. If he is to come to a more affirmative experience as he nears the end of life, it will not be because he has ignored the actuality of old age and approaching death.

With "Old Lady's Winter Words" a change in style is evident. The change is reflected in the use of a persona and in the new rhythms. The lines are no longer long and flowing but are short, often three-beat, restrained and classic in the manner of Yeats. This new style dominates the poems of these two volumes. Yeats was a strong influence on Roethke both in terms of concerns–though their resolutions seem quite different–and in stylistic matters.

In "Four for Sir John Davies" both Sir John Davies and Yeats are called on–Davies through the title and through the image of the dance and Yeats through the last stanza of the first section of the poem:

I take this cadence from a man named Yeats;
. . . .
Yes, I was dancing-mad, and how
That came to be the bears and Yeats would know.

John Davies's "Orchestra," written in 1596, portrays the dance as a universal enterprise in which all opposites are reconciled. This is applied on the one hand to the universe itself, which is seen as engaging in an intricately ordered dance that results in the harmony of the spheres. On the other hand it is applied to the union of man and woman, and the suitor describes this universal participation to Queen Penelope in an attempt to persuade her to dance with him.

For Yeats the concept of the dance was also important. Richard Ellmann reports that the two symbols that most fully expressed Yeats's understanding of the equilibrium of the Thirteenth Cycle of his *Vision* were the dance and sexual intercourse. Thus, there is a parallel between Davies's well-ordered Elizabethan world and the possibility for quite a different order that Yeats describes in *A Vision.* The equilibrium expressed in the dance and in sexual union also involves for Yeats a reconciliation of opposites. In "The Double Vision of Michael Robartes" the dancer moves between the Sphinx (the intellect, the mind) and the Buddha (the heart, the body) and in doing so brings both into a balance. Here, as in the image of the dancer and the dance at the end of "Among School Children," the dancer brings together the changing and the changeless, the form and the actualization, and so creates a moment of equilibrium. The dance symbolizes the coming together of the body and the spirit through a very physical action that yet involves more than the body; or, said another way, it is a physical and spiritual activity in which those two elements are inextricably and necessarily bound together.

Roethke draws on these poets and pays tribute to them by entering their world of the dance. He does not live in the orderly world supplied by Davies's Elizabethan harmony or Yeats's private vision. And he does not deal with either the dance or sexual union in just the way they do, though the idea of reconciliation of opposites—the physical and the spiritual, the temporal and the eternal—is an important aspect of his work as well. But Roethke's world is much more open than theirs; it lacks their rigid structure and so their greater certainty. The world that he is interested in as his dancing room is a world of light and dark, a world of ambiguity, at least as humans perceive it. He can only ask the questions and perhaps propose his own answers, but he cannot know, finally, if his perceptions are correct. Thus, "Four for Sir John Davies" is a poem of many questions and few absolute answers:

what is desire?–
The impulse to make someone else complete?
. . . .
The world is for the living. Who are they?

It is a world of contradictions, where there is "Incomprehensible gaiety and dread" and where "The flesh can make the spirit visible," while at the same time "The visible obscures." The images of light and dark further suggest the reality of a world that is made up of the body and the spirit, the living and the dead, the bears and Yeats. It is a world that contains all the ambiguity of the world we know, yet somehow, in spite of the apparently discordant elements, it is one world, one related process in which all the elements participate; and it is only when they are all present that a wholeness is achieved. The spirit and the flesh serve to reveal and realize each other; in fact, it becomes very difficult to ascertain where one begins and the other leaves off. For brief moments the union of man and woman, body and spirit, light and darkness is complete. But more often these elements are in conflict, and the poet must struggle to bring them together.

Roethke describes his state as being "dancing-mad" and says that the bears and Yeats would understand this–the bears because of their natural, unrestrained response to life and Yeats because of the sometimes violent, wrenching process of reconciliation, in which extremes are blended but also brought to their peak (for example, in "Crazy Jane Grown Old Looks at the Dancers" and in the "life-in-death" and "death-in-life" of the dance in "Byzantium"). There is a hint of madness in such a world because of the openness and intensity of it. For Roethke being "dancing-mad" involves the desire both to embrace his world and to fling himself beyond it, to become wholly a person, a man of both flesh and spirit, and to lose himself in an impersonal, changeless eternity. He throws himself totally into life, into his dance, his love, not knowing which of these things it will lead to. Being dancing mad is having the passion to realize himself, to open himself to what is without knowing who he really is or what reality is. Thus, he has no dancing master; he must stumble along, discovering as he does what the dance is and where it will lead him.

Sam Keen in *Apology for Wonder* uses the dance as the symbol for the Dionysian mode of life–life open to possibility and wonder. The dance

> is flux, movement, a dynamic power which assumes form for a moment and then changes. There is no end-point, no complete product. . . . Everything is a fraction, incomplete without its counterpart. In the dance of life, male and female, work and play,

> creativity and fallowness, day and night, and life and death belong together in a *rhythmic* unity. Identity is in movement.

But to live with this constant movement and not be overwhelmed by it another element is needed–wisdom:

> *The wise man knows what time it is in his own life and in the life of the community....* Thus, the wise man is able to give himself gracefully to seemingly contradictory experiences, because he knows that they belong to different seasons of life, all of which are necessary to the whole.... The wise man is a dancer; he hears the music issuing from his situation, he is sensitive to his partners, and he moves boldly to commit himself to the rhythmic patterns that emerge in the dance.... The sense of timing which is the essence of wisdom comes only when one trusts oneself to the dance.

The wisdom of the dancer in Roethke's poem emerges as he explores with his partner the regions of the body and the spirit, searching out the rhythms of this dance, which he trusts has a pattern but which can be discovered only through participation and openness.

As we look at the poem itself, we see this exploration through the image of the dance. The reference to Davies's universal harmony sets up both the possibility of an order and the fact that it cannot be found in the same way Davies found it. There is a lightness to the tone that reveals the way the poet views both his world and the dance:

> And I have made a promise to my ears
> I'll sing and whistle romping with the bears.

He will create his own music if the spheres are no longer humming, and he picks as his partner the clumsy, laughable bear. The dance, he says, is in the mind, and this subjectivity is important throughout the poem. Even of his bears he is uncertain; did he really see one

> slide
> Down a steep hillside on a cake of ice,–
> Or was that in a book?

Uncertain about the nature of the dance, he tries to fling himself (his shadow) beyond this world while at the same time his flesh and blood leap with song (though a wordless song). He lacks a dancing master "To teach my toes to listen to my tongue." And, finally, he mentions the "joyless motion of a stone." At every step there are discrepancies, apparent contradictions. How do toes listen? What motion does a stone have? What is created for us is a world that is not the orderly, predictable one of Sir John Davies, though the dance he heard continues yet. It is closer to the vision of Yeats, but it has a quality of lightness about it that that more serious world lacks. He refers in the final stanza to Yeats:

> I take this cadence from a man named Yeats;
> I take it, and I give it back again:
> For other tunes and other wanton beats
> Have tossed my heart and fiddled through my brain.

He has danced the dance of Yeats and other dances as well, but the partnership is still strong:

> Yes, I was dancing-mad, and how
> That came to be the bears and Yeats would know.

The second section, "The Partner," is a further exploration of the world of the bears and of Yeats, of that which is of the earth and that which would transcend it. The "lively dead" are important both in the specific forms of Davies and Yeats, those earlier dancers, and in the forms of his ancestors in general with whom he struggled in earlier poems. As in "Unfold! Unfold!" where the dead help, here they teach us "to be fond." The line preceding this one speaks of the physical contact of the love dance; this line brings in the dead, the past, who are a necessary part of the present love; and the next line, "Who can embrace the body of his fate?" incorporates the future through an image reminiscent both of Yeats and "The Visitant" (and thus of Jung's anima). All these must be present for this dance, and they are subtly interwoven in this moment of love. The section ends with reference to a ghost: "I gave her kisses back, and woke a ghost." Again we hear the voices from the past, the fathers, who both haunt and provide spiritual sustenance. The images of light and darkness appear in this section in two places: "Light altered light along the living ground" and "The body and the soul know how to play / In that dark world where gods have lost their way." The dark world is obviously the world we live in. And though a dark world, it seems not a wholly negative place, for although gods are not suited for it the body and the soul commingled are at home in it. It is within this dark place that light alters light—that is, "along the living ground," the earth.

In "The Wraith" the ambiguity continues as, with "Incomprehensible gaiety and dread," the lovers ask, "Did each become the other in that play?" It is the body that casts a spell and the flesh that makes the spirit visible. And, in a beautiful description of love and of the world in which the lovers dance that recalls both Auden and Hopkins, the poet says:

> In the rich weather of a dappled wood
> We played with dark and light as children should.

From their sensual cry at the moment of consummation, a shape leaps forth that possesses the mystery and insubstantiality of a wraith. The form it takes both is and is not the woman; it is

> A shape alone,
> Impaled on light and whirling slowly down

as they rise to meet the moon in their physical union.

In "The Vigil," the poet calls up Dante and his image of woman, Beatrice. Dante's vision is embodied in Beatrice, and she seems to be both a projection of his will—an anima—and the creator of that vision, as Dante "Shook with a mighty power beyond his will." The point that Roethke makes is again the indeterminate nature of the dance, the world of dark and light, the shape "impaled on light":

> All lovers live by longing, and endure:
> Summon a vision and declare it pure.

The subjectivity of such a vision is undeniable. But its truth is neither affirmed nor denied by this. The remaining stanzas of the poem attempt to describe the vision of these lovers, to describe what cannot be defined: "Though everything's astonishment at last," he says, again indicating the openness, the element of surprise in this world. His description of the entry into this openness reveals the beauty and danger of this "astonishment":

> We undid chaos to a curious sound:
> The waves broke easy, cried to me in white;
> Her look was morning in the dying light.

The next stanza begins, "The visible obscures. But who knows when?" Is it their love that is causing the light to die, or is their love creating a brightness in spite of the dying light? Whatever the case may be, the poet can make one affirmation:

> Things have their thought: they are the shards of me;
> I thought that once, and thought comes round again;
> Rapt, we leaned forth with what we could not see.

Both the things of the world and that which he cannot see are part of his reality. This much he knows, though he cannot see the way they are related. But with this understanding he sees the dance differently:

> We danced to shining; mocked before the black
> And shapeless night that made no answer back.

It is now their dance that belongs to the world of light, their dance, which is at once physical and spiritual. Thus he says in the last stanza, "We dared the dark to reach the white and warm." And the understanding of those who dance in this world of uncertainty and openness, light and darkness, is given:

> Who rise from flesh to spirit know the fall:
> The word outleaps the world, and light is all.

Because humans are spiritual beings, they may rise from flesh to spirit, but because they are also physical beings who have knowledge of their spiritual side they will fall. Thus, the poet must live in this world, but through his dance he can bring together these two elements, and when he does "The word outleaps the world, and light is all." It is a light, now, that goes beyond this "dark world"; but on the other hand the dark world has become a world of light, and it is here in this world of flesh and spirit that the dance is realized.

The final poem in this volume is the title poem, "The Waking," and it presents quite a different approach to the experience of reality. It is in the form of a villanelle, and the perfect structure of the poem coincides with the apparent acceptance and affirmation within the poem. The whole force of the poem is participation in the rhythms of nature that we cannot understand, but there is an unquestioning assertion that we can learn them by moving with them. In spite of the fact that the poem is based on this acceptance and affirmation, however, it is similar to "Four for Sir John Davies" in that the entire poem is filled with ambiguity. The two repeated lines that unify the poem are both subject to a dual interpretation:

> I wake to sleep, and take my waking slow.
> I learn by going where I have to go.

Although J. C. Maxwell dismisses the ambiguity of the second phrase by referring to a variation of this line ("And, lovely, learn by going where to go") which can mean only one thing, it seems clear to me that the ambiguity is essential to the poem. It is not the significance of the two meanings that is important so much as the fact that there can be two meanings. Other lines that complement this shifting nature of the reality of the poem are:

> We think by feeling. What is there to know?
> . . . .
> Light takes the Tree; but who can tell us how?
> . . . .
> This shaking keeps me steady. I should know.
> What falls away is always. And is near.

And the poem always returns to the refrain of one of the two above lines. Thus, we have a poem whose form is rigidly structured, and within this structure is a repetition, a return, and an organic connection between the various stanzas through this repetition. What we have in the words of the poem is both different and similar. The prescribed structure is complemented by the tone of affirmation, the unquestioning assumption of an order to which the words are directed and from which they take their form. On the other hand, however, the ambiguity that is present and the faith on which the order is assumed transform the structure into something much more open and experimental: "I learn by going where I have to go." Taken either way, this indicates a trust in the order of things that is not equaled by the "knowing." In this sense the poem is very much like the dance of "Four for Sir John Davies," where the pattern of the dance is believed to exist—and there is a dance—but where it can be discovered only by the dancing. The organic nature of the villanelle form is suited to this poem, as this world is organic as well. There is constant movement, change; and it is in and through this process that the meaning of the waking becomes clear.

"ANOTHER BEING, AT LAST"

The new poems of *Words for the Wind* explore more fully the various forms and dimensions of the love relationship. The intrusion of old age and death becomes more pressing, and these problems are confronted not just through a persona (as in "Old Lady's Winter Words") but in the voice of the poet narrator himself. The times of despair are greater as well, and the abyss, that region hovering between terror and joy, becomes more prominent. The love relationship is the vehicle for the struggle to reconcile the conflicting elements of existence–life and death, sensual and spiritual love, joy and despair. It is clear that life can have meaning in Roethke's world only as these elements are brought together; he can neither desert the things of this earth, of which he is one, nor deny the power of the spirit, of which he is also a part. And so he moves into the world largely through his love, seeking to discover the understanding that would make meaningful the existence of this strange human creature, who is body and spirit inseparably.

These poems move between the extremes of joy and despair. This not only makes sense in terms of the world Roethke is creating in his poetry–that undulating, unresolved process–but it may also be significant that this period of his life involved these extremes as well. He married Beatrice O'Connell in 1953, and his life with her was probably the first close extended relationship he had had outside his family. He also experienced several recurrences of his manic-depressive illness between 1953 and 1958. Two other events that added to this tumultuous period were the death of Dylan Thomas in 1953 and the death of Roethke's mother in 1954. David Wagoner in his selections from Roethke's notebooks, *Straw for the Fire,* has grouped together a number of entries from 1954-58 under the title "The Middle of a Roaring World," which reveal Roethke's concern with his illness and the connection he makes between it and poetic creation. During this period he began to realize that his bouts with mental illness were not isolated incidents but were something he would have to live with the rest of his life. And, according to Seager, he came at this time to accept this and to use these phases of illness as sources for his poetry.

At this time also he became interested in Kierkegaard and Paul Tillich, writers who also express these extremes of joy and despair. For Kierkegaard it is the "sickness unto death," the despair of the person who knows the possibility of spirit, that may lead to the joy of the spirit. It is when humans know and can face the abyss of total hopelessness that hope may come: "The decisive affirmation comes only when a man is brought to the utmost extremity, so that humanly speaking no possibility exists." In

Tillich the "courage to be" may grow out of the despair that comes with the recognition of nonbeing. Usually Roethke makes use of such sources only for rounding out or affirming his own view of the world, but occasionally his reliance on outside ideas becomes too great, and the poetry suffers. In "The Pure Fury," for example, he seems deliberately to paraphrase a passage from Tillich, perhaps to create the stance of the "intellectual man." But in the poetry it seems simply awkward and undigested. The passage in Tillich comes out of a discussion of nonbeing:

> Parmenides tried to remove it as a concept. But in order to do so he had to sacrifice life. . . . Plato used the concept of nonbeing because without it the contrast of existence with the pure essences is beyond understanding. It is implied in Aristotle's distinction between matter and form. . . . Jacob Boehme, the Protestant mystic and philosopher of life, made the classical statement that all things are rooted in a Yes and a No.

The second stanza of "The Pure Fury" uses this passage in this way:

> The pure admire the pure, and live alone;
> I love a woman with an empty face.
> Parmenides put Nothingness in place;
> She tries to think, and it flies loose again.
> How slow the changes of a golden mean:
> Great Boehme rooted all in Yes and No;
> At times my darling squeaks in pure Plato.

As in Tillich, so in this poem, the courage to face the reality of nonbeing leads to joy through despair. But by relying so heavily on Tillich's formulation of this understanding, Roethke's poem loses forcefulness.

Although the same extremes of experience are found in the earlier poetry in the cyclical movement from darkness and despair to affirmation and communion, in these poems this search takes on a more philosophical cast; here the joy and despair are more explicitly concerns of the spirit. The despair seems always to be a product of the confrontation of the affirmation of the world, including the things of the world and the self as a part of that world, with the reality of the loss of that world through separation or death–that is, through the threat of nonbeing. Joy, on the other hand, comes through affirmation of the other and the harmony that is felt with that person and with the world in spite of the inevitability of their separation. There is a sense of timelessness created in the moments of communion that remains when the moments have passed. This shared life comes through reaching out to the world, the other; and through this shared life the self is established more firmly and is given a reason for being and a protection against nonbeing. Joy also fills the moments of affirmation that come after a period of despair as the meaning of the world is reaffirmed.

The *Love Poems* are enclosed by the sense of a dream; the first poem is entitled "The Dream" and the final poem, "Memory." These poems are in one sense dimensions of the mind or the soul, as the individual struggles to understand the joy and despair of human life. "Motion" is a word that recurs throughout the poetry, stressing process and dynamic movement, as Richard Blessing notes throughout his study, *Theodore Roethke's Dynamic Vision.* In "The Renewal" the term is "Motions of the soul," and it is an understanding of this process that the poet seeks. But along with this inward process, there is also a motion outward that results in the formation of relationships. And both motions are necessary for the soul to find meaning in the world. "The Dream" leads out to its realization with an actual woman in "Words for the Wind" and "I Knew a Woman." The poet explores the meaning of the loved one in "The Voice" and "She," seeing her as an integral part of the natural process. But another dimension of a life of love is the conflict with nature that comes with the approach of old age, explored in "The Sententious Man" and "The Pure Fury." Further discontent that comes with the loss of the love relation is seen in "The Surly One" and "Plaint." With "The Swan" and "Memory" there is a movement back into the self and a tentative coming together of the inner and outer worlds.

Throughout the poems the joys and terrors of human experience are presented. It is largely with the other that the poet is able to face the questions of body and spirit and the approach of old age. The experiences with the beloved also lead to the more philosophical questions of the "motions of the soul," and these in turn lead back to the actual experience of the beloved. The fact that the lover and the love relationship are part of the natural order is the cause for both the joys and the terrors of the experience. And this fact is finally the reason for the acceptance of both joy and terror. The resolution of the conflict between them, when it comes, is possible because of a trust in that natural process.

"The Dream," like "The Visitant," creates a world that is both in and out of reality, that is a prelude to the experience of love of another and the capturing of that moment in the inner experience. Also as before, Jung's concept of the anima is important. The lover who is met in the dream is part of the speaker's self and part of the external world. The meeting that takes place is thus both within the self and with the other. And it is both a presentiment of what is to come and a statement that what is to come has always been. On all these levels what occurs in the meeting is revealed through the linking of the lover with nature, and what is realized is the opening out onto love.

Both the dream and a "deeper sleep" are described in the first stanza. The powers of sleep open the mind to those primordial images that were readily available to the child, and the poet finds in his dream what "The mind remembers from a deeper sleep." The original unity from which he separated himself as a child is touched on once again because of his closeness to the woman about whom he is dreaming. It is as if their first meeting were occurring in the moment of the dream, and at the same time it is as if it had occurred before that separation from the primordial unity in which all were one. The poet, then, is taking on the role of the adult who is touching the roots of his life, no longer as a child or through childhood but now through his relationship to another human being, through the experience of love.

The nature of the dream and that "deeper sleep" is given, of course, only indirectly; it is only through experiences in the external world and their analogues that we have knowledge of this deeper layer of experience. But the hints as to its nature are clear. While appearing to represent the unchanging, eternal roots of human existence, this primordial territory is at the same time in a constant state of movement and change. The lover is described as a part of the movements of nature:

> The water rippled, and she rippled on.
>
> She came toward me in the flowing air,
> A shape of change, encircled by its fire.

One dimension of change is ambiguity. Vulnerability and doubt seem necessarily connected with the experience of love. But there is also a kind of resolution in the last stanza, where the classically opposed elements of fire and water come together in the world of paradox and change. The lover "turned the field into a glittering sea," and the sea and the flame of love commingle as the dreamer

> played in flame and water like a boy
> And I swayed out beyond the white seafoam;
> Like a wet log, I sang within a flame.

In this moment—"eternity's confine," Roethke calls it, perhaps too obviously—the speaker finds both himself and the other and (which is at this point to say the same thing) feels the presence of love:

In that last while, eternity's confine,
I came to love, I came into my own.

That which was within is given expression through the meeting with the other, but what is realized is a reenactment or a preenactment; it is "shadows" that meet. The actual meeting of two people is presented both as a possibility and a memory in "The Dream."

"The Dream" follows a rather regular form. The lines are five beat and rhyme *aabbccdd* primarily as off rhymes. The five-beat line creates a flowing steadiness that is complementary to the dream state. The following poem, "All the Earth, All the Air," uses the three-beat line Roethke admired in Yeats and at which he himself became adept. This form is used to create a sense of playfulness and to bring us closer to the rhythms of natural waking life. In this poem Roethke creates a moment of joyful experience, which is necessarily passing, but he captures the delight of being a creature who partakes of such an existence. One example from this poem of the tender playing with the commonplace that Roethke does so well begins:

This joy's my fall. I am!–
A man rich as a cat,
A cat in the fork of a tree,
When she shakes out her hair.
I think of that, and laugh.

In "Words for the Wind" the three-beat line is continued and with it this touching humanness. However, Roethke combines this with his vision from "The Dream" so that we have the intermingling of the more universal anima and his flesh-and-blood lover. This is accomplished through the images he chooses to present and the forms they take. Along with the three-beat line is a rigid, though shifting, rhyme scheme that connects the four sections and moves them forward. There is also a change from an eight-line stanza in the first and last sections to a seven-line stanza in the second and third sections. The division is not complete, however, because the first and second sections are connected by having four stanzas, the third and fourth by having three. Thus, there is an underlying connection and various shiftings that create a sense of flow similar to that of "The Dream." The three-beat lines move quickly from one to another, so there is a flowing motion here as well. But the changes are more rapid and, again, more playful than the longer lines in "The Dream."

The poem "Words for the Wind" is one of Roethke's best expressions of the love of one person for another. Without losing his simplicity he also brings in two dimensions other than the love between a man and a woman: the world of nature in which the love occurs and is therefore essential and the world of spirit that is equally necessary to the creation of the experience of love. Thus, the two other dimensions are not extraneous additions but integral to the expression of love for another person.

Throughout the poem the loved one is closely associated with the things of nature, and the love seems to extend to these things as much as to a particular person. The poem begins, "Love, love, a lily's my care," and later the poet says:

> The dove's my will today.
> She sways, half in the sun:
> Rose, easy on a stem,
> One with the sighing vine.

Along with the importance of the things of nature in identifying the lover, there are also several parts of nature that have special significance for Roethke. The stone, the moon, the wind itself are archetypal images of renewed life that add the sense of universal experience to the particular. As in "The Dream" and the last poems of *The Waking,* paradox is also very important to this poem:

> Motion can keep me still:
> . . . .
> I stared, and a garden stone
> Slowly became the moon.

And again there are unanswered questions:

> Are flower and seed the same?
> What do the great dead say?
> . . . .
> What time's my heart?

A final element that becomes important in this poem is the presence of time. The moon is an indicator of the passage of time, the birds and fishes move north, the stars change their position; all create a sense of the passage of time. To nature this is cyclical time: the moon will continue to rise and wane, the birds and fishes will go south again, the stars will continue their circling indefinitely. But how do humans fit into this scheme? How is the lover to live in harmony with and acceptance of this natural cycle and at the same time rejoice in the particularity of his immediate love, which shall surely be destroyed by the passage of time? For one of the first times Roethke thus confronts this conflict that becomes central in much of the later poetry.

These various elements work together to create the "Words for the Wind"—words of love and joyous celebration, dedicated to the wind as the messenger of the spirit through the earth. The poem begins:

> Love, love, a lily's my care,
> She's sweeter than a tree.
> Loving, I use the air
> Most lovingly: I breathe;
> Mad in the wind I wear
> Myself as I should be,
> All's even with the odd,
> My brother the vine is glad.

The three-beat line and the casual language produce a spontaneous celebration of the loved one and of life. Because of love the speaker is open to the whole world and feels a comradeship with all living things. "The birds came down," he says, "And made my song their own." As before, the "great dead" are important to the living, who look to them for affirmation of love. Roethke turns to Phoebe, the goddess of the moon—that symbol of dying and resurrection, of eternity within constant change. A moment of aloneness occurs at the end of the first section as

> The shallow stream runs slack;
> The wind creaks slowly by;

and there comes the cry of a nestling, to which he cannot respond. But even then:

> A shape from deep in the eye—
> That woman I saw in a stone—
> Keeps pace when I walk alone.

The bridge is made between the concrete woman of his love and the spiritual substance he partakes of through that love. The stone shares as before in the primordial stability of the world, and the woman in the stone is at once Phoebe and the actual woman he loves. Throughout the poem his love seems to be at once for a singular person and for something more universal than that woman. It seems essential that both be present: the person is not sacrificed to the universal, but both are necessary to make the love experience possible.

The second section opens with a statement of the mutuality of living things:

> The sun declares the earth;
> The stones leap in the stream;
> . . . .
> Rose, easy on a stem,
> One with the sighing vine.

The image of the field becoming the sea from "The Dream" is repeated, but in this context as a simile it seems a more natural phenomenon:

> On a wide plain, beyond
> The far stretch of a dream,
> A field breaks like the sea;
> The wind's white with her name,
> And I walk with the wind.

The interrelatedness of things makes it possible for the imagination to see the transformation of one into the other. His "random joy" at life is given shape through passion, and he is now able to say,

> I cry delight: I know
> The root, the core of a cry.

He reaches into the heart, the beginnings of things, and through the lover finds there a calm, "Swan-heart, arbutus-calm." "Love has a thing to do," he says, and the poem is the revelation of that thing. The section closes with a further statement of his celebration:

> I bear, but not alone,
> The burden of this joy.

In section 3 there is a recognition of the presence of time, and various images give it and the love relationship meaning together. The poet begins with images of time in nature:

> Under a southern wind,
> The birds and fishes move
> North, in a single stream;
> The sharp stars swing around.

To stand back in this way to view the changing seasons of the earth is to

get a step beyond
The wind, and there I am,
I'm odd and full of love.

To acknowledge this movement of the earth and at the same time to embrace one's love is wisdom. And the words come from nature:

Whatever was, still is,
Says a song tied to a tree.

But the human question of time remains: "What time's my heart?" The answer is

I care.
I cherish what I have
Had of the temporal:
I am no longer young
But the winds and waters are;
What falls away will fall;
All things bring me to love.

This assurance in the face of approaching old age and death–and with them the loss of the lover–is far from the bitter cries of the old lady's winter words. The feeling of acceptance and fullness experienced here may be the final word Roethke gives, but it is not the only word. The protest against this harmony of nature, from which man would break free, continues through the poetry, though the poetry finds its way back to this tenuous moment of reconciliation as well.

The final section of "Words for the Wind" gives the reason for this moment of acceptance. The beloved is one with the things of nature:

The breath of a long root,
The shy perimeter
Of the unfolding rose,
The green, the altered leaf,
The oyster's weeping foot,
And the incipient star–
Are part of what she is.
She wakes the ends of life.

And because of this unity the lover can be who he is and rejoice in his being:

> Being myself, I sing
> The soul's immediate joy.
> Light, light, where's my repose?
> A wind wreathes round a tree.
> A thing is done: a thing
> Body and spirit know
> When I do what she does:
> Creaturely creature, she!

The wind and the tree intertwined; the spirit and body one—this is what it is to be a "creaturely creature." The final stanza expresses the immediate joy of loving another person within the fullness of the world. Sensuality is here fully combined with spirituality, and through the love achieved in this union the poet meets the other person as a Thou and finds in this meeting fullness of being:

> I kiss her moving mouth,
> Her swart hilarious skin;
> She breaks my breath in half;
> She frolicks like a beast;
> And I dance round and round,
> A fond and foolish man,
> And see and suffer myself
> In another being, at last.

"I Knew a Woman" continues the tone of this final stanza, celebrating the physical joys of love. It also takes up the question of time that was raised in "Words for the Wind." The structure of this poem is quite different, however. It has a very tight form, with iambic pentameter rhyming *ababccc.* But within this form Roethke is very playful with his language and attitude. He says in "The Swan,"

> I am my father's son, I am John Donne
> Whenever I see her with nothing on.

And in his playful and tender delight in the physical relationship he shares with this woman, he makes use of the form and tone of this ancestor through conceits and a delicately ribald humor.

The connection between nature and the beloved is still present, but there is an added sense of laughter that comes out in subtle ways through the rhymes and images. The poem begins:

> I knew a woman, lovely in her bones,
> When small birds sighed, she would sigh back at them;
> . . . .
> Of her choice virtues only gods should speak,
> Or English poets who grew up on Greek
> (I'd have them sing in chorus, cheek to cheek).

The first three stanzas describe the delights of love and praise the beloved for her charms and her initiatory powers. The beauty of the poem is in its details as, within the established form, it playfully and lovingly records the joys of physical love. The final stanza moves back a step and comments on the meaning of this experience. The poem raises the conflict between the time of nature—which is the cycle of birth, growth, decay, death, and new life—and the conflicting time of eternity, which would capture and preserve this experience. The poet begins by submitting to the time of nature; but through the image of the lover, and thus through love, he mixes the two subtly together. Sensual love is thus intermingled—almost confused—with a stasis that would apparently deny the possibility of this love that seems necessarily to be a part of nature and its time. The recurrent theme of motion is repeated as well—motion that seems to deny the stasis of eternity but that also participates in something that is unending. The stanza begins:

> Let seed be grass, and grass turn into hay:
> I'm martyr to a motion not my own;
> What's freedom for? To know eternity.
> I swear she cast a shadow white as stone.

The frolicking, sensual lover of the previous stanzas now seems to be transformed into something resembling Jung's anima and is closer to the "visitant" or the woman of the dream. But her corporeality is restored in the final image of the stanza:

> But who would count eternity in days?
> These old bones live to learn her wanton ways:
> (I measure time by how a body sways).

By linking the style of this poem with the metaphysical poets through the set form, the playful jests about sex, and the conceits themselves, Roethke reminds us of that time when body and soul were held together in a tenuous, paradoxical unity, which he tries to re-create in the world of "I Knew a Woman."

"MOTIONS OF THE SOUL"

With "The Sententious Man," "The Pure Fury," and "The Renewal," the poems shift emphasis. Although the lover remains important as a source of strength, what come to the fore are the moments of aloneness, the "terrible . . . need for solitude" ("The Pure Fury"), the ghosts one must face alone. The isolation and struggle that are part of these poems give greater depth and fullness to the more joyful love poems. Although the love poems are presented first, it is clear that this struggle lies beneath their joy. Human beings are first of all alone, and to reach another involves the necessarily threatening opening of oneself to that other and, in the process, looking deeply within oneself. In the *Northwest Review* issue devoted to Roethke, Coburn Freer and Arnold Stein both focus on the difficulties of relating to this other. Freer's essay, "Theodore Roethke's Love Poetry," stresses the difficulty of taking up the "burden of love." "Throughout the sequence [*Words for the Wind*], it seems that either alternative, acceptance of the woman or affirmation of his own separate individuality, will lead the poet very close to spiritual suicide." The essay stresses this conflict in the love poems, even though it closes, "although the burden of being loved was exhausting it was finally restorative." In "Roethke's Memory: Actions, Visions, and Revisions," Stein works sensitively with recaptured memories of the greenhouse and with their revisions from the notebooks, using the poems up to *The Far Field*, and finds an unhappy but apparently certain movement from the other to the solitary self:

> The conditions of life guaranteed that the world of the greenhouse had to be "lost." The personal imperative to lose the sense of participation may have been governed by as irresistible a certainty, but something in the human composition can accept as certain what it refuses to accept as necessary. "How terrible the need for solitude": that is a personal imperative which cannot once and for all be reconciled with the human desire to "see and suffer myself /

> In another being." . . . The poet chose to confront himself with solitude and with a loss of the "sense of kinship." The "we" disappears from the finished poem, the feeling of separation grows.

I acknowledge that both critics are dealing with an important area of conflict both in the poetry and in the nature of things, but this study obviously disagrees with their conclusions. I believe Roethke is able, from the greenhouse poems to the final dance, to create convincingly the experience of *the self with the other.*

The "Sententious Man" begins the inner search through his method of indirection ("My indirection found direction out") and aphorism. The poem begins, "Spirit and nature beat in one breast-bone–" and the questions of spiritual and physical love, spirit and body are again raised:

> We did not fly the flesh. Who does, when young?
> A fire leaps on itself: I know that flame.
> Some rages save us. Did I rage too long?
> The spirit knows the flesh it must consume.

Rage is a recurring theme in Roethke's poetry and is dealt with in many different ways. A few examples related to this poem are in "O, Thou Opening, O," "Old Lady's Winter Words," and "The Pure Fury." In the first poem he asks, "Where's the great rage of a rocking heart, the high rare true dangerous indignation?" The old lady, revolting against growing old and feeling impotent, cries,

> If I were a young man,
> I could roll in the dust of a fine rage.

And in "The Pure Fury," which, as the title indicates, is a poem devoted to rage, the following passage occurs:

> How terrible the need for solitude:
> That appetite for life so ravenous
> A man's a beast prowling in his own house,
> A beast with fangs, and out for his own blood
> Until he finds the thing he almost was
> When the pure fury first raged in his head
> And trees came closer with a denser shade.

The pure fury, the indignation, the rage, all seem to be connected with that ravenous appetite for life that must live with the inevitability of death. This is the struggle of the flesh to persist and of the spirit to consume the desires of the flesh with its own desire for being: "A fire leaps on itself" ("The Sententious Man"). The rage is a necessary and creative force, leading the poet to seek fuller being, but if he rages too long it can destroy him by overpowering his love for life.

Roethke describes the conflict as the life lived "near the abyss"—the harsh reality of a human being who stands, finally, alone and moves toward death, alienated from his world and unable to find meaning in it. "The Pure Fury" begins:

> Stupor of knowledge lacking inwardness—
> What book, O learned man, will set me right?
> Once I read nothing through a fearful night,
> For every meaning had grown meaningless.

It is not in books that meaning will be found. "Meaning" is not something that has been established and can be passed down, but it must be discovered—if it is to be found at all—at the edge of the abyss. This is quite different from the emphasis of most of the love poems, which are concerned not with the anguished isolation that seems here to be the necessary condition for a meeting of kindred beings but rather with the unity of living things or with the moment of their coming together that overcomes the separation.

This is related to Kierkegaard's faith that grows out of the sickness unto death, which is despair, only when it is clear that the overcoming of this despair is humanly impossible—and yet the possibility remains. It is Tillich's courage to be in spite of the lived reality of nonbeing. It is Buber's "turning" that results in the recognition of a Thou that may occur by "letting oneself sink and take root in the soil called despair by men, soil out of which arise self-destruction and rebirth," which would be the beginning of turning. It is the risk that depends on one's faith in an underlying order and goodness in things, which enables one to face the abyss—which may indeed mean destruction—and come forth from it with new life. This hope is expressed in "The Pure Fury" in the closing stanza:

> I live near the abyss. I hope to stay
> Until my eyes look at a brighter sun
> As the thick shade of the long night comes on.

In "The Sententious Man" a similar image of the struggle with darkness is given, but here there is movement into the light:

> There was a thicket where I went to die,
> And there I thrashed, my thighs and face aflame.
>
> But my least motion changed into a song,
> And all dimensions quivered to one thing.

The image of motion recurs in these poems at moments that go beyond the abyss. In "The Renewal" this term becomes the organizing force of the poem, and its meaning for Roethke becomes clearer. The same questions as in the two previous poems arise. The darkness of "The Pure Fury" is presented but passed beyond. The affirmations of the sententious man are reached, but his indirection is gone. The poem begins, "What glories would we? Motions of the soul?" This motion points to a life force that is both a perpetual vitality and a wisdom in which all things, whether stones or human beings, can share. The aim of the search in the previous love poems is here clearly expressed as "motions of the soul," which involve one's total participation in this life force and, through this, participation with others. In Buber's sense this power would be that third term through which the I-Thou relationship is made possible.

The poem begins with this possibility as a question and as a hope. Although the way to this meeting is uncertain, the poet is able to begin with an affirmation:

> The centaur and the sibyl romp and sing
> Within the reach of my imagining:
> Such affirmations are perpetual.

The centaur and the sibyl are archetypal forms from the deep inner world of the unconscious. They are also indicators of the powers of the life-giving imagination. As long as humans are able to imagine and to explore, the possibility for new understanding is present. In mythology these forms represent the body and the mind; and in the world of the unconscious these appear together in a single archetype. Aniela Jaffé describes this unity in the unconscious:

> Once the unconscious content is apprehended by consciousness, the pair is divided. The original parity of the opposites—the bipolar aspects of a single paradoxical archetype—retreats into a distance that consciousness can no longer reach. It is not even conceivable

> any more. How can spirit and nature be one? Or psyche and matter? In the place of prescient images of totality, veiled though they be from logical thought, there emerge clearly defined, independent concepts split off from it—a formidable achievement of human consciousness in its struggle to understand the world, yet fraught with the danger of psychic impoverishment through one-sidedness, and menaced by the loss of a unitary grasp of reality.

In this poem a resolution is sought through the imagination. The comment on the poetry itself is clear: it is the power of the imagination to create worlds of possibility out of which a new understanding of the self and the world may come. The song is very often for Roethke a symbol for poetry: "I teach my sighs to lengthen into songs." In a later poem entitled "The Song" the poet comes to a fissure in the ground and begins to sing:

> I sang to whatever had been
> Down in that watery hole:
> I wooed with a low tune;
> You could say I was mad.
> And a wind woke in my hair,
> And the sweat poured from my face,
> When I heard, or thought I heard,
> Another join my song
> With the small voice of a child,
> Close, and yet far away.
>
> Mouth upon mouth, we sang,
> My lips pressed upon stone.

The imagination, the song, is here united with that subterranean world of the centaur and sibyl, the world of the small child and anima. And the song that is produced comes from both the poet and the child, from the conscious and from the unconscious universal world. As the event that occurs in "The Renewal" comes about through the power of the imagination to respond to the voices deep within, so it seems the poem itself is a result of this process.

Thus, "The Renewal" affirms the power of the imagination to change the poet's sighs into songs. Yet he must also, "like a tree, endure the shift of things." The realm of song, of art, may be eternal, but the poet, while a part of this world, is also and just as basically a part of the shifting world of nature. His strength, then, lies not only in his ability to sing but also in his ability to emulate the solid yet changing tree of nature. These two aspects of being human are his sources of strength as he enters into the darkness that follows in this poem, and they must both, as in the love poems, be preserved in the struggle to discover the motions of the soul.

The second stanza reveals the dark night, the edge of the abyss wherein the soul risks destruction in order to find itself:

> The night wind rises. Does my father live?
> Dark hangs upon the waters of the soul;
> My flesh is breathing slower than a wall.

He asks if there is a sustaining power behind this darkness, and, still uncertain, he submits to this darkness and feels the primordial unity that envelops him with love while at the same time threatening to destroy his individual self:

> These waters drowse me into sleep so kind
> I walk as if my face would kiss the wind.

He feels his lifeblood being taken from him by a "raw ghost"—the forces of the unconscious that would draw him back to the mire. He has touched and been touched by the sources of love, of renewal, but now he must fight to bring that love up from the depths and to separate himself as an individual:

> I know I love, yet know not where I am;
> I paw the dark, the shifting midnight air.
> Will the self, lost, be found again? In form?
> I walk the night to keep my five wits warm.

In the final stanza the resolution and illumination occur:

> Dry bones! Dry bones! I find my loving heart,
> Illumination brought to such a pitch
> I see the rubblestones begin to stretch
> As if reality had split apart
> And the whole motion of the soul lay bare:
> I find that love, and I am everywhere.

The dry bones of Ezekiel's valley are called forth and with them the promise that the impossible is possible: those bones shall take on flesh and blood and spirit and shall live. Having come to the point of darkness and loss of self, having faced the abyss, the poet understands the true motion of the soul. The choice is not between nature and spirit, unity and individuality: in this moment of illumination he stands as an individual man of nature and yet is part of the universal spirit of love.

As this section of the poetry began with the prophecy of "The Dream," it comes to a close with "The Swan," which captures both the reality and the ideal, and with "Memory," which takes place "In the slow world of dream." It is the mind, the imagination, that encloses the love poems. Within them we found the sensual and the spiritual, the lovers' joyous reunion in both body and soul and the terrible isolation of despair. In "Memory" the poet returns to the world of the dream. As with the opening poem, there is the feeling of continuation: what is has always been. Within the mind the resolution of the conflicts is complete:

> In the slow world of dream,
> We breathe in unison.
> The outside dies within,
> And she knows all I am.

But when the speaker attempts to act within this world, as in the later poem "The Beast," he finds that this is a world of stasis:

> A doe drinks by a stream,
> A doe and its fawn.
> When I follow after them,
> The grass changes to stone.

This conflict between the soul's perpetual motion and the changing world of nature is resolved in "The Swan." Unlike "The Renewal," which brought the two worlds into one illuminating image, this poem explores another way of understanding how they are to be accepted together. The world of changing human love is revealed in the first stanza. Roethke asks,

> Must I stay tangled in that lively hair?
> Is there no way out of that coursing blood?

His answer to himself is to be delighted with what is, not to try to get beyond the moment to a safely unchanging eternity, because he has found that the moment itself has joy—even though it is certain that that moment will come to an end:

> We think too long in terms of what to be;
> I live, alive and certain as a bull;
> A casual man, I keep my casual word,
> Yet whistle back at every whistling bird.
> A man alive, from all light I must fall.
> I am my father's son, I am John Donne
> Whenever I see her with nothing on.

He is able, then, to accept the moment in all its love and all its transitoriness. He will embrace that which, though it leads to death, is filled with life. And through the glories of human love comes a vision of that other persisting world. Not by turning away from them but by embracing the other and the world, one comes to the world of the swan:

> *The moon draws back its waters from the shore.*
> *By the lake's edge, I see a silver swan,*
> *And she is what I would. In this light air,*
> *Lost opposites bend down–*
> *Sing of that nothing of which all is made,*
> *Or listen into silence, like a god.*

Jung's idea of the "psychoid archetype" may speak to the experience of this poem. Jaffé explains this as the "transcendental unity of psyche and world." There is an *"acausal orderedness"* underlying them, but in our experience "part of the archetype is still in the unconscious, hence the relativity of space and time characteristic of processes outside or beyond consciousness. But another part of it has broken through into consciousness, hence its originally unknowable psychoid unity splits into opposites that can now be recognised, into psychic and physical parallel events." The opposites are not made one, but each fills the other with life, resulting in shared joy.

"CREATURES"

The *Voices and Creatures* section of *Words for the Wind* begins rather darkly with voices that continue wrestling with the question of death in life. The powerfully felt presence of evil emphasizes guilt and isolation. The exception to this darkness and isolation is the voice of the child in "The Song," which joins the poet's voice in singing to and with the creative, communal forces of the earth. Thus, the child and earth images return as symbols of creativity. The creature poems with which the section ends are also filled with a great deal more light, for the poet turns again to the things of the world. As in some of the early greenhouse poems, the things of nature are at the center of the poems, although the human reaction to them is also important. These poems are also similar to the early poems in their reliance on imagery. As the lives of flowers and humans were commingled in the greenhouse poems, so here the close relation of creatures and humans is revealed. "Snake," "Slug," and "The Siskins" explore the worlds of these living things, and though each is different in its approach and tone in each the kinship the poet feels with the creatures—and thus the connectedness of all living things—is stressed.

"Snake" presents this creature in a single image as it is observed by the poet:

> I saw a young snake glide
> Out of the mottled shade
> And hang, limp on a stone:
> A thin mouth, and a tongue
> Stayed, in the still air.
>
> It turned; it drew away;
> Its shadow bent in half;
> It quickened, and was gone.

The description of the object is presented directly and simply: a single continuous movement as the snake appears, the image is caught for a moment, and then the snake is gone. The poet's reaction to his intimate vision of this strange, untamed creature of nature shows the kinship he feels despite the strangeness:

> I felt my slow blood warm.
> I longed to be that thing,
> The pure, sensuous form.
>
> And I may be, some time.

The "pure, sensuous form," the image cleansed of everything but itself, strikes a note of longing in the poet and, it seems, a note of recognition. The snake as a form in nature is connected with something deep within the unconscious aspect of human beings. The appeal of the snake comes, as Donoghue points out, in its being "nothing if not itself and nothing beyond itself." The poem hints at metempsychosis and reincarnation, but here, as in the following poem, such philosophical ideas seem too burdensome for the simple image that is presented; and the poet relies not so much on them as on a psychological reality that causes us to react to such an image because it *is* a part of our unconscious being.

In "Slug" the connection with the unconscious is equally important. "How I loved one like you when I was little!" The "young" snake is replaced by the "little" child; in both cases the beginnings of life indicate closeness to the unconscious. After establishing his presence in the scene as a child, the poet creates in the manner of "Snake" the image of the creature:

> With his stripes of silver and his small house on his back,
> Making a slow journey around the well-curb.
> I longed to be like him, and was,
> In my way, close cousin
> To the dirt, my knees scrubbing
> The gravel, my nose wetter than his.

The time of *The Lost Son* poems is recalled—the childhood world of closeness to and even unity with nature, that dissolved as the individual identity of the child became stronger. It recalls the world of the mire out of which consciousness grew but with which humans through their unconscious still have strong ties. When he was young, then, and still an integral part of this world, he intuitively felt and rejoiced in his close kinship with the slug. But now he complains about this "loose toe from the old life,/ The cold slime come into being," who eats the heart out of his garden. With seeming guilt for his destruction of what was a part of his past, he berates the creature for the way it dies:

> And you refuse to die decently!—
> Flying upward through the knives of my lawnmower
> . . . .
> And I go faster in my rage to get done with it.

But even now he pauses in his tirade to admire it for a moment:

> Or, poisoned, dragging a white skein of spittle over a path—
> Beautiful, in its way, like quicksilver—
> You shrink to something less,
> A rain-drenched fly or spider.

His heated rejection of the slug nevertheless expresses a sense of closeness and of regret. And in the final stanza, which is his triumphant justification for his rejection, we feel he is protesting too much. He begins this stanza with the same idea of reincarnation that was found in "Snake," and, as there, the image is placed too fully within this world, made too much a part of mowing the lawn on a Sunday afternoon, to make the Eastern philosophy very relevant–though the idea, to be sure, is similar:

> I'm sure I've been a toad, one time or another.
> With bats, weasels, worms–I rejoice in the kinship.
> Even the caterpillar I can love, and the various vermin.
> But as for you, most odious–
> Would Blake call you holy?

The poet is rejecting that aspect of his past and of his unconscious self that has its roots in the slime. But there is a note of tenderness and of intimate knowledge and connection that makes him even in the denial a close brother to the slug.

In the closing poem of the section, "The Siskins," these tiny birds, agents of lightness and of song, reveal a moment of life that moves beyond the questioning, dark side of life that has appeared in many of the poems of *Voices and Creatures.* As in the greenhouse poems, the image of the siskins is given as they are observed by the poet, and then at the end, as if he has been drawn into their movement, he describes his own, human feelings. He begins by placing himself in the poem:

> The bank swallows veer and dip,
> Diving down at my windows.

And of the siskins he says:

> And the small mad siskins flit by,
> Flying upward in little skips and erratic leaps;
> Or they sit sideways on limber dandelion stems,
> Bending them down to the ground;
> . . . .
> Or they fling themselves against tree trunks,
> Scuttling down and around like young squirrels,
> Birds furious as bees.

These intense little birds in their furious yet gentle activity ("they sit sideways on limber dandelion stems") seem to strike a note of understanding in the poet. Somehow he feels like them, the seemingly helpless birds who are often called mad as they rage in their tiny and quite delicate way against their world. Their fury is not the dark rage of "Pure Fury" but has been transformed into beauty by its appearance as a part of the natural order of things. The poet moves to his own involvement in this scene as he sees the birds moving together:

> These airy hippety-hop skippers,
> Light as seed blowing off thistles!
> And I seem to lean forward,
> As my eyes follow after
> Their sunlit leaping.

At the end of this rather dark section, he is able to join with these creatures and feel himself their "sunlit leaping" and rejoice once again in being part of this world. The questions of the self and the other (including the world), the spirit and the body, life and death are not resolved or forgotten—indeed they are intensified in *Meditations of an Old Woman*—but the return to the things of the natural world and the poet's connectedness with them emphasizes again that, in Roethke's poetry, the struggle with these questions can go on because of the rootedness of human beings in the earth.

"WET WITH ANOTHER LIFE"

In *The Dying Man* and *Meditations of an Old Woman,* Roethke again focuses on the question of life and death that appeared so often in the earlier poems of *Words for the Wind.* From the threshold perspective of two dramatic characters who stand at the boundary between these two worlds, Roethke again struggles with the spiritual and sensual, the eternal and temporal, the self and the world.

Although the two poems do not come to conflicting resolutions, their approaches to this boundary situation are quite different. *The Dying Man* is dedicated to W. B. Yeats, and Roethke deliberately utilizes Yeats's language and style in his tribute to this very important ancestor, modeling the poem on the structure of "Upon a Dying Lady," though transforming it for his own purposes. The poem moves from image to associated image in a sophisticated philosophical counterpart to the early childhood poems. Although the poem includes some striking images—especially the key image, "Eternity defined, and strewn with straw"—that seek to overcome the dualities of death and life, temporality and eternity, a sense of abstraction remains that prevents this from being one of Roethke's best poems. This may be the result of his attempt to emulate the exultation of the visionary experience of Yeats. Although they share the same world in many respects and both work to embody the vision that "Eternity is Now," Roethke's commitment is finally to the unifying power given in the concrete particulars of the earth, whereas Yeats finds this power in the realm of artifice.

Roethke seems much more at home in the world of *Meditations of an Old Woman;* perhaps because it embodies lived experience in the concrete world, this sequence contains some of his best work. The old woman muses on her life and approaching death, struggling with the question of how to find meaning in a world she loves but must soon leave. She feels her body growing old and dry but remembers the times of its fullness. She both adores and rages at the world because it is filled on the one hand with life and beauty and on the other hand with ugliness and death. She moves from her present to the past of her childhood, then to the dream world that has always been part of her life, and finally, to visions of the possible in which these other realms meet. The old woman explores the many parts of her life as she approaches death; she moves through darkness and through light, and she comes finally to affirm herself and her world in spite of the darkness and death that are present in it.

The form and content of these poems are interesting in their relation to the poetry of T. S. Eliot and Walt Whitman. Like Yeats, Eliot had a great influence on Roethke. However, Roethke says in a letter to Ralph Mills, "I came to some of Eliot's and Yeats's ancestors long before I came to them; in fact, for a long time, I rejected both of them. . . . So what in the looser line may seem in the first old lady poem ["First Meditation"] to be close to Eliot may actually be out of Whitman, who influenced Eliot *plenty,* technically." Along with the looser line Roethke shares with Eliot and Whitman what S. Musgrove describes as the "isolation of the image to the point where it becomes a consciously constructed and deliberately maintained symbol." James Miller points out that there are similarities between Eliot and Whitman in their use of catalogues and in the paradoxical conjunction of opposites that occurs so frequently in their poetry. Roethke is related to them in these two ways as well. Finally, the fact that they are all in some sense prophets through their dramatic poetry again unites them. Also, there are several phrases and images from Eliot, especially from the *Four Quartets,* that are used by Roethke apparently quite deliberately in *Meditations.* And the old woman herself seems to parallel the narrator in *Four Quartets* in her attempts to reconcile in her mind the opposing realities she senses in her world and in the final resolution she achieves. Roethke says of the *Meditations:*

> I wanted . . . to create a character for whom such rhythms are indigenous; that she be a dramatic character, not just me. Christ, Eliot in the Quartets is tired, spiritually tired, old-man. Rhythm, Tiresome Tom. Is my old lady tired? The hell she is: she's tough, she's brave, she's aware of life and she would take a congeries of eels over a hassle of bishops any day.

Here he gives two reasons for his use of the woman as a persona: first, to create a dramatic character, someone outside himself (though of course a part of himself) and, second, to create a contrast to the tired old man he sees in the *Quartets.* His old woman, enduring the same spiritual journey as the narrator of the *Quartets,* is anything but tired. Explaining why his dramatic character should be a woman, Ralph Mills states that he models this character after his mother. She also serves as a female counterpart of the "Dying Man." But a further reason–again in contrast to the Eliot of the *Four Quartets* who is the "intellectual man"–might be found in the view of women Roethke presents in the love poems. The feminine–Jung's anima–represents the emotional and sensual side of human beings rather than the intellectual and rational. To be sure, it is obvious in these two poetic sequences that Roethke's woman is very much a part of and concerned with the details of the earth and with intuitive responses, whereas the narrator of Eliot's poem deals more in abstract ideas and deliberately expresses his intellectual concern with ideas and their meanings. This is not to say that Eliot does not employ natural details or that Roethke's woman is not concerned with ideas and meaning, but their ways of approaching the world are basically different. It should also be noted that there are many points of similarity within the explorations of the old woman and the man of the *Quartets.* These will be pointed out in the examinations of the individual poems. In discussing the way in which he sees *Meditations of an Old Woman* as presenting an alternate vision of life to that in the *Four Quartets,* Ralph Mills says that Roethke "emphasizes, in contrast to [Eliot], the indeterminate character of human existence: the mixture of despair and gladness; of affection and hatred; of the sensuous and spiritual–and embraces them all."

The relation of these poems to the rest of the poetry is significant. The "looser" line that may have been influenced by Eliot and Whitman is closer in form to the early poems of *Praise to the End!* than to the more rigidly structured poems of *Words for the Wind.* The greater variation of rhythm and the movement away from rhyme also connect these poems to the early poetry. In addition, the structural and thematic organizational technique of cycles of light and darkness are common to both.

There is an even greater connection between these meditations and the poems that follow in *The Far Field.* Thus, we find in these poems a link with the early poetry and a transition to the final volume.

The differences between the *Meditations* and the long poems of *Praise to the End!* are, of course, great. Although they both are formed of longer, looser lines, in the early poetry these lines create the vision of the child. Thus, the images are primarily associative, often appearing disjointed. The rhythm also shows more abrupt changes, again in order to create the exuberant and fearful world of the child. This child, it will be recalled, is seeking to separate himself from his primordial unity with nature and to discover his identity as an individual consciousness. The world is new to him, and all his life lies before him. The old woman, on the other hand, is standing at the other end of that spectrum of life and death, individuality and unity. The approaching end to her separate consciousness, the end of individual life, confronts her. As a separate being she has learned to love the particulars of nature; now she must face the termination of that possibility. Her tone and rhythm are naturally more subdued, though she can rise in anger and can relive the carefree joy of youth. The images are more coherent, befitting one who has made her way through a lifetime in this world.

Both the youth of *Praise to the End!* and the woman of these poems are involved in a journey, a search for an understanding of themselves in their world. The child searches for his identity in this world largely through the wisdom of the unconscious, while the old woman, though in touch with her deeper self, begins her search through the conscious mind. For the boy it is his first journey, for the old woman, her last. For both, though, the journey involves a cyclical process of going forward and backward through periods of light and darkness. The journey for the child began with a reaching out to the things of nature. In the love poems of *Words for the Wind,* this I-Thou relation was extended to other human beings. The questions raised by the coming of consciousness and love of another person are still present in *Meditations of an Old Woman,* but there is also the movement into the third realm of relationship, the realm of the spirit and the meeting of the "eternal *Thou.*" Buber says of the relationship between these different I-Thou meetings: "Every particular *Thou* is a glimpse through to the eternal *Thou;* by means of every particular *Thou* the primary word addresses the eternal *Thou*. . . . The inborn *Thou* is realized in each relation and consummated in none. It is consummated only in the direct relation with the *Thou* that by its nature cannot become *It.*" The beginnings of the search for this "eternal *Thou*" are found in the *Meditations of an Old Woman,* and it becomes the primary goal of the poems to be discussed in chapter 4.

The "First Meditation" opens in a time of darkness for the old woman, and this despair may be the reason for the meditations. All nature seems to participate in the emptiness she feels as she observes in nature those things that complement her own mood:

> On love's worst ugly day,
> The weeds hiss at the edge of the field,
> The small winds make their chilly indictments.
> Elsewhere, in houses, even pails can be sad;
> While stones loosen on the obscure hillside,
> And a tree tilts from its roots,
> Toppling down an embankment.

In the second stanza the human element appears: "The spirit moves, but not always upward." The process of life continues, but, as in the cycles of *Praise to the End!,* the movement may be into darkness rather than light. It is in this state that she says, "But the rind, often, hates the life within." But the wish to give in to the feelings of lifelessness, to cease the process and the struggle, is thwarted by the ever-insistent life urge of the spirit. In the third stanza the old woman, having moved from describing natural objects to human objects, now describes herself in "the days of [her] slowness." "I've become a strange piece of flesh," she says, speaking of her old age. "What's left is light as a seed." Both physically and in the life force that motivates her, she has shrunk to almost nothing. Though light, however, a seed contains the germ of life. Her assessment of her situation is "I need an old crone's knowing." She seeks not the knowledge sought by the lost son or the rational knowledge that is a "hutch for grubby schoolboys!" ("I Cry, Love! Love!") but the intuitive knowing that will release her from "the dreary dance of opposites" ("What Can I Tell My Bones?") that plagues her as she contemplates her life in the face of death.

Her way of approaching this kind of understanding is seen in the second section, which begins in the realm of the imagination, the dream world. What she describes in this and the following section is the journey of the spirit. The description must be given through indirection and metaphor, for that is the way the spirit travels. She imagines herself riding

> Alone, on a bus through western country.
> I sit above the back wheels, where the jolts are hardest,
> And we bounce and sway along toward the midnight.

Moving for a moment away from particular details, she says, "All journeys, I think, are the same." In the universal meaning of this statement she aligns her journey with all others and thus gives it the dimensions of the archetypal quest. But she is concerned with more than the universal, and she describes the sameness in particular details, presenting the "drunken soldier, the old lady with her peppermints"; "And for a while we are all alone." Roethke also describes the feeling and the scenery of the journey; not for a moment are we to be left with the abstract notion of a "journey theme." Through the old woman's imagination he attempts to draw us in, to make us feel the ride, see the shapes flashing past; and he can do this, he assumes, because "All journeys . . . are the same." We have had this experience, and he can call upon it by presenting particular, vivid details.

There is also a journey within a journey; as one jounces along on the bus, staring at nothing, memories arise, and one journeys backward in time even as one moves forward in space. Expectedly, the old woman's journey within a journey is (as Roethke's would be) to the greenhouse world, where she remembers

> Two song sparrows, one within a greenhouse,
> . . . .
> And another, outside, in the bright day.

Singing as the work of the greenhouse goes on, they may represent in this journey the outer and the inner worlds, the present and the past singing in harmony–but also simply this memory of childhood greenhouse days:

> One sang, then the other,
> The songs tumbling over and under the glass,
> And the men beneath them wheeling in dirt to the cement
> benches,
> The laden wheelbarrows creaking and swaying,
> And the up-spring of the plank when a foot left the runway.

Once again, the accumulation of details prevents the image from becoming an abstract idea. The real world of the old woman remains at the center of the poem, and through it the meaning of the poem unfolds. Other memories come in at the end of the section–both personal memories and memories from the age-old collective unconscious shared by all people:

two horses plunging in snow, their lines tangled,
A great wooden sleigh careening behind them,
Swerving up a steep embankment.
For a moment they stand above me,
Their black skins shuddering:
Then they lurch forward,
Lunging down a hillside.

The journey is frightening, the black horses in their lunging forbode terror and disaster, but there is, nonetheless, a movement forward.

In the third section the reflections are narrowed down still more, and the relation of the spirit to the journey is made clear. With two extended metaphors Roethke describes this journey, relating it to the spirit only at the end. In his later poetry he frequently uses this technique, building up an image through particular details so that we are totally involved in the image itself and then relating it to the spiritual quest. In this particular instance the technique seems related to Eliot's description of the dark journey in "East Coker," where there is a similar use of the "as when" clauses followed by a statement about the spirit's journey. As in Eliot, a difficult, despairing journey is described. But where Eliot uses images of the theatre when the lights are extinguished and of an underground tube during the stops between stations, Roethke uses images of the crab and the salmon—once more the things of nature:

As when silt drifts and sifts down through muddy pond-water,
Settling in small beads around weeds and sunken branches,
And one crab, tentative, hunches himself before moving along the
bottom,
Grotesque, awkward, his extended eyes looking at nothing in
particular,
Only a few bubbles loosening from the ill-matched tentacles,
The tail and smaller legs slipping and sliding slowly backward—
So the spirit tries for another life,
Another way and place in which to continue;
Or a salmon, tired, moving up a shallow stream,
Nudges into a back-eddy, a sandy inlet,
Bumping against sticks and bottom-stones, then swinging
Around, back into the tiny maincurrent, the rush of brownish-
white water,
Still swimming forward—
So, I suppose, the spirit journeys.

The images are exquisitely vivid and convincing in spite of their apparent dissimilarity to the human spirit: the grotesque, almost laughable crab moving slowly, awkwardly backward (and we are reminded of Eliot's "Prufrock," though Roethke uses the image as a way to wholeness and vitality rather than a symbol of fragmentation and impotence); the beautiful salmon in its almost hopeless struggle upstream where, if it makes it, it will only lay its eggs and die. These are images of the spirit, beautiful and grotesque, graceful and awkward. The crab moves backward in order to go forward; the salmon moves forward to return to the place of its birth. The movement of the spirit is similar, and we are reminded of Roethke's statement, "To go forward as a spiritual man it is necessary first to go back." The journey begun in the poems of *Praise to the End!* continues, though on a different level, to the end of the poetry. We are also reminded of several phrases from the *Four Quartets* that reveal a similarity in the journeys: "In my beginning is my end. . . . In my end is my beginning" ("East Coker"); "And the way up is the way down, the way forward is the way back" ("The Dry Salvages"); "And the end of all our exploring / Will be to arrive where we started / And know the place for the first time" ("Little Gidding"). There are differences here, too, of course, in the way in which one travels and in what one expects to find at the end of the journey. Eliot's quest is primarily philosophical: the intellectual man is searching out the ways of his soul. Roethke creates an old woman who is living out the days of her search and who looks to the things she knows in nature to give expression to her feelings.

The image of the difficult journey is further described in the final section. The stanza begins with a possible reference to Eliot's *The Waste Land:* "I have gone into the waste lonely places / Behind the eye." What is beyond is not explosive and dynamic—in power neither to save nor to destroy:

> There are no pursuing forms, faces on walls:
> Only the motes of dust in the immaculate hallways,
> The darkness of falling hair, the warnings from lint and spiders,
> . . . .
> There is no riven tree, or lamb dropped by an eagle.

But in the journey of the spirit there is after the darkness and difficulty a time of stillness and the speech of nature:

The cerulean, high in the elm,

. . . .

And the far phoebe, singing,

. . . .

Or the whippoorwill, along the smoky ridges.

It is the old woman's world, the world of nature, where she finds her solace and sees "A flame, intense, visible," which moves without burning. It evokes the image of the burning bush and the still, small voice, but this is no appeal to Yahweh. She is meeting the natural world, and because of it she is able to say,

In such times, lacking a god,
I am still happy.

The second poem of the sequence, "I'm Here," follows the form of the first meditation in moving from a time of darkness and meaninglessness to an exploration of the past–her girlhood with its sensuality and imagination and its impatience–and then to another point of still joy. In addition, it contains a fifth section in which the old woman sees both the joy and the darkness and is prepared to meet whatever life or death will bring. The first stanza begins by asking,

Is it enough?–
The sun loosening the frost on December windows,
The glitter of wet in the first of morning?

These would once have been pleasing, life-giving images, but now the old woman feels separated from them and irritated by them:

Outside, the same sparrows bicker in the eaves.
I'm tired of tiny noises:
The April cheeping, the vireo's insistence,
The prattle of the young no longer pleases.

She is perplexed by "needles and corners" and asks, "Dare I shrink to a hag?" Dare I give up the struggle for new life and become a witch, separating myself from all other people and things?

The second section moves from the winter setting with the old woman imagining herself as a hag to the summertime girlhood when she was "queen of the vale." The images in this and the following section reveal the joys of romantic, idealistic girlhood, the rejoicing in oneself and in nature and feeling the intimate connection between the two. It was a time of openness and discovery of all things–touching, smelling, listening, seeing–as a new awareness of herself as body and spirit developed in accord with nature. She was at the same time "Flesh-awkward, half-alive" and "Bemused; pleased to be." But the old woman interrupts her thoughts with the other side of these feelings:

> So much of adolescence is an ill-defined dying,
> An intolerable waiting,
> A longing for another place and time,
> Another condition.

Although this sounds at the beginning more like Roethke than the old woman, the feeling is clear. The joy in the rose, the sunset, and the smells and feels of things carries with it an expectation, a longing for something undefined and never satisfied. So, the old woman says, we die to those moments of immediate joy as we reach for something more, as we seek out our individual consciousness, our separate and unique identity.

Section 3 includes other memories from childhood, and, in addition, the old woman's speculations on them become more important. The first image is a remembrance of one time (again the specificity of detail helps to make the woman real to us) when she bent to loose her dress from a rose briar, and

> The scent of the half-opened buds came up over me.
> I thought I was going to smother.

To the intensity of childhood feeling is added a sense of the mysterious, almost frightening power of the natural world. This memory opens the old woman's thoughts to the realm of the threshold–an area that is important in much of Roethke's work:

> In the slow coming-out of sleep,
> On the sill of the eyes, something flutters,
> A thing we feel at evening, and by doors,
> Or when we stand at the edge of a thicket,
> And the ground-chill comes closer to us,
> From under the dry leaves,
> A beachy wetness.

This is the subterranean, enticing world of the unconscious that is awakened at the edge of sleep or when the mysteriousness of nature is sensed. And, she says, the body, delighting in thresholds,

Rocks in and out of itself.
A bird, small as a leaf,
Sings in the first
Sunlight.

The sill, the threshold, that moment between sleep and waking–these borderline experiences are occasions for new life. The second memory from childhood describes this threshold in terms of a time of sickness. The adult might call it delirium, but for the child it was actual:

The whole place shook whenever I got a chill–
I closed my eyes, and saw small figures dancing,
A congress of tree-shrews and rats.

And these seemingly repellent creatures are to the child playful inhabitants of her world, romping and jumping,

Their forepaws joined together, like hands–
They seemed very happy.

The section closes with a short memory of wisdom given to the child by her grandmother:

In my grandmother's inner eye,
So she told me when I was little,
A bird always kept singing.
She was a serious woman.

Thus, this mysterious world is confirmed by the old wise one, and with it is an affirmation of life itself: the bird kept singing.

This memory returns her to the present, for she is the old wise one now. And her feelings of irritation in the first section gone, she is able to turn to the world with care and concern: "My geranium is dying, for all I can do." She is herself dying for all she can do as well. The days of childhood joy she has been remembering are simply gone. But she has found something else:

But these roses: I can wear them by looking away.
The eyes rejoice in the act of seeing and the fresh after-image.

Perhaps this is what adolescence sought—a way of preserving the immediate moment as well as rejoicing in it. Again she affirms the moment of stillness. She can admire the rose

> Without staring like a lout, or a moping adolescent;
> Without commotion.
> . . . .
> I prefer the still joy:
> The wasp drinking at the edge of my cup;
> A snake lifting its head;
> A snail's music.

The small things that caused her irritation and seemed an indication of lack of life at the first now bring her joy and are an affirmation of life.

Section 5 is the announcement to whatever may come that she is ready for it. She will not deny life; she feels upheld by it, and so she can face the darkness:

> It's not my first dying.
> I can hold this valley,
> Loose in my lap,
> In my arms.
>
> If the wind means me,
> I'm here!
> Here.

The third meditation is entitled "Her Becoming," and the movement from the final stanza of "I'm Here" is clear. She has prepared herself for her becoming and is now involved in a kind of waiting for whatever the wind will bring. This poem, which is the middle poem of the sequence, is different in structure from the first two. Whereas they began with a time of darkness and moved into light, here the first section reaches a vision of possibility through a "shape, lighted with love" and a ghost from within. After a brief retreat and period of darkness in the second section, the third section renews that vision and reaches its climax through the memory of an experience from the past; it seems to be both the actual past of youth and the eternal past that is captured in the unconscious. The fourth section reaffirms the vision through an extended image of being fully alive, in which she adds to her statement at the end of the previous poem ("If the wind means me,/ I'm here!") the assertion "I become the wind."

"I have learned to sit quietly," she says at the beginning of the poem, but as she waits, watching the wind at play, her inner thoughts are as active and frolicsome as the wind:

> A mad hen in a far corner of the dark,
> Still taking delight in nakedness,
> In the sun, busy at a young body,
> In the rain, slackening on a summer field;
> In the back of my mind, running with the rolling water,
> My breast wild as the waves.

The summer field and rolling water are images of vital life for Roethke, and though the old woman sits quietly her mind is on fire. A vision of "a shape, lighted with love," presents itself, and she responds "From the folds of my skin"–from the body, which, old though it is, can still sing, and its song joins in harmony with nature:

> The air still, the ground alive,
> The earth itself a tune.

This vision gives her a moment of acceptance and openness to herself and nature, and with this the images of the poem become more disjointed, and questions appear: "A face floats in the ferns. Do maimed gods walk?" And the world of the threshold appears:

> A voice keeps rising in my early sleep,
> A muffled voice, a low sweet watery noise.

This is the moment of possible renewal in which old patterns of organizing the world are broken down. There is a measure of chaos, but out of this may come new life. The voice she hears is that of the child–"A child at play, a wind-excited bird"; it is her past and the past of all living things, and she asks,

> Dare I embrace a ghost from my own breast?
> . . . .
> A ghost from the soul's house?

A sense of timelessness is created by this return of the past, and the final question of the section is "Who knows/ The way out of a rose?"–the rose, which is often in Roethke's poetry a symbol for the eternal and timeless.

The second section begins with the feared yet obvious question "Is it the sea we wish? The sleep of the changeless?" Is this the timelessness the old woman desires in order to hold off the approach of death? Is this the only meaning we can hope for? "Last night," she says, "I dreamt of a jauntier principle of order;/ Today I eat my usual diet of shadows." The darkness has reappeared with the daylight, and she asks, "What else can I steal from sleep?" She acknowledges that on the journey of becoming "We start from the dark." But she revolts against this darkness and against the conciliatory advice that suffering is good for the soul:

> Pain teaches us little.
> I can't laugh from a crater of burning pitch.

And when from out of the darkness she asks, "Is there a wisdom in objects?" her reply is "Few objects praise the Lord." She knows "the cold fleshless kiss of contraries," the dark world that is isolated from any real life.

But out of this darkness she is able to say in section 3, "There are times when reality comes closer," and the memory of an experience from girlhood is re-created in her. The memory is apparently of an actual experience:

> In a field, in the actual air,
> I stepped carefully, like a new-shod horse.

But it has about it a feeling of the unconscious or the imagination as well. It is one of those threshold moments that occur within the world of nature. It was this moment for which section 1 of this poem prepared. The field is often for Roethke a place of renewal (e.g., "A house for wisdom; a field for revelation," from "Unfold! Unfold!"). The horse, which appears often in the *Meditations,* in these poems is associated with the positive sensuality of youth, in this case the "raw tumultuous girl." The moment of revelation begins, then, not only with images of the natural sensual world but with this added emphasis on human sensuality as well. The woman indicates the revelatory nature of this experience of "reality":

> And then I ran—
> Ran ahead of myself.

In this moment of timelessness within time,

The light air slowed: It was not night or day.
All natural shapes became symbolical.

The lines narrow as the woman describes her flight from and to what she does not know. But in her terror she cries out to the "loved fox, and the wren"—to the living things she loves. The scene slows from tumultuous activity to a moment of silent stillness, and she asks, "Did my will die? Did I?" She has seen for a moment the timeless meeting with time; she has seen the flame, the fire of the eternal. And her response to it is to follow it with love. She accepts the darkness, the sighing—and the joy, the song. Both are a part of this revelation of love, and she is content now simply to be because she knows that she is:

I sigh before I sing.
I love because I am
A rapt thing with a name.

The final section reaffirms this moment of living:

I hum in pure vibration, like a saw.
. . . .
By swoops of bird, by leaps of fish, I live.
My shadow steadies in a shifting stream;
I live in air; the long light is my home;
I dare caress the stones, the field my friend;
A light wind rises: I become the wind.

Images of life and renewal fill this short section—the air, the light, the stones, the field, the wind—the elements of the natural world that fill the old woman with assurance of the eternal within the present time, and she becomes in this moment one with these life-giving sources.

A brief word should be said about the "mystical" nature of this vision, although the nature of mysticism in Roethke's poetry will be discussed at greater length in chapter 4. Roethke was familiar with the works of mystic writers such as Boehme and Eckhart and also with Evelyn Underhill's works on mysticism. In the *Meditations* he may have been following the steps of the "Mystic Way" Underhill gives in her works: awakening of self, purgation, illumination, the dark night of the soul, and union. The five poems generally follow this pattern, although it is subsumed to some extent by Roethke's naturally recurring cycles of darkness and light.

While the old woman's meditations ought not to be reduced to the five stages of the mystic way, it is interesting at least to note a few ways in which Roethke plays off of traditional mysticism while changing it to conform to his own view of the world. For example, if "I'm Here" corresponds to purgation, what occurs is not the usual overcoming of the senses. Indeed the old woman does come to a new understanding of the things of the world. But whereas she began the poem by being annoyed with them, she moves, by opening herself to the now past sensual joys of childhood and the ever-present past of the unconscious world, to a new delight in them. "Her Becoming," may illustrate the stage of illumination as well as the dark night and union, but when the old woman asks, "Did my will die?" the answer seems to be no. From what we know of the old woman, the traditional abnegation of self seems unlikely.

Although in the final poem, "What Can I Tell My Bones?" she indeed achieves a kind of union that is in many ways associated with traditional mysticism, she seems deliberately to reject orthodox forms of transcendence when she acclaims herself "A prisoner of smells" who "would rather eat than pray" and as she rejoices in the world she finds around her. There may also be a reference to Eliot's "Little Gidding" here in the alternate vision the old woman offers to the narrator of that poem, who is told at the end of his journey, "You are here to kneel / Where prayer has been valid." To the old woman natural objects are not only symbols of what lies beyond. They have life and meaning in themselves. James Miller, comparing mysticism in Eliot and Whitman, finds many similarities in the dramatizations of mystical experience in *Song of Myself* and *Four Quartets.* But one of the differences he points out is related to their ideas of purification, which for Whitman (in what Miller calls inverted mysticism) means celebrating the senses; Eliot remains within traditional mysticism, attempting to purge himself of his burden of sin through fire. Although the world Roethke has created contains within it premises different from Whitman's that lead him to celebrate the senses, here he seems closer to the older poet than to Eliot. Although his "burden of sin" appears in several poems in *Voices and Creatures,* it is not his dominant theme.

The "Fourth Meditation" is structured largely around darkness, aloneness, and the presence of the dead; but there is as well a vision of the *possibility* of light. What is presented is not the experience of revelation that was felt in the previous poems but a description of the "still-to-be-born"—the possibility of as yet unrealized experience. In the final section of the poem this hope moves the old woman to another of her fierce, undaunted affirmations of life in spite of the fact that it is only a hope. This poem is different from the others and from most of Roethke's poetry in that one section is devoted to "the other" who exists not in relation to the self but apart from the self–the world of society. The poem begins with an affirmation of the past:

> I was always one for being alone,
> Seeking in my own way, eternal purpose.

The old woman describes the times "At the edge of the field," "on sandy beaches or walking along green embankments" when she found this purpose in shells or night rain or ripples of water "Tilting back the sunlight." The poetry here is similar to what will be found in *North American Sequence*–elaborate descriptions of particular details of nature, through which comes a renewed sense of life. But this sounds like the greenhouse poems as well. Indeed throughout the poetry Roethke accomplishes his poetic aim by beginning with a very close look at what lies around him. The distinctiveness here and in the poems of *The Far Field* is the way he builds one detail upon another, sometimes leaving the description as it stands and sometimes using it as an extended metaphor.

The old woman begins with such a description of what once had "eternal purpose" for her but now yields only darkness: "Was it yesterday I stretched out the thin bones of my innocence?" Regretting the aloneness she once cherished, she says, "O the songs we hide, singing only to ourselves!" In this dark time "the vague life of the mouth no longer suffices." That is, the life of sensuality no longer is enough. The world is not rejected here; it is a question of the inner and outer worlds corresponding. The spirit and nature must both move together, and she feels now the lifelessness of the one and the separation from the other. So as she stands alone without the comfort of nature, "The dead make more impossible demands from their silence." The spirit does not receive comfort from the ancestors either. Thus, as the section ends, the life-giving signs of nature do not speak to her:

> The river moves, . . .
> A light wind stirs. . . .
> The shape of a lark rises from a stone;
> But there is no song.

In the second section the woman moves first to a consideration of what it is to be a woman. The answers, put in question form, begin rather neutrally, psychologically:

> To be contained, to be a vessel?
> To prefer a window to a door?
> A pool to a river?

But then these questions become more charged—negatively:

> To become lost in a love,
> Yet remain only half aware of the intransient glory?
> To be a mouth, a meal of meat?
> To gaze at a face with the fixed eyes of a spaniel?

Such a woman cannot be our old woman, who has the power to love and to hate passionately and who has known with full awareness the "intransient glory." But such is the way women are viewed: they become only objects to themselves and others.

This loss of selfhood is also present in the self-involved people she goes on to describe, for it is only when you have a self that you are able to reach out to others. These "ritualists of the mirror, the lonely drinkers, . . . those who submerge themselves deliberately in trivia, . . . What do their lives mean?" she asks. They teach their children silence and isolation. They know not the "sharp bones of the poor" or "the soul's authentic hunger." She bitterly describes them as

> Those cat-like immaculate creatures
> For whom the world works;

but, having a self, she is able to reach out to them nonetheless. She knows what they need, they who in their isolation from life "feel neither the tearing iron/ Nor the sound of another footstep—/ How I wish them awake!" she cries, and her prayer is for their awakening through the meeting of spirit and nature that she herself was not able to achieve at the beginning of the poem:

> May the high flower of the hay climb into their hearts;
> May they lean into light and live;
> May they sleep in robes of green, among the ancient ferns;
> May their eyes gleam with the first dawn;
> May the sun gild them a worm;
> May they be taken by the true burning;
> May they flame into being!

She sees a vision of these "gentle and beautiful still-to-be-born" who have within them the possibility for greatness, for spirit in tune with nature. Her love of these creatures, who have clearly fallen far short of their possible glory and who have survived almost in spite of themselves, takes her beyond herself to embrace all humanity:

The descendants of the playful tree-shrew that survived the archaic
killers,
The fang and the claw, the club and the knout, the irrational edict,
The fury of the hate-driven zealot, the meanness of the human
weasel;
Who turned a corner in time, when at last he grew a thumb;
. . . .
A lion of flame, pressed to the point of love,
Yet moves gently among the birds.

In the final section of the poem a change has occurred in her. The reason is not given, but it is clear. By stretching herself out to others, she has come to herself again: "The small fish keep heading into the current"; the struggle continues in nature and continues in her. Now she can say,

I'm in love with the dead! . . .
On a dark day I walk straight toward the rain.

The darkness is not gone, but she can now face it:

By singing we defend;
The husk lives on, ardent as a seed.

And she ends again with her affirmation of life, of body and spirit, the living and the dead:

Is my body speaking? I breathe what I am:
The first and last of all things.
Near the graves of the great dead,
Even the stones speak.

The final meditation is entitled "What Can I Tell My Bones?" The question is, on the one hand, the very simple one of what can I say to my body? After all this struggling with life and death, what word of assurance can I offer to my bones that must surely turn to dust? The title plays off the passage in Ezekiel where the bones are assured of new life and also the second section of Eliot's *Ash Wednesday,* where the scattering and dissolution of the bones is the necessary ascetic prelude to renewal of the spirit. The poem begins in darkness, in the world that is "always late afternoon." There is a tone of sadness, of despair, of tiredness. In the second section this despair turns slightly toward courage. Though the darkness remains, the old woman's spirits pick up as she tries to fight her way through the meaninglessness. In the final section this courage becomes an acceptance that opens out into affirmation of herself and her world.

The poem opens, "Beginner,/ Perpetual beginner"; the recurrent struggle to start over and over again is facing her once more. This may be close to Eliot's statement in "East Coker" that "each venture/ Is a new beginning," but it quite obviously also refers to the way of approaching life that has been found throughout Roethke's poetry: "To go forward . . . you must first go back." The cycles of light and darkness are for Roethke's poetic world the way life is lived. And the old woman is now tired. To begin again, the soul

> stirring sluggishly,
> In the least place of its life,
> A pulse beyond nothingness,

seems almost too much to ask. But in a moment of renewed spirit, a striking out once more for life, she asks in a couplet,

> Before the moon draws back,
> Dare I blaze like a tree?

This is, however, the only sign of life in the section. For her now the world is "always late afternoon," there is a "slow wind," she hears "the weeds' vesperal whine," and she feels she is lost in "Longing for absolutes that never come."

Throughout the meditations the old woman has reached for that further moment, that greater meaning, which if it were achieved would put an end to the cycles of light and darkness, joy and despair, and would move her into a realm of pure being. But that moment does not come. There are no absolutes. The world is constantly changing, renewing itself and decaying—and she with it. But such indeterminacy now threatens her existence:

> And shapes make me afraid:
> The dance of natural objects in the mind,
> The immediate sheen, the reality of straw,
> The shadows crawling down a sunny wall.

The intermingling play of nature and spirit, inner and outer world, darkness and light, that she has sought she now turns away from. And in answer to the question of the title, she says,

O my bones,
Beware those perpetual beginnings,

for they seem to lead nowhere. They are "songs from a spiral tree," which turn round and round and are never concluded. She is caught in the contradictions she cannot understand that lead to impotent anger or sad despair:

Fury of wind, and no apparent wind,
A gust blowing the leaves suddenly upward,
A vine lashing in dry fury,
A man chasing a cat,
With a broken umbrella,
Crying softly.

It is as if the woman's spirits were finally broken, but in the second section her good sense returns, and she lashes out in bitterness at the folly of those who try to console her and at her own self-pity. The reference to Eliot ("Little Gidding") in the first statement is clear:

It is difficult to say all things are well,
When the worst is about to arrive.

She will not turn aside from the horror of her death, but, on the other hand, she will not waste her moments of living in self-pity:

It is fatal to woo yourself,
However graceful the posture.

She faces the reality she knows:

Loved heart, what can I say?
When I was a lark, I sang;
When I was a worm, I devoured.

As a person,

The self says, I am;
The heart says, I am less;
The spirit says, you are nothing.

She must begin from here. The movement upward will come, if it comes, from her way of addressing the heart—"Loved heart." Love, which is her "wound" because it makes her care, will also be her salvation.

The nagging question of her bones returns: "Mist alters the rocks. What can I tell my bones?" She sees through the life cycles of nature her own decay:

> The wide streams go their way,
> The pond lapses back into a glassy silence.

And she asks, "The cause of God in me—has it gone?" Will the life of the spirit ebb and decay like her body? And then, glancing toward Ezekiel and Eliot, she asks, "Do these bones live?" and adds her own question, "Can I live with these bones?" This struggle to deal with life and death does not lead her to seek escape from this world; rather she prays, "O to be delivered from the rational into the realm of pure song." It is not release from the world she cries for in this dark time but a release from the rational and the abstract that prevent her from experiencing immediate existence. In this way her bones could live, and she could live with her bones. With this new understanding the section closes, still in the darkness, but it is now a darkness that has meaning and hope. The poem narrows to two three-line stanzas that describe her search through the dark:

> To try to become like God
> Is far from becoming God.
> O, but I seek and care!

She rejects the mystical oneness with God wherein her own identity would be lost, and she affirms her ability to reach out, to love:

> I rock in my own dark,
> Thinking, God has need of me.
> The dead love the unborn.

The rocking reminds us of the body rocking "in and out of itself" in "I'm Here" and gives the hope that the movement in darkness portends a movement into light. Buber in *I and Thou* criticizes the kind of mystic union that involves total dependence of the person on God and seems to be a denial of one's own self:

> You know always in your heart that you need God more than everything; but do you not know too that God needs you—in the fulness of His eternity needs you? How would man be, how

> would you be, if God did not need him, did not need you? You need God, in order to be–and God needs you, for the very meaning of your life.

And in the final statement the ancestors are again life-giving as the old woman reaffirms the continuity of existence and of love.

The final section opens with the barest note of possibility:

> Weeds turn toward the wind weed-skeletons.
> How slowly all things alter.
> Existence dares perpetuate a soul,
> A wedge of heaven's light, autumnal song.
> I hear a beat of birds, the plangent wings
> That disappear into a waning moon;
> The barest speech of light among the stones.

And this slight hope is to her a reassurance of life she can accept. "I no longer cry for green in the midst of cinders"–she will accept the darkness if it comes–"Or dream of the dead, and their holes"–she will not long for nonbeing. Although this is not as she had thought it would be, she says, "Mercy has many arms." She affirms her existence within this world: "A prisoner of smells, I would rather eat than pray." And in answer to her previous despairing statement, "I know the cold fleshless kiss of contraries," she is now able to say, "I'm released from the dreary dance of opposites." She is at one with her world. "I live in light's extreme," she says, presenting an image of her new vision filled with joy and love:

> The sun! The sun! And all we can become!
> And the time ripe for running to the moon!
> . . . .
> My spirit rises with the rising wind;
> I'm thick with leaves and tender as a dove,
> I take the liberties a short life permits–
> I seek my own meekness;
> I recover my tenderness by long looking.
> By midnight I love everything alive.

With Eliot, for whom "humility is endless" ("East Coker"), the old woman knows the "wisdom of humility," and with both Whitman and Eliot, the value of love. Miller points out in his discussion of *Song of Myself* and *Four Quartets* that in both "it is love that pervades, informs, and gives meaning to the world and universe, and it is spiritual love that is fulfilled in the supreme achievement of mystic insight or in the 'total' release of death." In Roethke's poem as well love is the power that is made possible through the old woman's new insight, and it is love that takes "the darkness from the air" and brings new life. "I'm wet with another life," she says in a beautiful image of rebirth that has its roots in the early greenhouse poem "Cuttings (later)." "Yea, I have gone and stayed."

In the final, short stanza the indication that this represents the mystic stage of union is reinforced by the line "What came to me vaguely is now clear." The insight experienced in the stage of illumination–which for the old woman was a total unity of herself and the wind ("Her Becoming")–is modified and more clearly understood. To love and to move with the life of nature–in this there is no loss of self but renewal of life. And the poem ends,

> What came to me vaguely is now clear,
> As if released by a spirit,
> Or agency outside me.
> Unprayed-for,
> And final.

Buber describes this resolution as well as the struggle of the old woman through her meditations:

> It is a finding without seeking, a discovering of the primal, of origin. His sense of *Thou,* which cannot be satiated till he finds the endless *Thou,* had the *Thou* present to it from the beginning; the presence had only to become wholly real to him in the reality of the hallowed life of the world.

The world of Roethke's poetic creation, from the greenhouse to the vision of the old woman, almost parallels Buber's way of perceiving the world and living in it and loving it. In the final group of Roethke's poems, those of *The Far Field,* this same struggle for the eternal Thou within the "hallowed life of the world" continues in its many forms and several resolutions. All of them, though, involve the life of the spirit as it seeks within this world, in darkness and light, the Thou that gives shared life and meaning to the world.

CHAPTER FOUR

THE SEARCH FOR THE SPIRIT

Roethke's final volume of poetry, *The Far Field,* continues the search begun in *Meditations of an Old Woman* for a reconciliation between the body and the spirit, the joys of change and the longing for permanence, the meaning of life and the reality of death. Roethke has moved fully into that realm of the spirit described by Buber—the search for the "eternal Thou" in which all other relationships acquire their full meaning. His search has two primary focuses that have been present through much of the poetry—the world outside him, the rich and ever-changing world of nature, and the world within, the microcosmos of self and soul. Because the two realms are counterparts of one another, it is the same search. Roethke does not use the world as a way of giving form to the invisible workings of his mind; rather, he sees in both the same process at work. Thus, by exploring the one he can discover something of the other.

The poems of this period take two major forms. One resembles *Meditations of an Old Woman,* having long, flowing lines and no fixed pattern of rhyme or rhythm. This form is developed in *North American Sequence,* and through it Roethke explores the regions of the continent, including all that he can within the expansive embrace of his poetic world. *Sequence Sometimes Metaphysical* best illustrates the other main form, which depends on extreme concentration of imagery. The structure is more firmly set, the lines are shorter and their rhythms more regular and pronounced. Here Roethke attempts to create the intensity of an experience in a compact moment. The aim is to discover in its barest form the unity and relatedness of all things. In both cases the search is for a pattern, an order, that will give meaning and wholeness to experience.

The end of this spiritual quest, the meeting of the final "Thou," occurs in several ways. To some extent Roethke is using forms of the mystic experience to create the moments of meeting—either from his knowledge of such mystics as Boehme and Eckhart and, as mentioned above, Evelyn Underhill's study of mysticism or from his own experience. Regarding his personal understanding, he makes the following statement in his prose piece "On 'Identity,'" which although he is referring to someone else expresses his own thoughts as well: "One could sense a real hunger for a reality more than the immediate: a desire not only for a finality, for a consciousness beyond the mundane, but a desire for quietude, a desire for joy. Now this desire is what the drunkard, the saint, the mystic hankers for in varying ways." Discussing "A Field of Light," he explores further:

> The second part of this feeling, the "oneness," is, of course, the first stage in mystical illumination, an experience many men have had, and still have: the sense that all is one and one is all. This is inevitably accompanied by a loss of the "I," the purely human ego, to another center, a sense of the absurdity of death, a return to a state of innocency.
>
> This experience has come to me so many times, in so many varying circumstances, that I cannot suspect its validity: it is *not* one of the devil's traps, an hallucination, a voice, a snare. I can't claim that the soul, my soul, was absorbed in God. No, God for me still remains someone to be confronted, to be dueled with: that is perhaps my error, my sin of pride. But the oneness, Yes!

Whether or not Roethke is calling on his own experience, what the poems create is clearly a dramatized event, not a confession. His poetry has led him to a point where the various conflicting elements of his poetic world converge into a harmony and wholeness; and insofar as traditional mystical experience is a useful form for presenting this poetically Roethke makes use of it. But he is not bound by these traditional forms and often departs significantly from the "mystic way."

But more must be said. If we are to consider Roethke's poetry of the earth to be an affirmation of the immanent, how are the experiences of mysticism, which seem necessarily to transcend this world, part of this poetry? Underhill defines the mystical experience in several ways: "In mysticism the will is united with the emotions in an impassioned desire to transcend the sense-world, in order that the self may be joined by love to the one eternal and ultimate Object of love." She also says that mystics "have succeeded . . . in establishing immediate communication between the spirit of man, entangled as they declare amongst material things, and that 'only Reality,' that immaterial and final Being, which some philosophers call the Absolute, and most theologians call God." Roethke says in his notebooks that he wants a "rampant, triumphant, fleshly mysticism, the full spasm of the human, not simply beauty and darkness."

A necessary part of the mystic way is the abolition of individuality, the act of "unselfing," but Underhill claims that no European mystics, in contrast to Oriental mystics, see as their goal the annihilation of the self: "The doctrine of annihilation as the end of the soul's ascent . . . is decisively rejected by all European mystics . . . for their aim is not the suppression of life, but its intensification, a change in its form. This change, they say in a paradox which is generally misunderstood, consists in the perfecting of personality by the utter surrender of self." But she notes that to the normal consciousness such a state would *seem* to involve loss of self because it would be impossible for one who has not experienced the state to understand this paradox.

Buber and Underhill describe two types of mystical experience in similar ways but come to different conclusions about the role of the self in each. In the first, described by Buber, the being takes "its stand directly in itself as though it were in the divine One. . . . [This is] the identification of the human with the divine." Underhill describes this as "the metaphysical mystic, for whom the Absolute is impersonal and transcendent, [and who] describes his final attainment of that Absolute as *deification*, or the utter transmutation of the self in God." In the second type, Buber says, "it is imagined that God enters the being that is freed from *I*, or that this being is merged in God. . . . [This is] unification." Underhill calls this the "Spiritual Marriage" of the soul with God and says it is experienced by "the mystic for whom intimate and personal communion has been the mode under which he best apprehended Reality."

Buber claims that in both cases relation is destroyed because it is necessary to maintain the I and the Thou as separate entities to create an authentic relationship. He does go on to say that there can be a sense of the soul's becoming a unity. This happens within the self rather than between man and God and is the necessary preparation for the meeting with another, but it is not an end in itself. In the experience of unification described above he says there can be a meeting that overcomes duality; however, the I is not lost in the One, but both feel the force of the relation itself:

> What the ecstatic man calls union is the enrapturing dynamic of relation, not a unity arisen in this moment of the world's time that dissolves the *I* and the *Thou*, but the dynamic of relation itself,

> which can put itself before its bearers as they steadily confront one another, and cover each from the feeling of the other enraptured one. . . . The relation itself in its vital unity is felt so forcibly that its parts seem to fade before it, and in the force of *its* life, the *I* and the *Thou*, between which it is established, are forgotten.

For Buber this extreme moment of reality, which for Underhill is the supreme goal of all mystics, is not terribly important: "Here is one of the phenomena of the brink to which reality extends and at which it grows dim. But the central reality of the everyday hour on earth, with a streak of sun on a maple twig and the glimpse of the eternal *Thou*, is greater for us than all enigmatic webs on the brink of being." Underhill does say that in the stage of illumination the world of nature takes on new beauty: "The self then becomes conscious of the living reality of that World of Becoming, the vast arena of the Divine creativity, in which the little individual life is immersed. Alike in howling gale and singing cricket it hears the crying aloud of that 'Word which is through all things everlastingly.'" But it is only what is perceived as being transcendental within the world that attracts the mystic. The aims of true mysticism, says Underhill, "are wholly transcendental and spiritual. It is in no way concerned with adding to, exploring, re-arranging, or improving anything in the visible universe." The author of the fourteenth-century mystical writing *The Cloud of Unknowing* describes the "work of the soul" in this way: "Lift up your heart to God with a meek stirring of love, seeking God Himself and none of His created things. . . . You must then do whatever will help you forget all the beings whom God has created and all their works." As Underhill says, "The Unitive Life, though so often lived in the world, is never of it. It belongs to another plane of being, moves securely upon levels unrelated to our speech." And Buber, speaking of both forms of the mystic experience he has described, says of "union":

> What does it help my soul that it can be withdrawn anew from this world here into unity, when this world itself has of necessity no part in the unity—what does all "enjoyment of God" profit a life that is rent in two? If that abundantly rich heavenly moment has nothing to do with my poor earthly moment—what has it then to do with me, who have still to live, in all seriousness still to live, on earth?

Of the identification of the human and divine he says, "In so far as the doctrine contains an affirmation about true being—however the matter stands with its content of truth, which cannot be ascertained in this life—

it has nothing in common with one thing, with lived reality; for it is bound to reduce this too to the world of appearances." Buber's answer to mysticism as he defines it is to say, "But we with holy care wish to foster the holy good of our reality, that is gifted to us for this and perhaps for no other life that is nearer truth."

It seems clear that Roethke's poetry is not the traditional account of mystical experience. He does employ certain characteristics of the mystic way to describe his search for reality, and thus Underhill's work on mysticism is useful in discussing the poetry. But he and Buber oppose the mystics on two points: the goodness and the reality of the I-Thou relationship and of the created world. Although he explores forms of unity and absorption and though he occasionally longs for those extreme moments on the boundaries of reality, he finally comes back to these indisputable truths of "lived reality." Through the struggles and joys of relationships within this world he comes in this final volume to wholeness and meaning.

"THE ROSE IN THE SEA-WIND"

North American Sequence is a series of six rather long poems that are similar to *Meditations of an Old Woman* in their loose, expansive lines that conform to the rhythms of everyday speech. Now, however, the protagonist making the journey into himself and his world is a man—the man who began in the greenhouses, the lost son who found his selfhood through the living things of nature, who delighted in the joys and sorrows of human relationships, and who now seeks to explore the dimension of the spirit. As the title indicates, this quest-journey takes place within the varied landscapes of America. The setting is important both in being the natural world, where much of Roethke's poetry is set, and in being America. In most of his poetry he explores the American landscape because it is what he knows. But here he specifically emphasizes the fact that this is the land of which he is a part. He thus inevitably aligns himself with Walt Whitman, for whose poetry the American landscape was both backdrop and substance, and he deliberately calls on Whitman in "The Abyss," the first poem of *Mixed Sequence*. In establishing specific, different places as the setting for each poem, he also brings Eliot's *Four Quartets* into dialogue with these poems. As in *Meditations,* he occasionally refers to lines or images from Eliot's poems that reveal the poets' common search as well as their different paths. Like the *Meditations* these six poems constitute a dramatically conceived organism. As in the early poetry, there is a constant movement forward and back "with a little progress being made each time." The sequence begins with "The Longing" and moves with alternations between land and water, between interior meditation and exterior relationship, to the final vision of harmony and joy in "The Rose"—Eliot's symbol, Dante's symbol, but also uniquely Roethke's symbol for wholeness of life.

"The Longing" begins in darkness and meaninglessness. It is from this state that the poet longs to escape, and thus the longing becomes the impetus for the whole sequence. The poet describes his dark condition through the natural, the social, and the personal worlds:

> On things asleep, no balm:
> A kingdom of stinks and sighs,
> Fetor of cockroaches, dead fish, petroleum,
> Worse than castoreum of mink or weasels,
> Saliva dripping from warm microphones,
> Agony of crucifixion on barstools.
>   Less and less the illuminated lips,
>   Hands active, eyes cherished;
>   Happiness left to dogs and children—
>   (Matters only a saint mentions!)
> Lust fatigues the soul.

The life of the spirit is in a state of deadness. At such a time the eye perceives the world in all its stagnation and mundaneness and asks the question "How to transcend this sensual emptiness?" "The spirit fails to move forward" in this world where "The great trees no longer shimmer." The poet cannot answer by deserting the very world wherein he has found his life. The "sensual emptiness" must be overcome not by going beyond the world but by filling it with meaning.

In the second section the stigma is removed from the external world and placed within the self: "A wretch needs his wretchedness. Yes." It is his own inability to see beyond the lack of "motions of the soul" that confines his vision to the darkness of the world. But knowing this, he is at least able to move to a vision of possibility:

> How comprehensive that felicity! . . .
> A body with the motion of a soul.

Through this image the two elements that struggle with each other throughout the poems of this sequence are brought together. At this moment the answer is not to move beyond the body, not to see it as "sensual emptiness," but to bring it into harmony with the gracefulness of the soul. Here this unification is still only a vision, not a reality.

Although he says in the previous section, "(Dreams drain the spirit if we dream too long)," he adds here "A dark dream," which contains images of the rose, the moon, the sea. These are images of light, but he is still in his darkness, able only to look on, not to participate in the light. The image of the rose, which recurs as a touchstone of wholeness and possibility throughout the poems and is the culminating image of the sequence, is now present but beyond the reach of the poet: "The rose exceeds, the rose exceeds us all." This is surely different from the image in the early poem "Praise to the End!" in which he said: "The weeds exceed me"; there he was in darkness with no sign of hope. Here hope in the form of the rose is present, but there is not yet any contact with it. It stands as a bright light above the "sensual emptiness" and "wretchedness" but is still seen only through the darkness.

The vision of the dark dream also reminds us of the paradoxical statements of mysticism in which the vision of the Godhead is described both as "Divine Light and Divine Dark" because of its utter discontinuity with our normal ways of describing things. In this poem "A great flame rises from the sunless sea," an unearthly vision to which the poet responds,

> I'd be beyond; I'd be beyond the moon,
> Bare as a bud, and naked as a worm.

To be beyond the moon seems clearly to indicate a movement outside the cycles of nature and becoming, beyond joy and despair, darkness and light. But this is not possible even for the mystic who must live with both the world of "Being and Becoming." In addition, Roethke uses this vision not as a final resting place of union but as the beginning of the movement into light. The images he uses for this beginning are the simple things of nature, the bare bud and naked worm:

> Out of these nothings
> —All beginnings come.

A vision of possibility is thus revealed out of his darkness, and in the third section he has begun his search. He states here the way and the goal that will both be present throughout the sequence. The way is through delight in the world:

> I would with the fish, the blackening salmon, and the mad
> lemmings,
> The children dancing, the flowers widening.
> . . . .

> I would delight in my hands, the branch singing, altering the
> excessive bird.

Through this way he "would unlearn the lingo of exasperation, all the distortions of malice and hatred." The process of unlearning, of beginning again—as in the images of the bud and the worm—is very important. Just as it was necessary to go back to the beginnings of life in order to gain self-awareness, it is also necessary to do this as a spiritual man. He expresses the goal of this process: "I long for the imperishable quiet at the heart of form." The meaning and the realization of these words constitute the rest of the poems of the sequence. He affirms again that this search is to take place in this world:

> This ambush, this silence,
> Where shadow can change into flame,
> And the dark be forgotten.

It is a world of darkness and light, joy and despair, but here it is possible to discover the light. "I have left the body of the whale, but the mouth of the night is still wide," he says, referring to Jonah and thus hinting at a grace that has brought him closer to the light.

The final lines of the poem evoke America. In this place of dryness and slaughter, in the Dakotas, the land of the dead buffalo, a "country of few lakes," the beginning must be made. He refers to "East Coker," Eliot's poem of beginnings, which says,

> Old men ought to be explorers
> Here and there does not matter.

Roethke asks, "Old men should be explorers?" In contrast to Eliot, who aligned himself with his English ancestors, Roethke identifies himself with North America: "I'll be an Indian." This reinforces the idea of beginnings, reminding us of the first explorers of America. It is also, of course, a daring, dangerous choice in which the particularities of "here and there" do indeed matter. As Eliot was concerned in his poem with language, Roethke also makes a subtle reference to it, repeating the rich Indian names with no struggle for articulation: "Ogalala?/ Iroquois."

James McMichael observes that the choice of Iroquois over Ogalala is a decision for the lakes rather than the plains. I do not think, however, it is necessary to interpret this as a choice for a place whose qualities "speak much better for the external world" but rather as a movement toward the water environment of the next poem, which will be followed by an alternating movement back to the interior. Thus, the poet begins his journey in a place of dryness, death, and danger, begins out of the darkness of the longing. From the place on the Dakota plains the next poem, "Meditation at Oyster River," moves into a region of water. The remaining poems, "Journey to the Interior," "The Long Waters," and "The Far Field," alternate between places of land and of water. "The Rose" begins with water and ends by bringing the land and the sea together. It is not possible to assign a simple symbolic scheme to these two elements. I disagree with Hugh Staples's idea, expressed in his often very insightful article, that water imagery generally represents that which is to be strived for and earth imagery that which is to be transcended. He sees water as the source of new life and movement. Although this is true, water is also used to symbolize the changeless, the loss of individuality and growth. As the old woman in "Her Becoming" says, "Is it the sea we wish? The sleep of the changeless?"

The alternation between these two life forces is itself important. It provides the structure of the cycles through which the poems move. If we are to assign a general meaning to these cycles, it would seem close to Underhill's description of the worlds of becoming and being that the mystic brings into reconciled harmony in the unitive life. Possibly the watery regions may indicate what is eternal in human life, and the earthy regions may be concerned with the process of growth and decay. However, even these terms are not fixed, and occasionally the land imagery indicates the unchanging (e.g., "The Long Waters," section 1). In any case, Roethke, unlike Staples and the mystics, will not affirm one over the other. Both earth and water are necessary parts of a dialectical structure through which there is movement forward from the longing in the first poem to the moment of the rose in the sea wind in the last.

"Meditation at Oyster River" begins in a time of twilight. Like the tide that moves in gently and ceaselessly, the lines are long and flowing. The poet passively observes the quiet coming of the tide and the evening, his only action being to climb higher up the cliff away from the incoming tide. The images of nature are subdued; the rocks are "elephant-colored," the ripples "blue-black." There is little sound; "Even the gulls quiet," and the waves slap "lightly against a sunken log." In the earlier poems these may have indicated despondency or the low ebb of the spirit, but here the setting simply indicates this quiet in-between time. "The wind slackens," which is usually a sign of the fading of the spirit, but because it is "A twilight wind, light as a child's breath," it serves this time of meditation. Images of life and death combine and cancel each other out. The poet retires to his higher ledge and prepares to turn his attention inward:

The dew revives on the beach-grass;
The salt-soaked wood of a fire crackles;
A fish raven turns on its perch (a dead tree in the rivermouth),
Its wings catching a last glint of the reflected sunlight.

Through these images the poet moves in the second section into himself. He has been a passive observer of this twilight, in-between time of nature, and now he regrets his lack of participation in the natural world and sees the self as isolated and fearful in its aloneness:

The self persists like a dying star,
In sleep, afraid.

Roethke seems to be referring to the mystic's desire for loss of self, for annihilation in the undulating waves would overcome the isolation. References to death follow immediately; this is what the self fears in sleep and what it would escape through conjunction with the ceaselessly flowing river. But the images following the introduction of death are contradictory:

Death's face rises afresh,
Among the shy beasts, the deer at the salt-lick,
The doe with its sloped shoulders loping across the highway,
The young snake, poised in green leaves, waiting for its fly,
The hummingbird, whirring from quince-blossom to morning-
glory.

These are images of the earth, where indeed death's face is seen. He should want to flee these images, but instead he says, "With these I would be." There is, then, an affirmation of this earthy realm, this changing world, which includes the face of death. He adds:

And with water: the waves coming forward, without cessation,
The waves, altered by sand-bars, beds of kelp, miscellaneous
driftwood,
Topped by cross-winds, tugged at by sinuous undercurrents
The tide rustling in, sliding between the ridges of stone,
The tongues of water, creeping in, quietly.

He brings together the alternating images of the worlds of becoming and being, desiring both and idealizing neither. Although the face of death in the world of nature clearly shows the negative side of that world, the water imagery is not all serenity. There is struggle here as well. With both he would be.

Having moved from passive observation of the twilight world into active assertion of his commitment to the fullness of life, Roethke moves in the third section to the process, the way of reaching for the goal he established in "The Longing." Part of the technique of unlearning is to return to images from the past. They not only have power over the poet with which he must come to terms, they also serve as a source of strength and wisdom, a power for him. Having affirmed in the in-between moment both the land and the water and having accepted the danger of both, he achieves a state of harmony within himself that is a necessary preparation for the return to the past:

> The flesh takes on the pure poise of the spirit,
> Acquires, for a time, the sandpiper's insouciance,
> The hummingbird's surety, the kingfisher's cunning.

In this moment of meditation at Oyster River he reçalls other waters, "the first trembling of a Michigan brook in April," the beginning motion of a "tiny rivulet," a "wrist-thick cascade" that announces the stirrings of spring. He moves from these tiny yet significant and beautiful beginnings to the

> Tittebawasee, in the time between winter and spring,
> When the ice melts along the edges in early afternoon.
> And the midchannel begins cracking and heaving from the
> pressure beneath.

It is the same time of beginning, of reawakening after the deadness of winter, but on two very different scales. Of the tiny rivulet he says,

> Its spray holding a double rain-bow in early morning,
> Small enough to be taken in, embraced, by two arms.

There is the rainbow of promise and hope, the possibility of intimate embrace. Of the large river, beginning to break from its ice-locked prison, he says:

> And I long for the blast of dynamite,
> The sudden sucking roar as the culvert loosens its debris of
> branches and sticks,
> Welter of tin cans, pails, old bird nests, a child's shoe riding a
> log,
> As the piled ice breaks away from the battered spiles,

And the whole river begins to move forward, its bridges
shaking.

The concentration and multiplicity of images and the long, gathering lines build toward this violent release of new life. Both images are beautiful and life-giving, and both indicate corresponding states of the spirit as it strives for a reawakening to life. It comes gently, almost imperceptibly, as the Michigan brook, and it comes violently, thunderously, as the Tittebawasee. These images announce new beginnings in the poet, stirrings, full of vitality but also danger, that have always been in him and are now coming to life after a long winter.

In the final section of this poem we are returned with shorter, gentler lines from the dramatic power of the released river to his present moment at Oyster River in a time of quiescence and silence. Now, however, he is more than a passive observer. He has entered into this quiet, twilight moment of nature:

Now, in this waning of light,
I rock with the motion of morning;
In the cradle of all that is,
I'm lulled into half-sleep
By the lapping of water,
Cries of the sandpiper.

The cradle indicates a kind of passive participation, and the half sleep implies a lack of positive activity by the spirit, but both also indicate rebirth. From this harmonious flowing with the things of nature, a spiritual activity does result; he is not simply lost in the flow of the world:

And the spirit runs, intermittently,
In and out of the small waves,
Runs with the intrepid shorebirds—
How graceful the small before danger!

We are reminded of the tiny siskins of *Words for the Wind* and feel both the beauty and danger in their undaunted flight.

Through this meditation the spirit has begun its movement forward. The emphasis of the poem is on beginnings, but the reminder of danger is still present. The poem closes with lines that speak again of beginnings and of the poet's acceptance of his place in the world. Although previously he cried to be beyond the moon, he now rejoices in the beginning of the moon's new cycle:

In the first of the moon,
All's a scattering,
A shining.

"Journey to the Interior" begins,

In the long journey out of the self,
There are many detours.

The detour in the attempt to reach out beyond the self is a journey inward into the past and into the depths of the psyche. As the previous poem indicated, it is a dangerous journey, announced here by uneven rhythms and described as

washed-out interrupted raw places
Where the shale slides dangerously
And the back wheels hang almost over the edge
At the sudden veering, the moment of turning.

But the "detour" seems to be a natural part of the route of alternation that has characterized the poet's journey from the beginning. This is the time of turning back and daring to face the danger of the past and the deep interior life. The interior is as well, of course, the center of the continent, and thus his journey is to the heartland of America.

In the first section are two images of the danger of this journey. The car on a dangerous detour, struggling to stay on the road, is surrounded by

wind-bitten buttes, the canyons,
Creeks swollen in midsummer from the flash-flood
roaring into the narrow valley.
Reeds beaten flat by wind and rain,
Grey from the long winter, burnt at the base in
late summer.

The second image is of a path narrowing as its winds toward a stream, crossing

Through the swamp alive with quicksand,
The way blocked at last by a fallen fir-tree,
The thickets darkening,
The ravines ugly.

The washed-out road, the winding, blocked path, and on every side danger—these are the challenges that must be faced, and they seem to lead only to dead ends.

In the second section the danger is approached from another angle. As the previous poem turned to the past for the images of the two rivers in their spring reawakenings, now the poet remembers from his youth an experience of danger and exhilaration which evokes the countryside of his past. The interior of America and his remembered past flash before him as he imagines

> how it was to drive in gravel,
> Watching for dangerous down-hill places, where the wheels
> whined beyond eighty—
> . . . .
> A chance? Perhaps. But the road was part of me, and its ditches,
> And the dust lay thick on my eyelids,—Who ever wore goggles?—

In contrast to the detours of the first section, this one seems to be chosen deliberately and with great love for the passing, intimate countryside that you see only on a detour and love for the danger—partially self-created—of the detour itself. The images he evokes of the countryside—and so, we would think, of his interior life—are mixed. There is a great deal of death and dryness, but they are a part of the life of the plain, and he seems to accept them:

> The cemetery with two scrubby trees in the middle of
> the prairie,
> The dead snakes and muskrats, the turtles gasping in
> the rubble,
> The spikey purple bushes in the winding dry creek
> bed—
> The floating hawks, the jackrabbits, the grazing
> cattle—
> . . . .
> And the sun comes out of a blue cloud over the Tetons.

All of them flow past him; "I am not moving but they are," he says, creating the sense of the memory dream. In this same mode of apprehension he sees the grassy plain as the wavy sea, and he rises and falls with these waves. Thus the image of water is brought into the dusty region of the detour. It seems, however, that with the rising and falling of the waves he moves away from the immediacy of the memory. The section begins with a specific recollection of dangerous and exciting driving and moves to the description of all that flows past:

> I rise and fall, and time folds
> Into a long moment;
> And I hear the lichen speak,
> And the ivy advance with its white lizard feet–
> On the shimmering road,
> On the dusty detour.

In the final section of the poem the images are difficult to decipher. The rising and falling motion seems to have rocked "the flesh to sleep." And the soul, then, is at a "still-stand" and at ease. His vision is of

> the flower of all water, above and below me, the
> never receding,
> Moving, unmoving in a parched land, white in the
> moonlight.

Staples points out that "still-stand" would be translated in German as "stagnation," which has more negative connotations. In any case, in the "never receding,/ Moving, unmoving" we do come to a moment of stasis. But in this moment of time "when the small drop forms, but does not fall," he seems to move beyond his "still-stand"; the soul seems actively to gather together the images of darkness and light, life and death. Even in the dry place with the dusty wind and the midnight cries, he can see the heart of the sun, a flicker of fire, hear a slight song. Even though he feels the presence of death, he delights in this world, and as he does so the body reawakens and joins the soul in its quest. He is still in this suspended moment of time,

> Neither forward nor backward,
> Unperplexed, in a place leading nowhere.

But this detour has revealed the wholeness of his past in its beauty, terror, and danger and, by comparison, the wholeness of his present inner self. Now, having understood and successfully avoided the pitfalls of his journey, he can say:

> As a blind man, lifting a curtain, knows it is morning,
> I know this change:
> On one side of silence there is no smile;

> But when I breathe with the birds,
> The spirit of wrath becomes the spirit of blessing,
> And the dead begin from their dark to sing in my sleep.

He has not lost his way on this journey to the interior. He has returned to the past of his youth both as experience and landscape and has entered those dangerous, yet beautiful interior regions of the mind. But he has not remained either in the past or the unconscious. He has rejected the "eternity" that would come through disavowing the reality of the present in which he has accepted his full humanity as both body and spirit and his interior region with all its beauty and terror. He is now prepared to move back to the refreshing waters as the spirit again travels forward.

The next poem, "The Long Waters," begins with a delight in the things of the earth to which the poet returned at the end of the previous poem. The tone is light, carefree:

> Whether the bees have thoughts, we cannot say,
> But the hind part of the worm wiggles the most.

Delighting with butterflies in "the language of smells and dancing," he says,

> Therefore I reject the world of the dog
> Though he hear a note higher than C
> And the thrush stopped in the middle of his song.

By contrasting himself to the dog he asserts his own uniqueness as a human being with powers of consciousness and of spirit, and he renounces the desire to flee the struggle that accompanies these powers. The image also reveals his acceptance of his limitations as a human being. It seems he has learned humility:

> And I acknowledge my foolishness with God,
> My desire for the peaks, the black ravines, the rolling mists
> Changing with every twist of wind,
> The unsinging fields where no lungs breathe,
> Where light is stone.

He is referring at least in part to his temptation in the previous poem to seek out such places, which symbolized the eternity that would deny the present. And so he returns "where fire has been,/ To the charred edge of the sea." As in the water imagery in "Meditation at Oyster River," if the sea does represent a kind of changeless eternity it is not one that is beyond the hazards of this world. Here a little grass pokes out of the scorched earth. There is only a faint sign of life in the midst of a waste land. This is also the place "Where the fresh and salt waters meet"–the ever-changing streams of fresh water making their way to the constancy of the sea.

In the second section the poet calls on "Mnetha, Mother of Har," a figure from Blake's mythology whose name suggests Athena and the Greek word for memory–thus, "wisdom founded on memory." But the poet seems to be asking not so much for her wisdom as to be under her care like Har, a pathetic creature who lives in perpetual innocence and ignorance in his self-centered world. Indeed she will protect him "From the worm's advance and retreat, from the butterfly's havoc" but at the cost of what it is to be really human. Realizing this, he asks,

> But what of her?–
> Who magnifies the morning with her eyes,
> That star winking beyond itself,
> The cricket-voice deep in the midnight field,
> The blue jay rasping from the stunted pine.

"Her" seems to refer to Mnetha and emphasizes her own closeness to nature in a more positive way. This recalls for him through memory both the love of a woman and the love of the natural, ever-changing world. Such memories as "The dry bloom splitting in the wrinkled vale" or "The first snow of the year in the dark fir" fill him with pleasure great enough to bear the risk of living in the world of change. He concludes that, "Feeling, I still delight in my last fall."

Once again, then, there is movement backward and forward. In the first section the poet moves into the world, rejecting the extremes of spirituality that would take him beyond the human into the world "Where light is stone." In the second section he rejects a second option that would take him into the less than human. In both cases he returns to the world to affirm the changing but meaningful natural human reality. Now, in the third section, at the center of the sequence of poems, the poet can make an affirmation by cataloguing the things of nature in his particular place and time. It begins, "In time when the trout and young salmon leap for the low-flying insects." He lists plant, bird, and human life under the controlling "in time" in an attempt to reveal the fullness of this moment when "These waves, in the sun, remind me of flowers." And then he lists the flowers, both living and dead, in settings of beauty and "Down by the muck." This is his world. This is his place of affirmation. In the closing stanza of this section he gives the meaning of these catalogues:

> I have come here without courting silence,
> Blessed by the lips of a low wind,
> To a rich desolation of wind and water,
> To a landlocked bay, where the salt water is freshened
> By small streams running down under fallen fir trees.

He affirms the world in spite of death, decay, and times of darkness. He affirms things in their reality, their wholeness. Like the old woman he can embrace the world.

The fourth section creates an image that leads to a memory in which this moment is reaffirmed. The image is of "the vaporous grey of early morning," another in-between time, in which

> A single wave comes in like the neck of a great swan
> Swimming slowly, its back ruffled by the light
> cross-winds,
> To a tree lying flat, its crown half broken.

This single wave, this particular of nature, singled out from the totality for special observation and contemplation, recalls to him

> a stone breaking the eddying current,
> Neither white nor red, in the dead middle way.

As he imagines the wave to be like a swan, a noble, graceful symbol of the spirit, so he sees the stone, also a sign of spiritual renewal, placed squarely in the midst of the swirling water. This is for the spirit a place

> Where impulse no longer dictates, nor the darkening
> shadow,
> A vulnerable place,
> Surrounded by sand, broken shells, the wreckage of
> water.

The steady, enduring stone in the midst of the rushing water brings together the unchanging eternal and the constantly altering temporal. In this moment neither the less-than-human impulse nor the greater-than-human shadow rules. Thus, it is a vulnerable place—the place of living fully within the earth.

In the final section the renewal at the side of the long waters is once again emphasized. The humility acknowledged in the first section is reaffirmed, and the image of the child, tragically and wrongly sought in Har, is repeated now not as something to escape to but as an ever-present source of strength, indicating the continuity and rootedness of human life. The section begins with the extended simile that works so well for Roethke in these poems:

> As light reflects from a lake, in late evening,
> . . . .
> As a fire, seemingly long dead, flares up from a
> downdraft of air in a chimney,
> Or a breeze moves over the knees from a low hill,
> So the sea wind wakes desire.
> My body shimmers with a light flame.

The awakening that occurs in the presence of this breath of life does not exclude the body or desire. It is now possible for the poet to bring them into harmony with the eternal spirit. This sense of the eternal is given as a vision from sleep, from the depths of the psyche. In it appear

> the child, the swaying vine branch,
> The numinous ring around the opening flower,
> The friend that runs before me on the windy headlands,
> Neither voice nor vision.

All are parts of the self just as the self is part of the world. In the final stanza the poet repeats the lesson of humility and reveals what he has now become:

> I, who came back from the depths laughing too loudly,
> Become another thing;
> My eyes extend beyond the farthest bloom of the waves;
> I lose and find myself in the long water;
> I am gathered together once more;
> I embrace the world.

The self is lost–but found again. He is gathered together, yet he embraces the world. This is not a unity that destroys the individual self-in-the-world of the poet. Rather there is a meeting, a coming together in which the self in its wholeness stands in relation to the eternal Thou and the meaning of the world is fully affirmed.

The title of the following poem, "The Far Field," indicates the movement once again into a region of land. As in the "Journey to the Interior," this poem also begins with a recounting of the journeys the self must take: "I dream of journeys repeatedly." Also as before, the journeys are not easy and often end in bleak dead ends. The first image Roethke gives is "Of flying like a bat deep into a narrowing tunnel." Using this natural analogy for the route of the human spirit, the poet creates the blind, fruitless journey that leads to the dead end. Then he moves abruptly from this natural image to one of a journey in a car and extends this image through the rest of the section, building detail on detail of failure and futility:

> Of driving alone, without luggage, out a long peninsula,
> . . . .
> Alternate snow and sleet, no on-coming traffic,
> And no lights behind, . . .
> The road changing from glazed tarface to a rubble of
> stone,
> Ending at last in a hopeless sand-rut,
> Where the car stalls,
> Churning in a snowdrift
> Until the headlights darken.

These two images of futility, of "end places," lead into the second section that begins "At the field's end," a place of isolation and decay. We discover that, as in "Journey to the Interior," this too is a journey into the past. This end place is

> Not too far away from the ever-changing flower-dump,
> Among the tin cans, tires, rusted pipes, broken machinery.

And Roethke says it is here, "in the shrunken face of a dead rat . . . And the tom-cat . . . Blasted to death by the night watchman," that "One learned of the eternal." Again Roethke uses the technique of building image on image and then reaching unexpectedly the statement toward which the images have been building. Finding the eternal in such a place seems to indicate two things. First, what has seemed so desirable and salutary may in fact be something quite different. And although the eternal may then seem to be loathsome, it is another important lesson in unlearning. It is at the end places of the earth at the time when it is not expected and in a way that is shocking that one comes upon the eternal. Therefore, these journeys into the dark and lonely places are not futile. The vision comes at the edge of the abyss.

The second part of this section moves from images of death to images of life. Though he "suffered for birds, for young rabbits caught in the mower," he admits,

> My grief was not excessive.
> For to come upon warblers in early May
> Was to forget time and death.

In the remainder of the section the poet presents two ways of trying to face the harsh truth of the field's end. The first is through watching and rejoicing in the birds; as Roethke used the analogy of the bat to describe the flight of the human spirit, now he uses analogies of other natural things to describe birds, which are

> Moving, elusive as fish, fearless,
> Hanging, bunched like young fruit, bending the end
>   branches.

These life-giving images persist in spite of the fact of death.

The second possibility for facing the image of the eternal in death recalls two earlier poems, "River Incident," from *The Lost Son,* and "Snake," from *Words for the Wind,* in that they all contain symbols of reincarnation. Through the imagination and the memory—both the conscious and the unconscious memory that leads down through all living things to the roots, the mire—the poet brings himself close to the common origins of all living things. He imagines his life energy projected through different forms in both the past and the future; and while asserting his eternal life through various forms he nevertheless achieves a sense of delight and playfulness in this prospect rather than a heavy seriousness:

> —Or to lie naked in sand,
> In the silted shallows of a slow river,
> Fingering a shell,
> Thinking:
> Once I was something like this, mindless,
> Or perhaps with another mind, less peculiar;
> Or to sink down to the hips in a mossy quagmire;
> Or, with skinny knees, to sit astride a wet log,
> Believing:
> I'll return again,
> As a snake or a raucous bird,
> Or, with luck, as a lion.

He reveres all of life, delighting in the prospect of sometime filling the forms he loves—the snake, the bird, the lion. He has no desire to move upward in the scale of spirituality; indeed there is no such scale. This view of life contrasts with Eastern reincarnation and also with Pierre Teilhard de Chardin's idea of the progressive movement of the world toward and beyond human spirituality. He rejoices in all of life, each living thing possessing its unique, beloved wholeness.

From these two possibilities he is able to answer his earlier vision of the eternal in this poem as well as to understand correctly now his earlier longing for the peaks and far fields in "The Long Waters":

> I learned not to fear infinity,
> The far field, the windy cliffs of forever,
> The dying of time in the white light of tomorrow,
> The wheel turning away from itself,
> The sprawl of the wave,
> The on-coming water.

Neither eternity nor temporality is to be feared because both are enveloped by the same process of life.

From this point of acceptance and courage the poet is able to move forward: "I feel a weightless change, a moving forward." As before, such movement comes not by willing or seeking; in a moment of reconciliation it simply happens. Now the movement begins

> As of water quickening before a narrowing channel
> . . . .
> Or when two rivers combine.

We have returned to the water, and Roethke reveals the movement of the spirit by describing the fullness and actuality of the life of the river. What the poet comes to is

> a still, but not a deep center,
> A point outside the glittering current;
> . . . .
> My mind moves in more than one place,
> In a country half-land, half-water.

Malkoff raises the question at this point of the nature of the moment of tranquility and wholeness. Is it, he asks, similar to Eliot's mystical intersection of the timeless in time; or is it more an aesthetic experience where the still center lies in the imaginative mind, as Louis Martz would assert; or is it an existential realization of the self in its wholeness? Malkoff points out that these areas are not mutually exclusive for Roethke and refers to his prose essay "On 'Identity,'" in which Roethke says,

> I take it that we are faced with at least four principal themes: (1) The multiplicity, the chaos of modern life; (2) The way, the means of establishing a personal identity, a self in the face of that chaos; (3) The nature of creation, that faculty for producing order out of disorder in the arts, particularly in poetry; and (4) The nature of God Himself.

It is true that these elements are all interrelated and are all part of this moment in the world of the poem. It seems, though, that their crucial point of relatedness lies in the understanding of order that Roethke searches out and comes to affirm in his poetic world. And that order appears to lie finally in the givenness of the world as Roethke has conceived it in the poetry. This moment of wholeness comes for human beings—and perhaps we could say the poem comes for the poet—when the imagination and the memory are able to perceive this order of which they are a part. Having come to this point at the end of section 3, the poet is able to affirm his death, even to be renewed by the thought of it, insofar as it is for him an evidence of the wholeness of life. And he is able to say,

> What I love is near at hand,
> Always, in earth and air.

In the final section the poet once again affirms his life and death, now through his association with the sea; and he calls himself a "sea-shape," reminding us of ever-changing, ever-renewing Proteus. He pictures himself as an old man in robes of green, the color of the living earth that promises renewal. Roethke moves in the next two stanzas first to the image of a person in all his splendor, then to the world in all its splendor; and the order seems appropriate since it has been the pattern that when the self comes to its wholeness it is able to move out to the world. Thus, he begins with the self:

> A man faced with his own immensity
> Wakes all the waves, all their loose wandering fire.
> . . . .
> He is the end of things, the final man.

Roethke calls up Stevens's "major man" of "Notes toward a Supreme Fiction," thus exulting the imagination in man. Stevens was important to Roethke, but it seems that Roethke moves beyond–or Stevens might say is still behind–the fictive world of Stevens's imagination. To be sure, they shared a "rage for order," but I am convinced that Roethke's poetry –that is, both the poetic world he creates and the act of creating that takes place in the world–puts more stress on a created order that lies outside the poet's mind and enables his creation to take place. It is the discovery of this order that is the act of creation within the poem. As Meredith says of the greenhouse poems, "Instead of ordering experience, these poems attend on experience with the conviction that there is order in it . . . *revealed* order." Thus, in "The Far Field" he moves from the "final man" to the world of which that man is a part, where

> All finite things reveal infinitude:
> The mountain with its singular bright shade
> . . . .
> The after-light upon ice-burdened pines;
> Odor of basswood on a mountain-slope,

and with these, and treasuring them, is

> The pure serene of memory in one man,–
> A ripple widening from a single stone
> Winding around the waters of the world.

This moment of serenity in which the finite and the infinite are revealed together and through each other is the prelude to the final conjunction of these poles of life in the last poem of *North American Sequence,* "The Rose." An image of hope and possibility, the rose appeared first in the opening poem, "The Longing." It now symbolizes the fulfillment of that longing in "the imperishable quiet at the heart of form." The poem begins,

> There are those to whom place is unimportant,
> But this place, where sea and fresh water meet,
> Is important.

Eliot also uses the rose as his culminating symbol in "Little Gidding." But Roethke, asserting again the importance of the particulars of this world, separates himself from Eliot and his more philosophical approach and describes the details of *this* place, the birds and the landscape, to show why it is important. Its significance lies in the marvelousness and uniqueness of the living things themselves.

The time is sunset and, as in "Meditation at Oyster River," it is a time of growing stillness as night comes on. In "Oyster River," however, there was a sense of isolation and emptiness in the passive observation of the stillness. Now silence itself is a part of the reality of the place and is accepted along with the sounds of the waves and the birdcalls. The poet has learned to affirm both sound and silence and is no longer isolated from them. The poem moves to the first person in the third stanza:

> I sway outside myself
> Into the darkening currents

and the poet becomes a part of the place rather than moving to a higher rock as he did at the time in his journey when meditation was necessary. The section ends with a question that both rouses the memory of a past moment of wholeness with this place and anticipates a coming moment:

> Was it here I wore a crown of birds for a moment
> While on a far point of the rocks
> The light heightened,
> And below, in a mist out of nowhere,
> The first rain gathered?

Having firmly established the particularity of the external world, the poet moves into this new moment of vision by opening the second section with an extended simile of a journey. Throughout the poems there have been particular journeys, and the sequence itself is a journey across North America from "The Longing" to "The Rose." But where the specific journeys mentioned before were filled with danger and often led nowhere or to death, the poet now has reached the point where the journey is wholly graceful:

> As when a ship sails with a light wind–
> The waves less than the ripples made by rising fish,
> The lacelike wrinkles of the wake widening, thinning out,
> . . . .
> The stern high, dipping like a child's boat in a pond–
> Our motion continues.

In contrast to the constant, peaceful motion of the ship is the rose. In the following stanza this focal symbol is revealed in all the particularities of its place in the natural world. This has been Roethke's intention throughout the poetry: not to use the natural world as a steppingstone to something that lies beyond it nor as a useful poetic device to clothe his philosophy but, rather, to present the actual details of the real world in which, we might say, he meets the eternal Thou. The rose does stand for a wholeness and realization of being in his poetry, but that is only because to have come the journey with him through the poem and to see this rose in the sea wind is to experience the meeting and to know the wholeness. And so the rose stays, constant in a world of change, amid thorns and weeds, moving with the waves yet remaining as they recede, at this place where the eternal sea and the flowing stream come together. But this is a paraphrase, and the rose depends upon the experience:

> But this rose, this rose in the sea-wind,
> Stays,
> Stays in its true place,
> Flowering out of the dark,
> Widening at high noon, face upward,
> A single wild rose, struggling out of the white embrace of the
>   morning-glory,
> Out of the briary hedge, the tangle of matted underbrush,
> Beyond the clover, the ragged hay,
> Beyond the sea pine, the oak, the wind-tipped madrona,
> Moving with the waves, the undulating driftwood,
> Where the slow creek winds down to the black sand of the shore
> With its thick grassy scum and crabs scuttling back into their
>   glistening craters.

In the final stanza of this section the power of memory recalls the roses of the greenhouse and brings together the early poems of *The Lost Son* with these poems as parts of one continuous journey:

> And I think of roses, roses,
>
> . . . .
>
> And my father standing astride the cement benches,
> Lifting me high over the four-foot stems . . .
> And how those flowerheads seemed to flow toward me,
>   to beckon me, only a child, out of myself.

Those earliest poems recorded the child's coming to a realization of himself as an individual through the I-Thou relationship he felt with the living things of nature and with his family:

What need for heaven, then,
With that man, and those roses?

But as he grew out of himself and away from his father and into the world that brought darkness and sorrow and finally the approach of death, there was a need for something more. This moment of the rose in the sea wind is the assurance that he has found it.

Having come to this point in which the eternal and temporal, the past and present, are enfolded, the poet reaches out to the land wherein this moment has been reached. He uses the forms of sound and silence that were established in the first stanza of this poem to reveal his unity with this land:

What do they tell us, sound and silence?
I think of American sounds in this silence.

He has perhaps Whitman in mind as his counselor as he unfolds the sounds of America that are a part of this moment of the silence of the rose. The poet seeks both to find himself in all the land from which his poetry has come and to bring all that land into his poetry. Of course, the canvas of Whitman's painting is much vaster; he includes far more details of America in *Song of Myself.* Perhaps because Whitman includes so very much, Roethke's catalogue seems more convincing. In the multiplicity of details Whitman's images often become universals, and perhaps this is what he sought. In Roethke's poem the sounds of America retain their particularity. His sweeping panorama is never created at the cost of losing the song of this thrush and the whistling of that killdeer. What is especially surprising is that he is able to include not only the sounds of nature, which we know he can do, but also the sounds of society, which he seldom does convincingly. Here they move together in harmony, the catbird and the bulldozer; and all are contained within the moment of the rose, all are part of that affirmation. He moves from the sounds of nature to those of society and then says, "I return to the twittering of swallows above water." He is back at the place of the opening of the poem, and now with the fullness of the rose and of America there is

that single sound,
When the mind remembers all,
And gently the light enters the sleeping soul,
A sound so thin it could not woo a bird.

His response to this moment, which may justly be called a moment of grace, is almost a prayer: "Beautiful my desire, and the place of my desire."

In the final stanza of this section sound and silence again come together, this time in the poet's mind as he thinks "of the rock singing, and light making its own silence / . . . in early summer" in moonlight; or he thinks of

> that lonely time before the breaking of morning
>
> . . . .
>
> While the moon lingers,
> And a drop of rain water hangs at the tip of a leaf
> Shifting in the wakening sunlight
> Like the eye of a new-caught fish.

The images of beginnings in nature are recalled in the mind and give shape to the awakening of the poet.

At the conclusion of this sequence we return to another image of the rose as a way of affirming that life in this world contains within it the possibility for wholeness of the self and movement to the other. The first stanza once again affirms the reality of this world with its light and its darkness:

> I live with the rocks, their weeds,
> Their filmy fringes of green, their harsh
> Edges, their holes
> Cut by the sea-slime.

In this imperfect though wondrous world the rose exists. As he comes to it, there is a moment of self-realization and a wholeness that contains the contradictory realities of life:

> Near this rose, in this grove of sun-parched, wind-warped
> madronas,
> Among the half-dead trees, I came upon the true ease of
> myself,
> As if another man appeared out of the depths of my being,
> And I stood outside myself,
> Beyond becoming and perishing,
> A something wholly other,
> As if I swayed out on the wildest wave alive,
> And yet was still.

His response to this vision that defies time is not to escape to it but to find in it meaning for the life lived in time:

> And I rejoiced in being what I was:
> In the lilac change, the white reptilian calm,
> In the bird beyond the bough, the single one
> With all the air to greet him as he flies,
> The dolphin rising from the darkening waves.

He moves from rejoicing in who he is to his meeting with the world through the image of the rose:

> And in this rose, this rose in the sea-wind,
> Rooted in stone, keeping the whole of light,
> Gathering to itself sound and silence–
> Mine and the sea-wind's.

In this final stanza the polar elements, so often at odds throughout the poems, now come together in a supreme moment of meeting. The longing has been satisfied, and the goals that Roethke expressed in "On 'Identity'" and which are also affirmed by Buber are attained: the poet has reached quietude and joy.

"THE ABYSS"

The next two sections, *Love Poems* and *Mixed Sequence*, were not arranged by Roethke, and although there are groups of poems that move together in each the sequences as wholes lack unity. The love poems contain a simplicity and openness that follow naturally from the vision of the rose at the end of the previous sequence. The first poems reveal a lyrical quality and a young girl's undarkened innocence. The final poems, also songlike, reveal a personal quality not often found in the poetry. All Roethke's poetry is personal, of course, in the sense that he makes himself the protagonist of his poetry; further, much of the material for the poetry actually does come from his life. But here he reveals his present life and the love relationship he shares with his young wife. The poems are quite simple; they are songs filled with tenderness. They are not the best of Roethke's poetry, but they reveal his individual humanity more than any others.

In the final love poem, "Wish for a Young Wife," Roethke is speaking–sadly, tragically, as it turns out–his own thoughts to his young Beatrice.

As in the other less personal love poems he uses the things of nature to address and describe the beloved, so it is here. The poem is a song, almost a prayer:

My lizard, my lively writher,
May your limbs never wither,
May the eyes in your face
Survive the green ice
Of envy's mean gaze;
May you live out your life
Without hate, without grief,
And your hair ever blaze,
In the sun, in the sun,
When I am undone,
When I am no one.

Mixed Sequence includes poems that deal with a variety of subjects: the spiritual quest of the poet, portraits of creatures and people, and insanity. The opening poem, "The Abyss," is itself a mixture of poetic styles and ideas. It seems clear that Roethke is aware of certain mystical doctrines as he writes; and the poem is to some extent the journey of the dark night of the soul and the movement into the unitive life. In William Heyen's discussion of Roethke's use of Underhill's five-step mystic way in "The Divine Abyss," he makes the excellent point that critics who accuse Roethke's poetry of leaping to an unearned affirmation fail to consider that "the happiness achieved in any Roethke poem . . . is not one based on reason, on step-by-step logical confrontations with dissatisfaction, on rational duels with and victories over disquieting thoughts." In most of the poems the movement to "joy is sudden and the realization of happiness is logically unfounded, is intuitive. . . . The mystical experience itself is ineffable, does not proceed reasonably."

The mystery of the abyss seems connected with Boehme's "Unground" insofar as it is darkness that is also the source of light. But it is also Kierkegaard's abyss, the point of despair to which one must come before salvation and, related to this, Tillich's nonbeing against which the courage to be asserts itself and thus strengthens itself. The abyss is also that dark region, so often found in Roethke's poetry, out of which all life comes; it is the mire, the slime, the underness of things. And it is the threat of return to nothingness, nonbeing. But through facing it steadfastly one comes, as Tillich says, to "the experience of the power of being." To be able to face it, to have the courage to be, is in itself an indication of faith in the ability of being to encompass nonbeing.

In the face of this abyss the poem moves with more drastic shifts than usual from despair to joy. The technique shifts sharply as well, the opening section reminding us of the poems of *Praise to the End!* with their irrational, associational quality and the second section moving abruptly into a style closer to that of *Meditations of an Old Woman*. Through all this Roethke's struggle with the world remains constant. His love of the things of the earth and his fear of losing them are accompanied by a longing to transcend them and all that their finitude implies.

The abyss confronts him with an acknowledgment of his shortcomings. In a traditional act of purgation he calls into question the imagination and the senses (the poetic act and the world). But through his appeal to Walt Whitman, the poet for whom purgation meant not the denial of the senses but the celebration of them, he demonstrates his deviation from the traditional mystic way:

> Be with me, Whitman, maker of catalogues:
> For the world invades me again,
> And once more the tongues begin babbling.
> And the terrible hunger for objects quails me.

The appeal to Whitman may indicate first the affirmation with Whitman that the world is not to be left behind; in his hunger for objects is his life. But as a maker of catalogues Whitman also presents a way of placing the things of the world into a pattern and so controlling them. In this sense the "invasion" can be stopped through the act of imaginative transformation. Thus the imagination and the world are affirmed rather than transcended.

Nonetheless, there is a tension throughout the poem between transcending this world ("How can I dream except beyond this life?") and becoming wholly a part of it (as he says of the tendrils, "I envy . . . their eyeless seeking."). He must live on the edge, hovering between the two and partaking of both. As he accepts this, he comes to a moment of "half-rest" in which the mind ceases its busy questioning:

> Knowing slows for a moment,
> And not-knowing enters, silent,
> Bearing being itself,
> And the fire dances
> To the stream's
> Flowing.

The paradoxical experience of the mystics comes to him; through not knowing he begins to know, as the fire and the water move in harmony. Rosemary Sullivan notes Roethke's comments on "not-knowing" in the notebooks and its connection with *The Cloud of Unknowing:* "'What is there to know? Not-knowing. We think by feeling, what is there to know? The answer is unknowing, the unknowing of the cloud of unknowing' (Notebooks, Reel 14, no. 204). Obviously the source of his terminology is the fourteenth-century mystical tract, *The Cloud of Unknowing,* which describes how the state of being can be approached through contemplation: 'Contemplation is just this unknowing knowing, this blind seeing, this presence which is unfelt . . . the earnest of the unmentionable, ineffable glory which is to come.'" Roethke creates a time of darkness—"I rock between dark and dark"—where there is acceptance and calm, where there is faith in spite of not knowing. Roethke has brought together the darkness of the underworld, the origins of things from which the lost son moved, and the darkness of the mystics' dark night of the soul. In this moment, at least, what lies behind and what lies ahead, which are both sources of life within this world for human beings, come together and pronounce the words that express the truth of much of Roethke's poetry:

"Adore and draw near.
Who knows this—
Knows all."

The things of nature are again sources of life in which he can rejoice. Using the mystical description of the unitive life, the "Spiritual Marriage," he says in language and images that are now explicitly religious:

I am most immoderately married:
The Lord God has taken my heaviness away;
I have merged, like the bird, with the bright air,
And my thought flies to the place by the bo-tree.

Being, not doing, is my first joy.

Evelyn Underhill says the first aim of the mystic is "Being, not Doing," and here Roethke has created not only the realization of this in the protagonist of the poem but also the fullness and joy of the moment of being itself.

Also found in this section are portrait poems of people, creatures, and plants. The poems about people are quite good, especially "Otto," and are important in that they add to the fairly small "social" dimension of the poetry. As is usual in Roethke's poetry, however, the creatures and flowers of the earth are best explored. In "The Lizard" and "The Geranium" Roethke establishes a relationship with a particular living thing. We find out a great deal about the poet even though his attention focuses on the external object, but these living things do not seem to be an excuse for the poet's thoughts. We get a sense of genuine interest in and caring for these creatures of nature. He may move beyond their individuality to a larger world, but their present uniqueness is equally important.

"The Lizard" opens, "He too has eaten well"–immediately bringing into conjunction the reptile and the human observer, who has presumably also eaten well. This is reinforced by the recognition that

> his world and mine are the same,
> The Mediterranean sun shining on us, equally.

The lizard is observing him as carefully as he is watching the lizard:

> His head, stiff as a scarab, turned to one side,
> His right eye staring straight at me.

We see that place is important again–it is the "Mediterranean sun"–and a detailed description of this strange creature, brought in this moment into a one-to-one meeting with the poet, establishes its individuality. The sense of some interchange occurring between these two living things who share the same place in the sun is heightened by the poet's asking "(Would a cigarette disturb him?)" and by the observation of the lizard's reaction:

> At the first scratch of the match
> He turns his head slightly.

He retires half beneath "A dried strawberry leaf" but keeps "One round eye still toward me." A butterfly appears,

> But the eye of the tiny lizard stays with me.
> One greenish lid lifts a bit higher,
> Then slides down over the eye's surface,
> Rising again, slowly,
> Opening, closing.

The repeated mention of the lizard's eye, culminating in this precise description of its silent opening and closing–a detail so small, so easy to miss—brings our focus squarely and fully upon this tiny, insignificant creature who now stands as a total, individual life in relation to our own.

At this point in the final stanza Roethke takes us beyond this lizard and this moment in the Mediterranean sun to a time long before human origins. It is as if he has used a telephoto lens on the lizard's eye, blinking slowly at us, and then pulls away, further and further back, leaving the history of mankind behind and finally encompassing a region we have never seen before, scarcely thought about in our deepest sleep. He does this not by moving to abstract, universal language; rather, through the particulars of this time and this place there emerges a time beyond human time which for this brief moment, in a lizard's eye, the poet can experience:

> To whom does this terrace belong?—
> With its limestone crumbling into fine greyish dust,
> Its bevy of bees, and its wind-beaten rickety sun-chairs.
> Not to me, but this lizard,
> Older than I, or the cockroach.

"The Geranium" emphasizes the mutuality of living things. The geranium is undeniably a part of the household, and in fact, it is the possibility that the geranium is too much in touch with the poet that finally terminates the relationship. This is not a flower of the greenhouse but one that has lived with a different kind of human care:

> gin, bobbie pins, half-smoked cigars, dead beer,
> Her shriveled petals falling
> On the faded carpet, the stale
> Steak grease stuck to her fuzzy leaves.

The geranium is given definite human characteristics but retains her separateness, suffering in this strange, unworthy apartment. The poem begins with both the poet's care for this run-down plant that seems to mirror his own condition and also, viewed through his perceptions, the plant's care for and reliance on him:

> When I put her out, once, by the garbage pail,
> She looked so limp and bedraggled,
> So foolish and trusting, like a sick poodle,
> Or a wizened aster in late September,
> I brought her back in again
> For a new routine—
> Vitamins, water, and whatever
> Sustenance seemed sensible
> At the time.

The ability of the plant to respond, as well as the similarity of their seedy states, is expressed in the second stanza:

> The things she endured!–
> The dumb dames shrieking half the night
> Or the two of us, alone, both seedy,
> Me breathing booze at her,
> She leaning out of her pot toward the window.

What finally ends it all is the poet's perception, whether imaginary or real, that

> she seemed almost to hear me–
> And that was scary.

It is not clear to the keeper of the geranium or to us just how much he is projecting himself onto the plant–for indeed they are similar–and how much the geranium is actually able to respond to him. This mystery is left undisclosed. What is clear is that though he said nothing "when that snuffling cretin of a maid / Threw her, pot and all, into the trash-can," he felt a deep loss, as if a part of him had gone with the geranium or as if a vital relationship had been destroyed:

> But I sacked the presumptuous hag the next week,
> I was that lonely.

A final poem from this sequence should be mentioned because, although it does not present new techniques or approaches, it does reveal an attitude of calm, peaceful acceptance that has gradually become more prevalent in the poetry. For a moment in "The Manifestation" the poet has moved beyond the darkness and the struggle and even beyond the intensity of the moment of vision, into a region of serenity. The poem consists of one stanza of eight lines and a second stanza of three lines. It begins, "Many arrivals make us live," and the rest of the stanza is the unfolding of the meaning of that statement. Five images are given that describe growing things as they begin or as they are renewed or as they continue their steady progression through the earth. We sense life in these images, and in sensing it we are called back to life ourselves. These images are not only of things that are obviously life-giving–the bird and the sprouting seed–but also of the mole and the worm. All living things are a manifestation of life. But there is another dimension as well. These images not only describe how we gain new life from observing and participating in it through these other forms of life, but they also are analogies for the forms of life, the new arrivals, that are within us. We learn to live not only through the bird, the skipping, graceful spirit, but also through the mole, that underground, unconscious world within us. The arrivals are described in this way:

> the tree becoming
> Green, a bird tipping the topmost bough,
> A seed pushing itself beyond itself,
> The mole making its way through darkest ground,
> The worm, intrepid scholar of the soil.

The poet then asks, "Do these analogies perplex?" and proceeds to give four more images, this time of nature itself:

> A sky with clouds,
> The motion of the moon, and waves at play,
> A sea-wind pausing in a summer tree.

Each of these presents a careful conjunction of being and becoming, of enduring and changing, of stillness and motion. As the world of nature is sustained through the commingling of these contradictory elements, so are we.

The final stanza is a simple, unquestioning affirmation. It contains three associationally related statements that, though they can stand alone, have all been worked toward in other poems:

> What does what it should do needs nothing more.
> The body moves, though slowly, toward desire.
> We come to something without knowing why.

The fulfillment of who we are is all we can do. As we discover that we are living creatures who have within us the power of love and sympathy and the power of spirit, then we can move toward desire—toward, not away from, the world we live in and the people and creatures of that world. And the wholeness and peace we discover in that meeting is a manifestation we did not even know enough to ask for—"Unprayed-for,/ And final."

THE STRUGGLE WITH DARKNESS

In the poems of *North American Sequence* the poet turned his attention outward in order to arrive at a moment of inward peace and understanding. In *Sequence Sometimes Metaphysical* the process is reversed, and there is an intense concentration inward. Rather than attempting to encompass all America within their bounds, and with it the spirit, these poems seek to strike straight into the heart of the spirit and there uncover its secret. The tightly constructed poems often rhyme and the rhythms are usually regular.

Roethke notes in his essay "How to Write Like Somebody Else" that one of the differences between him and Yeats is his use of end-stopped lines in the pentameter (which occurs in many of the poems in this sequence). He goes on to give his reasons for this: "It is part of an effort, however clumsy, to bring the language back to bare, hard, even terrible statement." Although these words may be applied to many of Roethke's poems, they are clearly a touchstone to a poem such as "In a Dark Time" as well as several others in this sequence.

In a symposium on "In a Dark Time," Roethke says of the poem, "It is the first of a sequence, part of a hunt, a drive toward God." It is important to see this poem as a part of a sequence, and, unlike the two sequences that have just been discussed, Roethke did arrange this one. Thus we can assume that the poems do work together, beginning with the intense, mystical struggle of "In a Dark Time" and moving through the sequence to the quiet affirmation of "The Right Thing" and "Once More, the Round." "In a Dark Time," then, is a stage on the journey, one way of trying to find one's true identity and to reconcile the conflicting elements within the self and between the self and the world.

The poem clearly involves some sort of mystical experience. Though it may not follow traditional forms of the dark night of the soul, Roethke himself says he uses certain terms out of mystical literature. Also, when describing the poem in the symposium, he gives the indication that the writing of the poem was itself a kind of mystical experience: "This was a dictated poem, something given, scarcely mine at all. For about three days before its writing I felt disembodied, out of time; then the poem virtually wrote itself, on a day in summer, 1958. . . . I was granted an insight beyond the usual, let us say. To speak of it further is a betrayal of the experience." In addition to this mystical aspect the poem portrays a psychological experience. The "shadow-side" is faced, and through the following period of dissociation, which is close to madness, the self is finally united and made whole with an almost terrifying intensity. Finally, Roethke seems to be revealing here the poetic image of a statement he makes in "On 'Identity'" when speaking of the oneness described earlier: "I can't claim that the soul, my soul, was absorbed in God. No, God for me still remains someone to be confronted, to be dueled with: that is perhaps my error, my sin of pride. But the oneness, Yes!"

In the final stanza of "In a Dark Time," such a dueling accompanies the oneness. The traditional goals of mystic unity seem not to be present. Where the mystic union would have at its forefront the supreme virtue of infusion of divine love and subsequent peacefulness that would come through complete humility in putting off self, Roethke's moment of vision, though intense and vital, possesses an unsettled quality, a quality of openness and mystery, that is almost terror. The soul is free in a "tearing wind." The image is hopeful but not unambiguous and not, certainly, the final, all-answering moment of the mystic union. In addition, the soul seems to be challenging God as well as becoming one with him; the sense of humility and loss of will to another is not present.

The form of "In a Dark Time" is quite rigidly controlled. The stanzas consist of regular iambic pentameter rhyming or off-rhyming *abbacc.* Kunitz comments on the style in this way:

> "In a Dark Time" is marked by a style of oracular abstraction. The vocabulary is plain, predominantly monosyllabic; the pentameters are strictly measured and often balanced; the stanzaic units, with their formalized combination of true and off-rhyme, adhere to a tight pattern. If these fiercely won controls were to break down at any point, the whole poem would collapse in a cry, a tremendous outpouring of wordless agitation.

This contraction and concentration make it essential that the form give control to the intensity; this is unlike the poems of *North American Sequence* where the loose, flowing form was appropriate for the method of expansive incorporation.

Within this controlled form the poem opens "In a dark time." Roethke seems close to the mystical doctrine that such a period of darkness and despair is necessary for the final movement toward illumination and union. Seeing in the dark is a common metaphor in mystical expression. The object of mystical contemplation always remains ineffable and unavailable to the light of conscious reason, and so it appears as "darkness" or "nothing" to our usual sight. Darkness is also a necessary preparation for putting aside the light of reason in order to be able to see with other eyes. In both senses "In a dark time, the eye begins to see." *The Cloud of Unknowing* describes this experience of darkness:

> You will find that there is at the start but a darkness; there is, as it were, a cloud of unknowing. . . . No matter what you do, this darkness and this cloud is between you and your God and because of it you can neither see Him clearly with your reason in the light of understanding, nor can you feel Him with your affection in the sweetness of love. Be prepared, therefore, to remain in this darkness as long as must be, crying evermore for Him whom you love. For if you are ever to feel Him or to see Him, it will necessarily be within this cloud and within this darkness.

This experience is also described as "nothing":

> Leave this everywhere and this something alone and choose this nowhere and this nothing. Do not be concerned if your mind cannot reason about this nothing; for certainly I love it much the better. It is so valuable a thing in itself that no one can reason about it. This nothing can be felt more easily than it can be seen, for it brings a blinding darkness to those who look at it for even a little while.

And so in Roethke's poem "In a dark time, the eye begins to see." At the edge of the abyss, when the soul knows only despair, the movement upward *may* begin. But what the eye sees and the soul must face is the "shadow-side," the other self, which represents all that one tends to deny about oneself. Thus, it is close to Jung's description of the shadow. It is this other self that the poet must face and join with if he is to move toward the spiritual illumination and psychological wholeness he seeks. He identifies himself as "A lord of nature weeping to a tree." As Roethke points out, the irony lies not in his weeping but in the lack of self-understanding in one who sets himself up as superior to the natural world. When he is able to see the things of nature as his equals, he finds in the tree and other living things his greatest consolation and strength as he faces his dark time:

> I live between the heron and the wren,
> Beasts of the hill and serpents of the den.

In the second stanza he finds consolation by identifying himself with and calling on a group of ancestors who share his intense seeking into that world beyond the rational that often results in the condition the rational world calls madness:

> What's madness but nobility of soul
> At odds with circumstance?

With such as these he takes his stand and gains his courage as he plunges into the darkness of the soul. Paradoxically "The day's on fire!" in this darkness. His mind is ablaze with the intensity of mystical revelation. But what he feels intensely is "the purity of pure despair." His shadow is pinned against the wall, unable to unite with the other self. The ego must traverse "That place among the rocks"–the place of the decisive moment, and he asks, "Is it a cave, / Or winding path? The edge is what I have." The images of the cave and winding path are found in earlier poems, and again they seem to signify the unknown, which must be explained and which will most likely lead to a dead end. Thus, the edge, the abyss, is what must be faced.

In the third stanza the mystical correspondences between the world of nature and the divine invade him like a storm:

> A night flowing with birds, a ragged moon,
> And in broad day the midnight come again!

Birds, the perpetual singers, which for Roethke are harbingers of the spiritual, fill the night. The moon is ragged, a strange image seeming to denote a cloudy unreality, and day and night intermix as the sense of time is lost. "A man goes far to find out what he is," the poet says. He goes so far as to surrender to the spiritual storm, as in "The Renewal," risking the loss of the self in order to find the self. And the self is indeed temporarily lost in this darkness outside space and time:

> Death of the self in a long, tearless night,
> All natural shapes blazing unnatural light.

In this night of brightness the soul perceives, in stanza 4, the darkness of itself. Having experienced both a sublime moment of vision and the depths of darkness within, the soul is torn as it stands at the threshold not knowing in which direction to turn:

> My soul, like some heat-maddened summer fly,
> Keeps buzzing at the sill. Which I is *I*?

The answer comes as the poet recognizes himself for what he is–neither divine nor spiritless but "A fallen man." Then he can climb out of his fear both of the unnatural blazing of God and of the heat-maddened fly, and the selves can finally join together in a whole being. Thus psychological wholeness is achieved; and, just as immediately, spiritual wholeness comes, and a daring, dangerous freedom is his:

> The mind enters itself, and God the mind,
> And one is One, free in the tearing wind.

Roethke says of these final, complex lines:

> The lines say, "The mind enters itself": this suggests (visually at least) an androgynous act, a hole disappearing into itself, "crawling into your hole and pulling your hole after you," the folk saying has it. An unpleasant image. It is stock myself, and maybe stock mystical doctrine. And perhaps the next part of the line, by itself—"and God the mind"—is right out of the hymn books, though it is usually the heart He enters, if we believe the hot-gospelers.
>
> But the next line? "And one is One." This seems a genuine double, at the least. In the Platonic sense, the one becomes the many, in this moment. But also—and this is what terrified me—the one not merely makes his peace with God . . . he—if we read One as the Godhead theologically placed above God—transcends God: he becomes the Godhead itself, not only the veritable creator of the universe but the creator of the revealed God. This is no jump for the timid, no flick from the occult, no moment in the rose garden. Instead it is a cry from the mire, and may be the devil's own.

Roethke is close here to Richard of St. Victor, who says of meditation, "God enters into the mind" and "the mind also enters into itself." His experience also seems similar to the "divine unground" of Boehme: that which exists before the Trinity and which is, above all, freedom. This is the freedom of both the mire and the spirit and may be a symbol for the meeting place of the origins and the goal of Roethke's poetry. On the other hand, Roethke's statement may be closer to Tillich's description of the "God above God" that evokes an absolute faith, creating "the courage that takes the radical doubt, the doubt about God, into itself." From a certain traditional viewpoint such radical doubt could be seen as a "cry from the mire," but for Tillich it is the only affirmation possible in the face of radical despair. Tillich says that this state of being grasped by the God beyond God is "the situation on the boundary of man's possibilities." It is this boundary, this opening of possibilities, that seems to be the point Roethke has reached. The individual is not lost but is given freedom–dreadful freedom–in the tearing wind of this world.

The poems that follow in this sequence turn in several directions, all of them searching for the resolution that will bring wholeness and triumphant meaning to life despite the continuing presence of death. "In a Dark Time" sought these things through that intensely blazing moment beyond time; "In Evening Air," while affirming both the things of nature and the transcendent moment that might come through nature, cannot overcome the approaching darkness that marks the end of the day lived within the natural world. In "The Sequel" the poet turns his back on these changing, dying joys and discovers that he now lives in a day of darkness. Finally, in "The Motion," having returned to affirm himself as a man in the world, he is able once more to begin to hope. In "Infirmity" many of these ways of approaching the world come together, and the poet approaches an understanding and a resolution that are both realistic and affirmative. The poem is filled with the rage Roethke mentioned in earlier poems; this may be a saving rage (see "The Sententious Man"), because he is able to move beyond it in the final two stanzas to accept and affirm the world in its paradoxical beauty.

He begins with the bitterness and sarcasm of an old man who feels the approach of death in this body. He is bitter because his only cause for rejoicing is through the destruction of all he loves. In what can by now be seen as a pattern in Roethke's poetry, he turns to the living things of nature for consolation and finds in his relation to them a coming together of the temporal and eternal. In this relationship he is able to affirm and accept his life and his death.

In the first stanza the poet challenges his own deepest affirmations by doubting the meaning of song–that creative utterance rising from bird and poet alike which has been for him a sign of the linking and fulfilling of the physical and spiritual. Now he says,

> In purest song one plays the constant fool
> As changes shimmer in the inner eye.

We are reminded of the old woman's grandmother, who said a bird always kept singing in her inner eye. But while that was a sign of vitality and promise, this image is of meaningless chaos. The purity and changelessness one searches for in song are mocked by the constant changes at the very heart of things. The poet's only reply to this world is an ironic affirmation of himself–and that was never enough in Roethke's poetry:

I stare and stare into a deepening pool
And tell myself my image cannot die.
I love myself: that's my one constancy.

This narcissism is so appalling to him that he is brought momentarily out of his sarcasm to utter a cry of desperation: "Oh, to be something else, yet still to be!" Gone is the sense of possibility of the previous poem with its certainty that "our chance is still to be." In despair at what he is and doubting that anything else is possible, he turns in stanza 2 to call on Christ, the protector of the sick and lonely. But his appeal is that Christ "rejoice in my infirmity." That it will be the decay of his physical body that will bring on his divinity is hardly a reassuring truth to the man who has loved life in that body and who is now suffering the pains of its decay. His reluctant acceptance of such a proposition is shown as he gives vivid details of what is actually happening to his body; the reality of his life is this:

Sweet Christ, rejoice in my infirmity;
There's little left I care to call my own.
Today they drained the fluid from a knee
And pumped a shoulder full of cortisone.

With little left he cares to call his own, he is following the mystic way of putting aside the individual self. But obviously he is not doing it in the way the mystics had in mind. His saying "Thus I conform to my divinity" adds a further note of bitterness in his use of the word "conform" to describe his approaching spirituality. The only sign of life in the stanza comes in his final comparison of himself to a dying tree. He can understand and accept the workings of the world of nature much better than the paradoxes of abstract thought:

Thus I conform to my divinity
By dying inward, like an aging tree.

In the third stanza the tension between the decaying body and the influx of spiritual light becomes stronger:

a pure extreme of light
Breaks on me as my meager flesh breaks down.

The purity comes only as the "living eye" begins to fade. "The soul delights in that extremity," the poet says with double irony. The soul may well delight, but what of the body which is partner to the soul and which has been equally involved in this quest for wholeness of life? Also, can the soul really delight in this "extremity" since it is tied inseparably to and intermingled with the body? Can the soul stand aside and delight in what is perceived by the self—which has its identity, its wholeness in the body—as a painful loss of itself? The poet's rage breaks out again:

> Blessed the meek; they shall inherit wrath;
> I'm son and father of my only death.

This rage against the nature of things, in which he finds death as well as a world he loves, has been with him all along. He has sought an order that would do justice to the world even in the face of death and that would also take account of the life of the spirit that has found its joy within this world. Now he is filled with empty wrath as he feels the brightness of the light of the spirit, which he has sought so long, coming at the cost of the world he loves. He has in a sense willed his death if that is the price of spirit; thus, he is the creator and the receiver of his "only death."

This conflict continues into stanza 4. He tries to "conform" himself to his divinity by stilling these unquiet thoughts and concentrating on the movement of the eternal:

> A mind too active is no mind at all;
> The deep eye sees the shimmer on the stone;
> The eternal seeks, and finds, the temporal.

He seems to accept this long-sought goal as he affirms his passage from this temporal world to the embrace of the eternal. But though there is no obvious holding back from this embrace, the words themselves speak a deep sadness and regret:

> The change from dark to light of the slow moon,
> Dead to myself, and all I hold most dear,
> I move beyond the reach of wind and fire.

He has moved beyond the conflicts and the joys of "wind and fire." He has reached what he sought. But the deadness he feels seems to extend beyond his body; his soul itself appears to have died with the loss of all he loves.

With a rapid shift he turns from the realm of the eternal to the living world of nature and of song:

> Deep in the greens of summer sing the lives
> I've come to love.

And rejoicing in this summer world, he finds,

> My ears still hear the bird when all is still;
> My soul is still my soul, and still the Son,
> And knowing this, I am not yet undone.

The separation from the world and the loss of self he dreaded have not occurred. He can still rejoice in the summer day and the vireo whetting its bill. What he feared in his eternity has not come to pass. "My soul is still my soul, and still the Son" refers, among other things, to the Son of God and the Incarnation. The meaning of the Incarnation—the eternal within the temporal—seems to be what he has discovered and experienced. The eternal may endure beyond the changing world, but it is discovered within this world and through the body. It is only by loving the one that he comes to the other. But if this is the nature of eternity, it is indeed difficult to attain; it requires the love and acceptance of the changing world and a recognition of the mutuality of all living things:

> Things without hands take hands: there is no choice,—
> Eternity's not easily come by.

It also requires the coming together of opposites, the acceptance of paradoxes, so that the body—the senses that have always brought him joy—becomes the loving means of moving to the spirit:

> When opposites come suddenly in place,
> I teach my eyes to hear, my ears to see
> How body from spirit slowly does unwind
> Until we are pure spirit at the end.

The rage and bitterness are now gone, and loving affirmation and acceptance take their place as, for this moment, symbolized by the Incarnation, the eternal and the temporal mingle and the spirit emerges from them both.

This moment of harmony is fleeting, as so often it is in Roethke's poetry; in the next poem the struggle with God is taken up again. It is called "The Decision," and once again the poet must determine to face the darkness in his search for wholeness. "The Marrow" continues this tone, exploring one of the bleak roads the man who takes this journey must travel. The poem begins in one of the periods of isolation and lack of vitality that often precede a movement to a state of renewal. In this poem, however, as in "The Decision," there is only a determination, a hope, for such a state rather than its actual accomplishment. This poem moves from inactivity and alienation to the renewal of the search for God and ends in a cry to that God for the knowledge that would bring him wholeness and meaning.

Through images of the natural world the opening section reveals the lack of life and the accompanying wish for death:

> The wind from off the sea says nothing new.
> The mist above me sings with its small flies.

Without a vital life within he can see only the lifelessness of nature without. The whole of nature seems to reprove him as, with additional images of devastation, he senses his own yearning to escape to death:

> From a burnt pine the sharp speech of a crow
> Tells me my drinking breeds a will to die.

Roethke uses the voice of the common, somewhat foolish man who yet can rise, later in the poem, to turn seriously to his deepest concerns and say, "Brooding on God, I may become a man." By making the protagonist of the poem painfully human, Roethke is advancing the possibility that it is not the hero who struggles with his God but simply the human being. He realizes that to seek too much of what lies behind the veil, to look directly at the face of God, would mean his destruction: "One look too close can take my soul away." Thus he seeks at least to become a man.

Having moved from the deadness of inactivity and bitterness to contemplation, he is now filled with the desire to overcome his aloneness and meaninglessness. The search for new life is expressed through the prayer of the third section. This cry to God becomes the central point of the search in this poem. It is a cry of both faith and despair. In the paradoxical way in which Tillich's God above God or Ground of Being is "the Yes [that] includes itself and the No which it takes into itself," Roethke calls to "Godhead above my God," affirming his faith in this source of life while asking at the same time, "Are you there still?" The despair and the affirmation go together; in his "half-death" he feels the dark closing in around him—the dark that the soul "once could melt . . .

with its small breath." Now he beseeches God in a way that reveals both the pride he feels in his capability to struggle with God and the humility he feels in the insurmountable distance between them:

> Lord, hear me out, and hear me out this day:
> From me to Thee's a long and terrible way.

Roethke reveals here in a quiet, bare, yet incredibly powerful way the core of the struggle, the search that is inherent in much of his poetry. This is the impetus to the journey that began in the greenhouse but was not yet verbalized. It continues throughout the poetry, taking its fully conscious form only in this final volume of poems. There is a note of desperation and faith. It is the cry in the darkness that lies behind and gives meaning to the joyful affirmations that fill the greater part of Roethke's poetry. It reveals the intimate experience with despair that refutes all claims of an easy optimism within the poetry.

In the final stanza this darkness is not removed but is given greater depth as the poet offers himself wholly before this power he believes he can meet through the despair. As though struck by a flash of lightning "When light divided on a storm-tossed tree," he is cut to the quick in his desire to open himself entirely to wholeness of being. In this moment he says, "I was flung back from suffering and love." He moves beyond the pain and pleasure of his individual self but still remains himself. Using biblical language, he says, "Yea, I have slain my will, and still I live." With another paradox he says, "I shut my eyes to see." Finally, in the last lines of the poem, we get to the heart, to the marrow, the very source of his life that he offers to his God, offers with a sense of humility that bespeaks atonement and a sense of fraternity that asks equality:

> I bleed my bones, their marrow to bestow
> Upon that God who knows what I would know.

As in "In a Dark Time," we feel a faith in the God above God who is far above him and a terrifying belief in his ability to face that Ground of his being and to take on the knowledge of Being. Although this remains only a prayer rather than the realization of "In a Dark Time," the same sense of faith and risk, of totally giving oneself and aspiring to become total in oneself, is present.

"The Tree, the Bird" begins with a gladness he achieved in "I Waited." In the midst of a stony field the poet experiences a deeply shared life with the things of nature. The union of commingled life with the tree and the bird, however, has an intensity that is almost more than he can bear. Yet he is able to affirm it with a terrible joy that brings us back to the ultimacy–in both its terror and its joy–that is found at the end of "In a Dark Time" and sought at the end of "The Marrow."

The poem opens with the poet "At ease with joy, a self-enchanted man." The stony fields, the snail, the light all seem in accord with him as he moves in a dreamlike world. As he says, however, it is an enchanted world; and it is with himself he is enchanted. As he sighs, sensing his loss of self by enchantment with self, he is able to stand outside his life, to open himself to what exists beyond him. Where before the night was brightened by the moon and he felt himself to be "a finger pointing at the moon," he now turns to the dark side of the tree:

> A leaf unaltered by the midnight scene,
> Part of a tree still dark, still, deathly still.

In this dark stillness he sees an image of double life, a willow

> Bearing its life and more, a double sound,
> Kin to the wind, and the bleak whistling rain.

This double sound is of the tree and the bird–that which is firmly rooted in nature and that which soars and sings like the spirit. Their coming together is not imaged as a carefree, gentle meeting but rather as an intense cry out of the midnight darkness:

> The willow with its bird grew loud, grew louder still.
> I could not bear its song, that altering
> With every shift of air, those beating wings,
> The lonely buzz behind my midnight eyes;–
> How deep the mother-root of that still cry!

The intensity, the incessant motion, the dark reunion are far from the calm and peacefulness he had hoped to find. And how frightening and awe-full the deepness of the cry. It reaches to his roots, his origins in the darkness from which he had thought he must escape. There is a coming together of the parts of life, of the body and spirit, which seems unworldly and strange because it is unexpected; but in this stanza the poet moves from terror to acceptance to a new kind of joy as he understands, as if for the first time, the "mother-root" that has been a part of his search since the beginnings in the greenhouse. In the final stanza the darkness disappears, and a new kind of day dawns:

> The present falls, the present falls away;
> How pure the motion of the rising day.

The image of the bird is given once more, but this time the dark terror is gone:

> The bird, the beating bird, extending wings–.
> Thus I endure this last pure stretch of joy,
> The dire dimension of a final thing.

As in the two earlier poems, "In a Dark Time" and "The Marrow," this final thing that man would become is not unambiguously desirable. There is a "dire dimension" to it, an extremity that takes man beyond himself and thus threatens the existence of the self. But for the tenuous moment a balance is held, and in that moment wholeness of being is experienced.

"WE END IN JOY"

Roethke's values are evident in the movement in three poems that evoke a sense of ultimacy: "In a Dark Time," "The Marrow," and "The Tree, the Bird." The extreme of being in "In a Dark Time" is filled with the purity of pure freedom; in "The Marrow" what is sought is pure knowledge; and in "The Tree, the Bird" the poet attains the purity of joy which is, finally, the goal toward which Roethke's poetry reaches. As he says in "The Moment,"

> What else to say?
> We end in joy.

The remaining three poems in *The Far Field* are a testimony to that joy. Having reached this final dimension in "The Tree, the Bird" through darkness and anguish, the poet is able to rejoice in what has been found. Although we may trust that this is not the final step in the recurring process of darkness and light–that if Roethke had lived there would have been more times of despair as well as joy–this is the final moment given in this final sequence and is indeed the region toward which all his poetry struggled.

In "The Restored" the battle is fought and won once more, but the two-beat lines that rhyme *aabb* create a sense of lightness, indicating that the desperation of the earlier poems is at least temporarily gone. The poem opens with the image of the soul dancing–the exemplification of harmony throughout Roethke's poetry. In addition, the soul takes the form of a bird, another example of grace-filled life. The enemy of the soul in this poem is that antagonist to the dance, reason. Insofar as it stifles life and deadens spontaneity, reason is a target of criticism in Roethke's poetry. Because of the gentle lightness of the verse in this poem, however, the attack on reason is more loving than vicious:

> In a hand like a bowl
> Danced my own soul,
> Small as an elf,
> All by itself.
>
> When she thought I thought
> She dropped as if shot.
> "I've only one wing," she said,
> "The other's gone dead."

The significance of rage, which was discussed in terms of several poems from *The Waking,* is further clarified here:

> When I raged, when I wailed,
> And my reason failed,
> That delicate thing
> Grew back a new wing.

This rage apparently has the power to save because it takes the place of the constricting reason that debilitates the soul. In the final stanza the poem returns to the vision of the soul dancing. The image of the stone gives the dance the semblance of eternity, and the normal calculations of time lose their meaning as high noon and midnight come together. The movement of the stanza is toward a "still point of light," which is again for Roethke an image of harmony and fullness of being:

> And danced, at high noon,
> On a hot, dusty stone,
> In the still point of light
> Of my last midnight.

The soul has been restored to its wholeness and is able to live at its fullest in this sacred dance.

Roethke uses the villanelle form in "The Right Thing," modifying it only slightly to suit his needs. The first and third lines of the poem are "Let others probe the mystery if they can" and "The right thing happens to the happy man." Roethke rearranges the repetition of these lines so that the two central stanzas do not contain the element of mystery, which then returns in the last two stanzas in a different way. To create this evolution in the understanding of mystery, it is also necessary for him to change the line containing the word "mystery" each time it appears. At the same time he follows the villanelle form in exact repetition of the third line. "The right thing happens to the happy man," then, is the stabilizing element of the poem; woven into this affirmation is "mystery" that evolves as the happy man moves closer and closer to himself.

The poem begins,

> Let others probe the mystery if they can.
> Time-harried prisoners of *Shall* and *Will*–
> The right thing happens to the happy man.

He has himself probed deeply into the mystery he has felt all around him from the moments in the greenhouse. Through the long struggle of the poetry he has now reached the point where he need ask no more, for he has found the mystery to be life-giving, and that is all he needs to know. In the second stanza he gives an example of the mystery:

> The bird flies out, the bird flies back again;
> The hill becomes the valley, and is still;
> Let others delve that mystery if they can.

Roethke expresses here the belief that is at the very heart of all his poetry–a faith in the created order. He has faced the roots of consciousness through his child poems of *Praise to the End!* trusting that out of the chaos of one's origins order will be revealed. He has faced the risk of reaching out to another, believing that a shared life rather than destruction of the self will result. He has faced the abyss of spiritual meaninglessness and despair, having faith that the yes of life is stronger than the no of nonbeing. Having taken these risks and having passed through the darkness, he is now able to affirm wholly the ever-changing, ever-renewing order of nature.

The third stanza opens with an affirmation that is also central to Roethke's poetry and that has its beginnings in the greenhouse poems: "God bless the roots!–Body and soul are one!" The roots of life both deep within the inner consciousness of human beings and within the depths of the natural world contain that unity and wholeness that humans must struggle through darkness and despair to rediscover as spiritual beings. The answer was in the greenhouse, but it could not be perceived in its wholeness without the long journey that led the poet through both joy and despair, light and darkness. Now a "happy man," he returns to the roots. Because he has been a "Child of the dark," now "he can out leap the sun." Because he has discovered the joys of his own individuality and the oneness of body and soul that constitute that individuality, he can enter into a wholeness with all other living things and so share in the unity of life:

> His being single, and that being all:
> The right thing happens to the happy man.

Such a man, the poet adds, turning to the communal aspect of life that is seldom found in his poetry, sustains those around him, "a solid figure when/ The self-destructive shake the common wall." Finally, he "Takes to himself what mystery he can." Through the affirmation that has occurred in the course of the poem, the mystery begins to reveal itself to the happy man.

In the final, four-line stanza the two recurring lines of the poem come together, and the mystery "is no more":

> And, praising change as the slow night comes on,
> Wills what he would, surrendering his will
> Till mystery is no more: No more he can.
> The right thing happens to the happy man.

This is more than acceptance of the natural order of things; it is affirmation both of life and of death. With an act of will he surrenders his will, and the meaning of the "happy man" fully reveals itself. In total accord with the rhythms of creation, he becomes a part of the mystery and by this act of affirmation is himself a revelation of the mystery. To participate in such a shared life with all of creation is, as in so much of Roethke's poetry, what it means to be a happy man.

This same feeling of revelation is present in the final poem of the volume, "Once More, the Round." However, the mystery is now made clear at the very outset: "What can be known? The Unknown." The unknown, the final goal of all our searching and the only thing we can know fully, is revealed in a dance of all creation in which the self and the other, the one and the many, the natural and the spiritual, body and soul, move together in a unity that raises each to its fullest life. The first stanza begins with questions and moves beyond them to an understanding and affirmation that require no answers:

What's greater, Pebble or Pond?
What can be known? The Unknown.
My true self runs toward a Hill
More! O More! visible.

Which is greater, the single entity or the encompassing waters? The question implies that the answer has been found or, perhaps, that there is no answer. Both pebble and pond are interrelated parts of creation; the one and the all need not, must not, cancel each other out. They in fact find their fullest life as they exist together. He who knows this has found his "true self." No longer at issue is the question "Which I is *I?*" of the opening poem of this section, "In a Dark Time." The true self will neither separate itself from the all of creation nor will it be lost in that unity. Thus, the poet is able to run without hesitation toward his goal of the spirit without fear of leaving behind the world he loves. It is within his world that more and more becomes visible.

This world that has been at the center of his poetry is once again affirmed in the second stanza. Also affirmed is his shared life with the things of creation, the I-Thou relationship of love that binds all together in the dance:

Now I adore my life
With the Bird, the abiding Leaf,
With the Fish, the questing Snail,
And the Eye altering all;
And I dance with William Blake
For love, for Love's sake.

Once again he lists with care the things he loves, and with the listing, as with the seeing, they take on meaning for his human consciousness. Calling on Blake, whose imaginative "Eye" has been present as a guide in much of the poetry, he celebrates both the creation and the act of creation. This human creation, the poem, has its roots in the created world and is for Roethke a way of discovering and giving joyous expression to the meaningful order he finds in the natural world; and that order is in Roethke's poetry based, finally, on love. That grounding of love enables him to conclude both this poem and the long struggle recorded in this volume of poetry:

And everything comes to One,
As we dance on, dance on, dance on.

Such an unquestioning affirmation of life in this world in its diversity and its ultimate oneness has come at the end of the long journey that began in the greenhouse. Although the poetry has taken various forms and concentrated on differing themes, there has been a consistent movement from the childhood struggle to gain identity to this final proclamation of the spiritual human being. What has gone before is not denied by this cosmic vision. The natural world, the place of humans, is present here as it was in the greenhouse poems. And though the ambiguity of joy mixed with despair in many of the previous poems is not present here, neither is it denied. The poet is still a participant in the "round," a joyful dance that is continuing and circular. Having journeyed with Roethke through his times of joy and despair, we cannot feel that he has reached a point of stasis, for that would deny the nature of life. Having discovered with Roethke that the light and the darkness are both meaningful, however, we can be certain that the darkness to come does not negate the joy of this moment of the dance. Together with the things and people of this created world, through happiness and anguish, he will "dance on, dance on, dance on."

CONCLUSION

Westward, hit a low note, for a roarer lost
across the Sound but north from Bremerton,
hit a way down note.
And never cadenza again of flowers, or cost.
Him who could really do that cleared his throat
& staggered on.

The bluebells, pool-shallows, saluted his over-needs,
while the clouds growled, heh-heh, & snapped, & crashed.

No stunt he'll ever unflinch once more will fail
(O lucky fellow, eh Bones?)—drifted off upstairs,
downstairs, somewheres.
No more daily, trying to hit the head on the nail:
thirstless: without a think in his head:
back from wherever, with it said.

Hit a high long note, for a lover found
needing a lower into friendlier ground
to bug among worms no more
around um jungles where ah blurt "What for?"
Weeds, too, he favoured as most men don't favour men.
The Garden Master's gone.

John Berryman, who knew the darkness and dislocation of life as Roethke did, though perhaps not the reunion Roethke affirmed, left us this "Strut for Roethke." It expresses his admiration for the "Garden Master's" care for the earth as well as his own bitterness and doubt about the pain both of living and writing poetry. He speaks to us of the man who began his search in the greenhouse and found there life and strength in the things of the earth that sustained him throughout his journey. Roethke was always trying to reveal through his poetry that final image of the unified vision that would be the truth; and when he succeeded it was, as Berryman reminds us, through an intuitive knowledge that did not depend on reason. Berryman identifies Roethke as "the Garden Master" who cared for the least things of nature more than most people are able to care about other people.

This loving concern for the things of the earth and the shared life that the poet experiences with them are at the heart of his poetry. From first to last he is the lover of the minimals of nature, of flowers and birds, weeds and slugs. With and perhaps because of these things he is the lover of the other human being and, finally, the lover of God. This love and his affirmation of life persist in spite of the very real darkness and despair that he also finds in this world. The natural world, then, is at the center of Roethke's poetry. He approaches this world with an intuitive understanding that is shared by human beings and flowers and birds but that is brought to expression most fully by the poet.

Such an understanding of the world begins, as we have seen before, with a faith in the ultimate meaning and goodness of things. This faith begins in the greenhouse poems where the child experiences the mysterious growth and creativity of the plants and the participation and parallel growth of the human being. He sees there too the underside of things—the weeds and roots which, though lacking the beauty of the sunlit blossoms, share equally in their life and are indispensable for growth and wholeness. This faith enables the poet to stand before the experiences of the world beyond the greenhouse and to open himself to their mystery even without the certitude that this faith will be justified—that is, that a meaningful, creative order will again be revealed. He submerges himself in the chaos of existence, accepting the possibility that only destruction will result and that there will be no poetry. Only by taking the risk of faith and entering into this experience of the life force will he discover whether it is creative or destructive. What is revealed in this quest is that the world is a place of constant, mysterious creativity. At every stage of the poetry this openness to the mystery of creation is repeated, and at every stage the poet comes to the discovery of a meaningful order that can be affirmed.

In order for the poet protagonist to come to an understanding of this mysterious order, he must have a strong sense of himself. He must confront the chaos of new experience as an individual; and it is to the individual that the order is revealed. Thus, the self is not lost in Roethke's world but is strengthened so that it is able to meet the other within the world. The possibility of meeting, then, which is for Roethke the result of a meaningful order within the world, depends on both the person and the other. Thus, nature is not neutral. It has the power to be responsive to the poet and to enter into relationship with him. Although this is, of course, different from the way two people may relate to each other, the fact of meeting is nonetheless a reality. Insofar as both forms of life share in the power of life, they are able to come together in what Buber describes as an I-Thou relationship and so to bear witness to a meaningful universe. Within Roethke's poetic world life by its nature possesses an urge toward reunification through meeting. Again, this is not a joining that destroys the individuality of each participant but rather a sharing of life that affirms each as an individual within the world as a whole. Thus, for Roethke part of the essence of life is the desire and ability to join with other lives. Insofar as living things fail in this endeavor, they experience the darkness of isolation and loneliness.

When the meeting does occur, it comes for Roethke through an attitude of love and faith, through awe and wonder at the fact of being itself both in its wholeness and in its individual, unique manifestations. That there is being and that there is this particular being elicit his responses of wonder and caring. The mystery at the heart of being remains, but through tender care he is able to join with the living things he loves in a relationship that takes him close to the heart of the mystery. Here he can joyfully affirm himself and his world.

This creative order within the world becomes the source of creativity for the poet. Through wonder and openness to the things of creation both in the outer world and in the inner world of the mind and emotions, the poet is able to create a work of art whose order corresponds to that which is given in the world. The "meeting" takes place both as the poet is able to engage his materials and bring them into the unity that is the poem and as the reader is able to enter into the world of the poem and share its life. The work of art, then, is not in conflict with the world. Neither, however, is it a copy of the world. The poem is possible (given Roethke's understanding of the world) because there is at the heart of things a meaningful order. Of course, the poem depends upon the creativity of the poet, but it also depends on the creativity of the world. Finally, it depends on the meeting of these two factors through the openness and loving concern of both.

With this belief in the nature of the world and of poetic creation, Roethke opens his poetry to a variety of forms and styles. Freedom of form is both possible and desirable. It is possible because the poet's trust in the given order of things makes him willing to open himself to the dangers of new forms. It is desirable because open form is a way of preparing for the moment of revelation, enabling the poet to lead the reader into a world that has a hidden form, the discovery of which is itself the revelation. He moves from poems that seem almost without form to those that follow an established, rigid form and from nonsense poems to metaphysical explorations. In every variation he discovers an order that can be affirmed; but because that order has many sides and remains, finally, mysterious, it must be approached in many different ways and from every possible angle.

Ong's statements about belief in art apply again as Roethke uses the device of association, trusting the reader's mind to follow him through "nonlogical" progressions by itself and then creating a world in which such trust is justified. Roethke thus breaks down the reader's usual perceptions of the world so that he or she may encounter the mysterious reality of his poetic world. His emphasis on the sounds of words and his subtle internal rhyme and off rhyme and alliteration also work to establish his mysterious world of meaning that defies explanation, of terror that is yet filled with wonder, of the immanent world of the earth that is also the realm of the spirit. The mystery, the chaos, is not banished or explained away. It is rather a part of the order and is, in fact, the source of the communication, the communion, that makes affirmation of this world possible.

Thus, Roethke's "primal intuition" about the nature of things–to return to Giles Gunn's description of a work of art–is that there is a meaningful order at the heart of things and that this order is based upon a relatedness, a shared life of all creation. His poetry develops from this belief and is an embodiment of it.

"THE GARDEN AND THE MAP"

Through the hypothetical creation that is his poetry, Roethke invites us to share in the experience of a world grounded in this primal intuition. Further, the power of the imaginative work itself and the fact that our lives are integrated wholes in which "aesthetic" experience cannot be discretely isolated from "religious" experience or "moral" experience stir us to consider what difference such a possible world might make to our actual world. The imaginative work asks us to reexamine our own grounding in the world, the way we understand things to be, the order that gives meaning and value to our own experience.

Two very important ways in which Roethke's poetry speaks to central concerns of contemporary experience are his understanding of the self and its relation to the other. The experience of his poetry reveals that in both depth and transcendence we are more than ego-selves. In terms of relation to others our being-in-the-world is an experience of relatedness not only to our several selves and our human kin but also to that larger realm of creation, the earth. The heart of this vision that speaks so significantly to our world is a mutuality, a boundless interrelatedness that cuts through the dualistic subject-object abstractions that continue to dominate the stories we tell about our world.

John Vernon has characterized two ways of being in and viewing the world by the metaphors of the garden and the map. He describes the map as

> that schizophrenic structure whereby areas of experience are extricated from each other and arranged in discrete spaces beside each other, often as opposites. . . . [The garden] refers to a structure the opposite of the map, one that unites opposites and enables all areas of experience to be accessible to each other.

As Raymond Benoit points out, for the romantics (who seem to inhabit Vernon's garden) there is a dual union in which both unity and dichotomy are undercut. There is no creative tension or dialogue when categories are simply divorced from one another and one side of the set is devalued and repressed or when they lose their uniqueness in an undifferentiated "one." "Division . . . is overcome while the difference between both is maintained."

Vernon uses Roethke's poetry as an example of the wholeness and freedom that come when "the garden embraces and transforms the map, temporalizes it, unfolds it in time. The garden is not total mergence and confusion, a scrambling of all things and all objects together, but unites mergence and separation, unity and multiplicity." The fact that Roethke was diagnosed as a "schizophrenic" illustrates Vernon's point exactly. It appears to him that a map culture is schizophrenic because it absolutely fragments existence. However, such a culture, which defines sanity by the ability to isolate parts of life from each other and the self from the world, sees as schizophrenic one who lives in a garden where these boundaries do not exist, where the self and the world, fantasy and reality, inner and outer are perceived as mutually interacting. He sees this same reversal of meaning occurring in each of the structures he finds in culture—the world, the body, objects, space, and time:

> In the map, the world is sealed off from the body, taking the form of a total Other, an absolute, blocklike not-me; but in the garden,

> the world and the body are united, and more important, united precisely where they are, in the world and in the body. Similarly, in the map, the body is sealed off from the self, whereas in the garden they are united; in the map, objects are inert and one-dimensional, whereas in the garden they are sacred and magical; in the map, time is spatialized and quantified, whereas in the garden it is qualitative and dynamic; and in the map, space is a thing-in-itself, a medium in which objects exist, a container, whereas in the garden it is a qualitative relationship between things, dynamized by time and by the temporal nature of the body.

The dissolution of these rigid boundaries, which is found throughout Roethke's poetry, allows the tentative intermingling of the self and not-self out of which emerges a new definition of self and its relation to others. This is clearly part of the movement in the modern period, as Dennis E. Brown describes it, from a traditional, bounded self to an exploration of the "real frontiers between self and not-self." Psychologically this involves a loosening of the grasp that ego consciousness imposes on the world in its desire to stake out for the self a narrow domain it can control. Roethke's self is open to the darkness of the depths, the unconscious world of the slime and roots, and to the darkness of the divine, the spiritual realm of the rose, both of which are mysterious and uncontrollable. In both cases the limited ego is overwhelmed and transcended, and a new, expansive self emerges as the poet learns, as David Miller says, to see in the dark. This does not mean that the ego-self uses its tools of light to dissipate the darkness but rather that the total self learns to live and grow in the depths of a darkness that illuminates. As Anthony Libby notes, "Because he tends to discover a paradoxical light within the darkness, not beyond it, his poetry . . . constantly involves images of dark light, 'bright shade,' 'shimmering' illuminations in shadow." "To submerge is to emerge, in Roethke's poems," Vernon adds, and submerging in a dark time gives the eye a new way of seeing, a new structure of consciousness that opens us to ourselves and to the powers of being in which our larger selves participate.

What we discover in the external world of the not-self is similar. Again, a narrow conception of self must be discarded as we come to acknowledge our holistic experience of interaction with the world. What we discover is never a disembodied or isolated "I" (as there is never only a single self) but an incarnate, intermingled being-in-the-world. Vernon says of Roethke's poetry that "the narrator and the world slip into each other's skins. . . . Roethke disperses himself, loses himself into even the most inanimate objects, stones and pebbles, and by that very dispersal finds himself fully and collects himself." Similarly, the world is never simply an isolated, objectifiable world. The disappearance of the boundaries between reality and dream, depth and transcendence, occurs with the world as well as the self. Richard Wilbur's poem "Thyme Flowering among Rocks" begins with the observation that to analytic Western minds "Here, where things are what / They are," a bed of thyme is simply that. However, as the poem progresses, we look more and more closely at the thyme itself until

> You
> Are lost now in dense
> Fact, fact which one might have thought
> Hidden from the sense,
>
> . . . .
>
> It makes the craned head
> Spin. Unfathomed thyme! The world's
> A dream, Basho said,
>
> Not because that dream's
> A falsehood, but because it's
> Truer than it seems.

Howard Nemerov's "Runes" (xi) reveal this mystery as well:

> A holy man said to me, "Split the stick
> And there is Jesus." When I split the stick
> To the dark marrow and the splintery grain
> I saw nothing that was not wood, nothing
> That was not God.

The implications of this view of the world for poetry are that it too must be involved in mutual interaction with all other processes of life, both natural and human. There can be no absolute boundaries between idea and image, word and thing. The activity of the poet is to discover the language that will bring to experience this always creative, always ambiguous interaction and communication between the living things of the earth. As Anthony Libby says of Roethke's poetry: "To see the world truly is to become it; the genuine immersion leads to a more than Romantic or animistic exchange of identities with things and beings." Dennis Brown says that Roethke's poetry "plunges the reader into the experiential real where things appear to breed language and language appears to invent things." Richard Wilbur's poem "Games Two" points to the place "Where word with world is one / And nothing dies." Nothing dies not because we have reached a stasis beyond time but because we have entered into an unending process of shared and mutually transformative life.

THE EARTH

Such an expanded view of the self and its relation to others and to the earth in Roethke's poetry offers us a possibility that just might be the case in our world. Living out of this experience in the poetry, we are called on to re-vision our relationship to the natural world in a way that may more adequately reflect our experience of our relationship to the earth. The necessity of this is clear as we realize that it is only recently that we have begun to question the post-Enlightenment understanding and treatment of nature. There has, of course, been a great deal of attention paid to nature since this time. But as Joseph Sittler points out, "in this process nature as a primal reality is subsumed under *nature as resource for historical transformation.* The central, operating factor in world-reflection since the Enlightenment has not been the world-as-nature; it has rather been the world-as-history, as this world, with man its primary agent, has been instrumentally anthropocentrized in fact." And this, as Sittler observes, is not to consider *creation.* We have also begun to question the assumption that with the use of reason we will be able to control this "nature" and make our world a perfect place in which to live. The hoped-for "progress" has not occurred. Twentieth-century science has become less concerned with the certainty supposedly achievable through reason and has become more concerned with exploring the mysterious interrelationships within the universe. And we in our culture have begun to realize that we are destroying the world and threatening our own survival rather than bringing about utopia. To such a situation Roethke's poetry offers new and vital possibilities for understanding and living in the created world.

Within this setting theologians too have become more concerned with elucidating a religious understanding of the earth. Too often, though, the concern has had to do only with humans and how the world affects them. Such a view remains within the anthropocentric understanding Sittler mentions and fails to be concerned with the things of the earth themselves. Daniel Day Williams, for example, begins with an understanding of God the creator that seems to hold great possibilities for developing a view of the world that shares the loving concern found in Roethke's poetry. He says that

> the Creator God of Christian theology is involved in basic structures which underlie everything that is, so that we ought to be able to find traces of His presence in this moving scheme of things. God is present to us as that reality which makes it possible for the world to exist, and for it to be a world in which living, conscious, responsible beings can find meaning, freedom, and worth in life.

And he goes on to say, "God the Creator we know as the power which binds the surging variety of life into richer and wider societies of mutual enjoyment and support. To be anything is to enter into social relations. Perhaps this is even true of electrons; it certainly is true of all living things, and supremely of men." He asserts the possibility of hope through the "good earth" and says that although there is a mystery of evil in the creation "there is the fact of the tender nurture of life." But in his list of the means in the world through which we experience God's grace—"the order of the stars and seasons, the rhythm of work and rest, the repeated miracle of birth, growth, death, and new life"—the specific *things* of the world themselves, the things that abound in Roethke's poetry, are missing. And although he says that "sheer control over life for the sake of control is self-defeating," it is clear that what he is concerned with is the fear that human beings are going to run out of "natural resources." He lacks a real concern for and a relationship with the things of creation.

Those theologians who do offer an understanding that does justice to the created world itself all seem to share two of the beliefs that are central to Roethke's poetry. They have a genuine concern for the unique living things of the universe, and they see those things as sharing in a process of interrelationships that bind not only human beings but all life together. Paul Tillich, for example, sets up a structure for understanding the world that is congenial to Roethke's poetic world. Understood in its full potential, he says, all of life forms a "multidimensional unity." Tillich is concerned here with the whole of creation, from the inorganic dimension of life (even Roethke's dirt!) to the historical dimension of human life. Each dimension contains within it the potential of all the other dimensions, and each depends on the actualization of the previous one for its own actualization. The actualization of the spiritual dimension of a person, then, is possible only because of the actualization of the inorganic. Thus, human beings are rooted firmly in nature and have a living connectedness with it.

The approach of process philosophy and theology is quite different from Tillich's, describing the life of the world as a sustained continuity rather than as the dialectic in Tillich, but there is a similarity in the attempt to deal fully with the created world. Alfred North Whitehead's process philosophy is predicated on a doctrine of internal relations, which asserts that all things depend on and share in the life of all other things. There is a togetherness that involves mutual immanence of one thing in another: "This community of the actualities of the world means that each happening is a factor in the nature of every other happening. . . . The whole antecedent world conspires to produce a new occasion." Each occasion "requires the whole universe in order to be itself." This unity in the universe is based on "the common fact of value-experience, as constituting the essential nature of each pulsation of actuality. Everything has some value for itself, for others, and for the whole."

The objection can be raised that such a view anthropomorphizes nature, attributing to it human feelings and values that are rightly the province of human beings only. But Charles Hartshorne asks at what point, then, shall we say that values enter the evolutionary schema? He goes on to say:

> What [science] is not doing and cannot do is to establish a dualistic materialism in which the sentient and intelligent arise out of mere bits of dead matter, human evaluations out of a nature devoid of values. *Human* values emerge, sure enough, but are there not simian values, amoebic values—and who dares to assign a first level of values?
>
> If the foregoing is at all correct, then the social point of view is the final point of view. All creatures are fellow creatures. Nothing is wholly alien to us or devoid of inner satisfactions with which, if we could grasp them, we might more or less sympathize. It is merely a question of how accessible to our perception and understanding the inner values may be.

The value that is common to all life is the urge toward self-actualization. This always involves a coming together into new creations, which he calls actual occasions, which are ever-transforming communities, whether of atoms or organisms or social groups. Value lies, then, in the actualization of community. "Our whole experience is composed out of our relationships to the rest of things, and of the formation of new relationships constitutive of things to come. The present receives the past and builds the future." We respond in such relationships, as Bernard Meland, a theologian within process thought, puts it, with "appreciative awareness," which involves a reaching out beyond the self. It is "a creative act of acquiring unto oneself real meaning of another self or of another object through a process of exercising empathy and identification in a circular movement which returns this feeling-into-another-centre-of-existence to one's own self-orientation." Through this act comes a kind of knowledge, a "knowledge by acquaintance." It is accompanied by a state of consciousness "in which bodily feelings, conveying the nexus of relationships, and conscious awareness, attentive to solitary concerns, merge; and, in fact, interpenetrate." Thus, feelings and awareness are brought together and transformed into a new unity so that the split between what we term body and spirit does not exist.

The process vision of value in shared life lying at the foundations of existence has clearly moved beyond the anthropocentrism that has dominated Western culture. As Hartshorne points out, in such a view "value" and "importance" are not reserved for human beings:

> We should learn to accept a contributory status in the living whole of reality, and shake off the illusion that each of us (or our group) is the inclusive whole of which other things are constitutents, contributing their values to us as the final consumers of all goods, the important ends of creation. . . . All experience is vanity of vanities, unless it contributes to an abiding whole of life that not only transcends us but transcends humanity altogether.

Whitehead echoes this sense of wholeness of life and speaks of "trust" as the mode of living in such a cosmos that parallels Roethke's attitude toward the world. It is the

> trust that the ultimate natures of things lie together in a harmony which excludes mere arbitrariness. It is the faith that at the base of things we shall not find mere arbitrary mystery. . . . It springs from direct inspection of the nature of things as disclosed in our own immediate present experience. There is no parting from your own shadow. To experience this faith is to know that in being ourselves we are more than ourselves: to know that our experience, dim and fragmentary as it is, yet sounds the utmost depths of reality: to know that detached details merely in order to be themselves demand that they should find themselves in a system of things: to know that this system includes the harmony of logical rationality, and the harmony of aesthetic achievement: to know that, while the harmony of logic lies upon the universe as an iron necessity, the aesthetic harmony stands before it as a living ideal moulding the general flux in its broken progress towards finer, subtler issues.

Whitehead's statement that "in being ourselves we are more than ourselves" and Hartshorne's affirmation, "All creatures are fellow creatures," point to the heart of Roethke's poetry. The many selves with their dark, mysterious sides must constellate if the larger self, which is more than the self, is to emerge. And at the same time this self, fellow of all creatures, is enabled to enter into relation with others and so to become itself as a part of the community of the earth.

In all these thinkers the whole of the world is seen to have worth in itself as part of God's creation. Human beings share in this worth, but it is not theirs exclusively or preeminently. This is in contrast to the schema Conrad Bonifazi sets up wherein he describes, following Teilhard de Chardin, the "personalizing" of the universe. According to Bonifazi's hierarchy, human beings not only fill the highest rank yet attained but also confer on lesser things their worth: "Only as things external participate in man's inner experience may they achieve their proper status." Humans with their "inwardness," he says, are able to free the things of the world from their "outwardness": "Endowing the outer world with inner fervour and granting inwardness to matter is to impose a new shape upon the world, to bestow upon environment its anticipated dimension . . . to communicate to things their awaited freedom." However, according to such men as Buber and Marcel and Heidegger, this inwardness is already inherent in the things themselves by virtue of their being living things. They do not have to be given anything by human beings in order to fulfil their being. It is humans who have trouble being what they are. Heidegger, in fact, makes the opposite movement when he says that the *presence* of things "hails" us as it opens the mystery of Being to us, Being that is not created by human beings but is wholly gratuitous.

Joseph Sittler, continuing this line of thought, defines grace as the "sheer *givenness-character* of life, the world, and the self–the plain *presentedness* of all that is." When human beings encounter grace, it is sheer gratuity that announces its presence: "By gratuity is meant a primal surprise, the need-not-have-been of uncalculated and incalculable givenness. 'Amazing' is the only adequate adjective; wonder is the ambience." Sittler also emphasizes the fact that such moments occur through–indeed human identity depends upon–relatedness. For Sittler, as for Heidegger, to be is to be with. Sittler quotes Joseph Haroutunian:

> We have no ontological status prior to and apart from communion. Communion is our being; the being we participate in is communion, and we derive our concrete selves from our communion. The old

> controversy between the realists and the nominalists about universals and particulars is incongruous with the ontology of communion. We have to do, not with universals, but with our neighbors, not with particulars, but with particular fellowmen.

Sittler says of "redeemed-life" that it is "given and matured in time and space and matter, among my fellow creatures, human and nonhuman."

Sittler also stresses the fact that the moment of grace through relatedness is found within the common. In our time, he says, "The movement is all in one direction–to announce the amazing in, with, and under the common; to beckon to wonder via the close and the usual." Sam Keen echoes this belief: "Revelation moves in what Tillich called a radically 'theonomous' direction. The ordinary is seen as holy." Indeed, "Reality as a whole is sacramental. Any tree, person, or event may become transparent to the holy power that informs every living thing." To come to such moments of revelation, he urges "the fullest possible participation in the present moment, . . . that we taste and see and feel the world, that we penetrate to the abiding dimensions of meaning and value that are within the immediate moment of experience. . . . It may well be that in recovering a wondering openness to our total experience we may discover that ours is a holy place."

The understanding and the feeling for life out of which Roethke's poetry grows have much in common with the beliefs of these theologians and philosophers. Insofar as through the poetic world of Roethke's creation we can appreciate the ways of experiencing life that they describe, we can, perhaps, come to a better understanding of the world we live in. His poetry "hails" us as we discover in the experience of it a relationship to the things of the earth that is life-giving. He reveals a shared experience of life within the created world that has a meaning that can endure through the darkness and despair that are also a part of that world. In spite of the darkness he reveals an affirmation of the immanent world that can say yes with joy to the shared life of all creation.

Theodore Roethke died in 1963 at the age of fifty-five. Doubtless there was much life yet to be shared, much poetry yet to be written. But what he did leave for us reveals a man who knew the joys and sorrows of life and who came, finally, to affirm both in his poetry. "Poetry can change your life," he says in the film "In a Dark Time." Through his poetry he reaches out to the world he loves, hoping to give it new life through sharing his joyous affirmation of the earth.

NOTES

Full publication information for the following references can be found in the bibliography.

INTRODUCTION

page
4 Roethke, *Selected Prose,* p. 39.
5 Auden, pp. 30-31.
6 Meredith, p. 41.
6 Roethke, *Selected Prose,* p. 39.
8 Buber, p. 101.

page
9 Gunn, *Literature,* p. 28.
9 Langbaum, *Poetry,* p. 233.
10 Roethke, from letter to G. Gaum, quoted in Seager, p. 138.

1. ROETHKE'S SHARED WORLD

11 Roethke, *Selected Prose,* p. 20.
12 Ong, p. 66.
13 Emerson, *Journals,* quoted in R. Lewis, *American Adam,* p. 6.
13 Emerson, "Experience," *Selections,* p. 269.
13 "American Adam": see Kramer, p. 143, and Spender, review, p. 22.
13 Roethke, *Selected Prose,* p. 40.
13 Tanner, p. 38.
13 Burke, p. 264.
13 Roethke, *Selected Prose,* p. 25.
13 Benoit, pp. 57–67.
14 Malkoff, *Roethke,* p. 6.
14 Ciardi, p. 410.
14 Mills, "Keeping the Spirit," p. 116.
14 Crane, p. 221.
14 Pound, p. 95.
15 Wilbur, *Walking,* pp. 16–17.
15 Wilbur, *Poems,* p. 117.
15 Ibid., p. 195.
15 Nemerov, p. 257.
15 Ibid., p. 246.
15 Ibid., pp. 471-72.
15. Burke, pp. 186–200.
16 La Belle, p. 4, and Blessing, pp. 5 and 92, for examples.
16 Rosenthal, pp. 15–16.
17 Bloom, pp. 462–63.
18 Wordsworth influence: see, e.g., La Belle, pp. 24–25. Also Benoit, chap. 3.
18 Seager, pp. 289-90.
18 Roethke in Ostroff, p. 49.
18 Seager, p. 264.
19 Snyder, p. viii.
19 Wilbur, *Poems,* pp. 195-96.

chapter one (continued)

page
19 Roethke, notebooks, 36 # 86, quoted in Blessing, p. 66.
20 Buber, *I and Thou,* p. 8.
20 Ibid., p. 15.
20 Keen, p. 24.
21 Ibid., p. 25, quoting Marcel, *Being and Having,* p. 117.
21 Marcel, *Mystery of Being,* p. 255.
21 "Nature" in Tenakh: Sittler, pp. 36, 24.
22 Bonifazi, *Theology,* pp. 182, 183, 194–96.
22 Sittler, p. 29.
22 Ibid., p. 37.
22 Ibid., quoting Galloway, p. 35.
22 "Cosmic Christ": Sittler refers, for example, to Col. 1:13–20 and Eph. 1:2–14 (pp. 43–48). He goes on to trace the development of this tradition in both Western and Eastern Christianity. See especially chap. 3, "Some Crucial Moments in Ecumenical Christology."
22 Bonifazi, *Theology,* p. 203.
23 Scott, p. 51.
23 Teilhard de Chardin, *Hymn,* pp. 19, 24.
23 Heidegger, *Poetry,* p. 94.
23 "Gelassenheit": see, e.g., Heidegger, *Discourse,* pp. 54–55.
23 Scott, pp. 73–74, citing H. Lewis, p. 210.
24 Scott, p. 74.
24 Roethke, *Selected Prose,* p. 24.

2. THE ROOTS OF THE POETRY

page
25 Roethke, *Selected Prose,* p. 39.
26 Abrams, pp. 183–84.
27 Ibid., pp. 190–91.
28 Seager, pp. 12–13.
28 Roethke, *Selected Prose,* p. 39.
41 Roethke, *Selected Letters,* p. 260.
41 Pearce, "Power of Sympathy," p. 179n, citing Kizer, p. 84.
41 Jung, *Two Essays,* p. 98.
41 Jung, *Archetypes,* pp. 163–64.
41 Jung, *Two Essays,* p. 173.
42 Jung, *Archetypes,* p. 160.
42 Bodkin, p. 72.
42 Jung, *Archetypes,* p. 170.
42 Roethke, *Selected Prose,* p. 37.
43 "Overcome time": see Eliade, *Myth,* chaps. 2 and 3.
44 Freud, p. 62.
44 Marcel, *Mystery of Being,* pp. 102–3.
45 Ibid., pp. 162, 168–69.
45 Bachelard, pp. xix–xx.
45 Heidegger, *Discourse,* pp. 44–45.
46 Scott, pp. 100–101.
46 Ibid., p. 87.
46 "Toads brooding wells": Although Roethke mentions in a letter to John Ciardi in 1949 that "in" should not be omitted, this reading remains in the *Collected Poems,* even though the other errors he mentions at this time *are* corrected. See *Selected Letters,* p. 151.
48 Eliade, "stones," p. 216; "trees," p. 267; "water," p. 188.
49 Sullivan, pp. 42, 43n, citing Jung, *Integration,* pp. 67, 73.
50 H. Williams, p. 52.
51 Malkoff, *Roethke,* p. 87.
51 Roethke, *Selected Prose,* p. 38.
53 Cassirer, p. 33.
55 Roethke, *Selected Prose,* p. 39.
57 Buber, *I and Thou,* pp. 25–26.
58 Ibid., p. 25.
58 Ibid., p. 63.
58 Ibid., p. 80.
62 Roethke, *Selected Prose,* p. 39.
63 Roethke, *Selected Letters,* p. 252. Also see La Belle, chap. 3.

3. TO BE FULLY HUMAN

page
72 Marcel, *Mystery of Being,* pp. 255–56.
74 Jung, *Archetypes,* p. 27.
74 Jung, *Aion,* p. 16.
76 Roethke and Yeats: Malkoff, *Roethke,* p. 115.
77 Ellmann, p. 166.
79 Keen, p. 156.
79 Ibid., pp. 197–98.
83 Maxwell, pp. 265–66.
84 Biographical references: see Seager, chaps. 12 and 13.
84 Roethke, *Straw for the Fire,* see esp. p. 87.
84 Seager, pp. 223–24.
84 Kierkegaard, p. 171.
85 Tillich, *Courage,* pp. 178–81.
85 Ibid., pp. 32–33.
95 Freer, p. 58.
95 Ibid., p. 66.
96 Stein, "Roethke's Memory," p. 31.
97 Buber, *I and Thou,* p. 61.
99 Jaffé, p. 25.
102 Ibid., pp. 33, 152.
103 Donoghue, p. 136.
106 Roethke's use of Yeats: see Mills, *Roethke,* p. 37.
107 Roethke, *Selected Letters,* p. 230.
107 Musgrove, p. 31.
107 J. Miller, pp. 129–31.
108 Roethke, *Selected Letters,* p. 231.
108 Mills, *Roethke,* p. 40. See also Roethke, *Selected Letters,* p. 211.
108 Mills, "Keeping the Spirit Spare," p. 122.
109 Buber, *I and Thou,* p. 75.
120 Underhill, pp. 169–70.
121 J. Miller, p. 125.
128 Buber, *I and Thou,* p. 82.
129 J. Miller, p. 135.
129 Buber, *I and Thou,* p. 80.

4. THE SEARCH FOR THE SPIRIT

page
131 Roethke, *Selected Prose,* p. 19.
131 Ibid., p. 26.
131 Underhill, p. 71.
132 Ibid., p. 4.
132 Roethke, notebooks, reel 14, no. 197, quoted in Sullivan, p. 126.
132 Underhill, p. 171.
132 Buber, *I and Thou,* p. 84.
132 Underhill, p. 415.
132 Buber, *I and Thou,* pp. 83–84.
132 Underhill, p. 415.
133 Buber, *I and Thou,* p. 87.
133 Ibid., pp. 87–88.
133 Underhill, p. 258.
133 Ibid., p. 81.
133 *Cloud of Unknowing,* trans. Progoff, p. 61.
133 Underhill, p. 414.
133 Buber, *I and Thou,* p. 87.
134 Ibid., p. 88.
134 Ibid., p. 89.
136 "Divine Light and Divine Dark": Underhill, pp. 171–72.
136 "Being and Becoming": ibid., p. 433.
137 McMichael, "Poetry of Theodore Roethke," p. 16.
138 Staples, p. 195. See Malkoff, *Roethke,* pp. 178–79, for a similar disagreement.
144 Staples, p. 199. Because of his familial background Roethke was familiar with German and occasionally used German words or phrases in his poetry.
146 "Mnetha": Frye, *Fearful Symmetry,* pp. 243–44.
152 Malkoff, *Roethke,* p. 185.
152 Roethke, *Selected Prose,* p. 19.

chapter four (continued)

page
153 Roethke's relation to Stevens: Roethke acknowledges his debt to this ancestor and honors him with "A Rouse for Stevens," a rowdy, rollicking song "(To Be Sung in a Young Poets' Saloon)," in which he cries, "Wallace Stevens —are we *for* him? / Brother, he's our father!"
153 Meredith, p. 41.
159 Heyen, pp. 1062–63.
159 Tillich, *Courage,* p. 177.
160 Whitman and purgation: J. Miller, p. 118.
161 Sullivan, p. 176, citing *The Cloud of Unknowing,* Clifton Wolters's translation, p. 38.

page
161 Underhill, p. 380.
166 Roethke, *Selected Prose,* p. 70.
166 Roethke, in Ostroff, p. 49.
166 Ibid.
167 Roethke, *Selected Prose,* p. 26.
167 Kunitz, in Ostroff, p. 41.
168 *Cloud of Unknowing,* trans. Progoff, p. 62.
168 Ibid., p. 224.
170 Roethke, in Ostroff, pp. 52–53.
170 Richard of St. Victor, in Underhill, p. 315.
170 Boehme, intro. by Berdyaev, pp. xxi–xxiii.
170 Tillich, *Courage,* p. 182.
171 Ibid., pp. 188–89.
175 Ibid., p. 180.

CONCLUSION

page
184 Berryman, p. 20.
188 Vernon, p. xii.
188 Benoit, pp. 16, 3.
188 Vernon, pp. 159–60.
189 Ibid., p. xiv.
189 Brown, p. 1243.
189 D. Miller, pp. 331–35.
189 Libby, p. 280.
189 Vernon, p. 182.
190 Ibid., pp. 185, 187.
190 Wilbur, *Walking,* pp. 33–35.
190 Nemerov, p. 216.
190 Libby, p. 285.
190 Brown, pp. 1246–47.
191 Wilbur, *Poems,* p. 147.
191 Sittler, p. 99.
192 D. Williams, p. 41.
192 Ibid., p. 52.
192 Ibid., pp. 163–64.

page
192 Tillich, *Systematic Theology,* Vol. 3, pt. 4: *Life and the Spirit,* pp. 12–16.
193 Whitehead, *Modes,* p. 225.
193 Whitehead, *Science,* p. 194.
193 Whitehead, *Modes,* p. 151.
193 Hartshorne, pp. 309–10.
193 Whitehead, *Modes,* p. 43.
193 Meland, p. 92.
194 Ibid., p. 93.
194 Hartshorne, p. 322.
194 Whitehead, *Science,* p. 18.
195 Bonifazi, *Theology,* p. 230.
195 Sittler, pp. 88, 104.
195 Heidegger, *Being,* see, e.g., pp. 153–63.
196 Sittler, p. 107, quoting Haroutunian, p. 150.
196 Sittler, p. 110.
196 Ibid., p. 105.
196 Keen, "Manifesto," pp. 47, 50–51.

SELECTED BIBLIOGRAPHY

WORKS BY THEODORE ROETHKE

The Collected Poems of Theodore Roethke. Garden City, N.Y.: Doubleday & Co., 1966; Anchor Books edition, 1975.

On the Poet and His Craft: Selected Prose of Theodore Roethke. Edited and introduced by Ralph J. Mills, Jr. Seattle: University of Washington Press, paperback edition, 1966.

Selected Letters of Theodore Roethke. Edited by Ralph J. Mills, Jr. Seattle: University of Washington Press, 1968.

Straw for the Fire: From the Notebooks of Theodore Roethke 1943-63. Selected and arranged by David Wagoner. Garden City, N.Y.: Doubleday & Co., 1972.

FILM

Myers, David. *In a Dark Time.* Distributed by Contemporary Films. Spring, 1963.

OTHER WORKS CONSULTED

Abrams, M. H. *Natural Supernaturalism: Tradition and Revolution in Romantic Literature.* New York: W. W. Norton & Co., Norton Library, 1973.

Auden, W. H. Review of *Open House. Saturday Review,* 5 April 1941, pp. 30–31.

Bachelard, Gaston. *The Poetics of Space.* Translated by Maria Jolas. Boston: Beacon Press, 1969.

Barbour, Ian G., ed. *Earth Might Be Fair: Reflections on Ethics, Religion, and Ecology.* Englewood Cliffs, N. J.: Prentice-Hall, 1972.

Benoit, Raymond. *Single Nature's Double Name: The Collectedness of the Conflicting in British and American Romanticism.* The Hague: Mouton & Co., 1973.

Berryman, John. *77 Dream Songs.* New York: Farrar, Straus & Giroux, 1964.

Blessing, Richard. *Theodore Roethke's Dynamic Vision.* Bloomington: Indiana University Press, 1974.

Bloom, Harold, *The Visionary Company: A Reading of English Romantic Poetry.* Rev. and enl. ed. Ithaca, N.Y.: Cornell University Press, 1971.

Bodkin, Maud. *Archetypal Patterns in Poetry: Psychological Studies in Imagination.* London: Oxford University Press, Oxford Paperbacks, 1963.

Boehme, Jacob. *Six Theosophic Points and Other Writings.* Translated by John Rolleston Earle. Introduced by Nicholas Berdyaev. Ann Arbor: University of Michigan Press, 1958.

Bonifazi, Conrad. *The Soul of the World: An Account of the Inwardness of Things.* Washington: University Press of America, 1978.

———. *A Theology of Things: A Study of Man in His Physical Environment.* Philadelphia & New York: J. B. Lippincott Co., 1967.

Boyers, Robert. *Excursions.* Port Washington, N.Y.: Kennikat Press, 1977.

Brown, Dennis E. "Theodore Roethke's 'Self-World' and the Modernist Position." *Journal of Modern Literature* 3, no. 5 (July 1974): 1239–54.

Buber, Martin. *Between Man and Man.* Introduced by Maurice Friedman. Translated by Ronald Gregor Smith. New York: Macmillan Co., 1965.

———. *I and Thou.* Translated by Ronald Gregor Smith. 2d ed. New York: Charles Scribner's Sons, 1958.

Burke, Kenneth. *Language as Symbolic Action: Essays on Life, Literature, and Method.* Berkeley & Los Angeles: University of California Press, 1966.

Cassirer, Ernst. *Language and Myth.* Translated by Susanne K. Langer. New York: Dover Publications, 1953.

Ciardi, John. "Poets of the Inner Landscape." *Nation,* 14 November 1953, p. 410.

Corrigan, Matthew. "A Phenomenological Glance at a Few Lines of Roethke." *Modern Poetry Studies* 2, no. 4 (1971): 165–74.

Crane, Hart. *The Complete Poems and Selected Letters and Prose of Hart Crane.* Edited by Brom Weber. Garden City, N.Y.: Doubleday & Co., Anchor Books, 1966.

Donoghue, Denis. "Roethke's Broken Music." In *Theodore Roethke: Essays on the Poetry,* edited by Arnold Stein. Seattle: University of Washington Press, 1965.

Eliade, Mircea. *Myth and Reality.* Translated by Willard R. Trask. World Perspectives, vol. 31. New York: Harper & Row, 1963.

———. *Patterns in Comparative Religion.* Translated by Rosemary Sheed. New York: Sheed and Ward, 1958.

Ellmann, Richard. *The Identity of Yeats.*. 2d ed. New York: Oxford University Press, Galaxy Book, 1964.

Emerson, Ralph Waldo. *Selections from Ralph Waldo Emerson: An Organic Anthology.* Edited by Stephen E. Whicher. Boston: Houghton Mifflin Co.; Cambridge, Mass.: Riverside Press, 1957.

Freer, Coburn. "Theodore Roethke's Love Poetry." *Northwest Review* 11, no. 3 (summer 1971): 42–66.

Freud, Sigmund. *Beyond the Pleasure Principle.* Translated by James Strachey. *The Standard Edition of the Complete Psychological Works.* Vol. 18. London: Hogarth Press, 1955.

Frye, Northrop. *Fables of Identity: Studies in Poetic Mythology.* New York: Harcourt, Brace, & World, Harbinger Book, 1963.

———. *Fearful Symmetry: A Study of William Blake.* Princeton: Princeton University Press, 1969.

Galloway, Allan D. *The Cosmic Christ.* London: Nisbet & Co., 1952.

Gunn, Giles B. *The Interpretation of Otherness: Literature, Religion, and the American Imagination.* New York: Oxford University Press, 1979.

———, ed. *Literature and Religion.* New York: Harper & Row, 1971.

Hamburger, Michael. *The Truth of Poetry: Tensions in Modern Poetry from Baudelaire to the 1960s.* New York: Harcourt, Brace & World, 1970.

Haroutunian, Joseph. *God with Us: A Theology of Transpersonal Life.* Philadelphia: Westminster Press, 1965.

Hartshorne, Charles. *The Logic of Perfection and Other Essays in Neoclassical Metaphysics.* LaSalle, Ill.: Open Court Publishing Co., 1962.

Heidegger, Martin. *Being and Time.* Translated by John Macquarrie and Edward Robinson. London: SCM Press, 1962.

———. *Discourse on Thinking.* Translated by John M. Anderson and E. Hans Freund. New York: Harper & Row, 1966.

———. *Poetry, Language, Thought.* Translated by Albert Hofstadter. New York: Harper & Row, 1971.

Heyen, William. "The Divine Abyss: Theodore Roethke's Mysticism." *Texas Studies in Literature and Language* 11 (summer 1969): 1051–68.

———, ed. *Profile of Theodore Roethke.* Columbus, Ohio: Charles E. Merrill, 1971.

———. "Theodore Roethke's Minimals." *Minnesota Review* 8, no. 4 (1968): 359–75.

Hoffman, Frederick J. "Theodore Roethke: The Poetic Shape of Death." In *Theodore Roethke: Essays on the Poetry,* edited by Arnold Stein. Seattle: University of Washington Press, 1965.

Jaffé, Aniela. *The Myth of Meaning: Jung and the Expansion of Consciousness.* Translated by R. F. C. Hull. New York: Penguin Books, 1975.

James, William. *The Varieties of Religious Experience: A Study in Human Nature.* Introduced by Reinhold Niebuhr. New York: Crowell-Collier Publishing Co., Collier Books, 1961.

Jung, C. G. *Aion: Researches into the Phenomenology of the Self* and *The Archetypes and the Collective Unconscious.* Translated by R. F. C. Hull. *Collected Works.* Vol. 9, pts. 1 & 2. Bollingen Series no. 20. New York: Pantheon Books, 1959.

———. *Two Essays on Analytical Psychology.* Translated by R. F. C. Hull. *Collected Works.* Vol. 7. 2d ed., rev. & aug. Bollingen Series no. 20. New York: Pantheon Books, 1959.

———. *The Integration of Personality.* Translated by Stanley Dell. London: Kegan Paul, Trench, Trubner, and Co., 1940.

Keen, Sam. *Apology for Wonder.* New York: Harper & Row, 1969.

———. *Gabriel Marcel.* Richmond: John Knox Press, 1967.

———. "Manifesto for a Dionysian Theology." In *Transcendence,* edited by Herbert W. Richardson and Donald R. Cutler. Boston: Beacon Press, 1969.

Kierkegaard, Sören. *Fear and Trembling and The Sickness unto Death.* Translated by Walter Lowrie. Garden City, N.Y.: Doubleday & Co., Anchor Books, 1954.

Killinger, John. *The Fragile Presence: Transcendence in Modern Literature.* Philadelphia: Fortress Press, 1973.

Kinnell, Galway. "The Poetics of the Physical World." *Iowa Review* 2, no. 3 (summer 1971): 113–26.

Kizer, Carolyn. "Poetry of the Fifties in America." In *International Literary Annual,* edited by John Wain. London, 1958.

Kramer, Hilton. "The Poetry of Theodore Roethke." *Western Review* 28 (winter 1954): 131–46.

Kunitz, Stanley J. *A Kind of Order, a Kind of Folly: Essays and Conversations.* Boston: Little, Brown & Co., 1975.

La Belle, Jenijoy. *The Echoing Wood of Theodore Roethke.* Princeton: Princeton University Press, 1976.

Langbaum, Robert. *The Modern Spirit: Essays on the Continuity of Nineteenth- and Twentieth-Century Literature.* New York: Oxford University Press, 1970.

———. *The Poetry of Experience: The Dramatic Monologue in Modern Literary Tradition.* New York: W. W. Norton & Co., Norton Library, 1963.

Lewis, H. D. *Morals and Revelation.* London: Allen & Unwin, 1951.

Lewis, R. W. B. *The American Adam: Innocence, Tragedy, and Tradition in the Nineteenth Century.* Chicago: University of Chicago Press, Phoenix Books, 1958.

Libby, Anthony. "Roethke, Water Father." *American Literature* 46 (November 1974): 267–88.

Liberthson, Daniel. *Quest for Being: Theodore Roethke, W. S. Merwin, and Ted Hughes.* New York: Gordon Press Publishers, 1977.

McClatchy, J. D. "Sweating Light from a Stone: Identifying Theodore Roethke." *Modern Poetry Studies* 3, no. 1 (1972): 1–24.

Malkoff, Karl. *Theodore Roethke: An Introduction to the Poetry.* New York: Columbia University Press, Columbia Paperback Edition, 1971.

McMichael, James. "The Poetry of Theodore Roethke." *Southern Review,* n.s. 5 (winter 1969): 4–25.

———. "Roethke's North America." *Northwest Review* 11 (summer 1971): 149–59.

Marcel, Gabriel. *Being and Having.* Translated by Katharine Farrer. Westminster, London: Dacre Press, 1949.

———. *The Mystery of Being.* Vol. 1, *Reflection and Mystery.* Translated by G. S. Fraser. Chicago: Henry Regnery Co., Gateway Edition, 1960.

Martz, Louis L. "A Greenhouse Eden." In *Theodore Roethke: Essays on the Poetry,* edited by Arnold Stein. Seattle: University of Washington Press, 1965.

———. *The Paradise Within: Studies in Vaughan, Traherne, and Milton.* New Haven: Yale University Press, 1964.

———. *The Poem of the Mind: Essays on Poetry, English and American.* New York: Oxford University Press, 1966.

———. "Recent Poetry: The Elegiac Mode." *Yale Review* 54 (winter 1965): 294–97.

Martz, William J. *The Achievement of Theodore Roethke.* Glenview, Ill.: Scott, Foresman, and Co., 1966.

Maxwell, J. C. "Notes on Theodore Roethke." *Notes and Queries* 214 (July 1969): 265–66.

Mazzaro, Jerome. "Theodore Roethke and the Failures of Language." In *Profile of Theodore Roethke,* edited by William Heyen. Columbus, Ohio: Charles E. Merrill Co., 1971.

Meland, Bernard Eugene. *Faith and Culture.* London: George Allen & Unwin, 1955.

Meredith, William. "A Steady Storm of Correspondences: Theodore Roethke's Long Journey Out of the Self." In *Theodore Roethke: Essays on the Poetry,* edited by Arnold Stein. Seattle: University of Washington Press, 1965.

Miller, David L. "Hades and Dionysos: The Poetry of Soul." *Journal of the American Academy of Religion* 46, no. 3 (September 1978): 331–35.

Miller, James E., Jr. *Quests Surd and Absurd: Essays in American Literature.* Chicago: University of Chicago Press, 1967.

Mills, Ralph J., Jr. *Contemporary American Poetry.* New York: Random House, 1965.

———. *Cry of the Human: Essays on Contemporary American Poetry.* Chicago: University of Illinois Press, 1975.

———. "Keeping the Spirit Spare." *Chicago Review* 13 (winter 1959): 114–22.

———. *Theodore Roethke.* University of Minnesota Pamphlets on American Writers, no. 30. Minneapolis, 1963.

Musgrove, S[ydney]. *T. S. Eliot and Walt Whitman.* Wellington: New Zealand University Press, 1952.

Nemerov, Howard. *The Collected Poems of Howard Nemerov.* Chicago: University of Chicago Press, 1977.

Ong, Walter J. *The Barbarian Within: And Other Fugitive Essays and Studies.* New York: Macmillan Co., 1962.

Ostroff, Anthony, ed. *The Contemporary Poet as Artist and Critic: Eight Symposia.* Boston: Little, Brown & Co., 1964.

Pearce, Roy Harvey. *The Continuity of American Poetry.* Corrected and revised. Princeton: Princeton University Press, 1965.

———. "The Power of Sympathy." In *Theodore Roethke: Essays on the Poetry,* edited by Arnold Stein. Seattle: University of Washington Press, 1965.

Phillips, Robert S. *The Confessional Poets.* Carbondale: Southern Illinois University Press, 1973.

Pound, Ezra. *Pavannes and Divisions.* New York: Alfred A. Knopf, 1918.

Progoff, Ira, trans. and intro. *The Cloud of Unknowing.* New York: Dell Publishing Co., Delta Book, 1957.

Ramsey, Jarold. "Roethke in the Greenhouse." *Western Humanities Review* 26 (winter 1972): 35–47.

Richardson, Herbert W., and Donald R. Cutler, eds. *Transcendence.* Boston: Beacon Press, 1969.

Rosenthal, M. L. *The New Poets: American and British Poetry since World War II.* New York: Oxford University Press, 1967.

Schumacher, Paul J. "The Unity of Being: A Study of Theodore Roethke's Poetry." *Ohio University Review* 12, no. 1 (1970): 20–40.

Scott, Nathan A., Jr. *The Wild Prayer of Longing: Poetry and the Sacred.* New Haven: Yale University Press, 1971.

Seager, Allan. *The Glass House: The Life of Theodore Roethke.* New York: McGraw-Hill Book Co., 1968.

Sewell, Elizabeth. *The Orphic Voice: Poetry and Natural History.* New York: Harper & Row, Publishers, Harper Torchbooks, 1971.

Sittler, Joseph. *Essays on Nature and Grace.* Philadelphia: Fortress Press, 1972.

Snodgrass, W. D. "'That Anguish of Concreteness': Theodore Roethke's Career." In *Theodore Roethke: Essays on the Poetry,* edited by Arnold Stein. Seattle: University of Washington Press, 1965.

Snyder, Gary. *Myths and Texts.* New York: New Directions, 1978.

Spender, Stephen. "The Objective Ego." In *Theodore Roethke: Essays on the Poetry,* edited by Arnold Stein. Seattle: University of Washington Press, 1965.

———. Review of *Words for the Wind. New Republic,* 10 August 1959, pp. 21–22.

Staples, Hugh B. "The Rose in the Sea-Wind: A Reading of Theodore Roethke's 'North American Sequence.'" *American Literature* 36 (May 1964): 189–203.

Stein, Arnold, ed. Introduction. *Theodore Roethke: Essays on the Poetry.* Seattle: University of Washington Press, 1965.

———. "Roethke's Memory: Actions, Visions, and Revisions." *Northwest Review* 11, no. 3 (summer 1971): 19–31.

Stepanchev, Stephen. *American Poetry since 1945: A Critical Survey.* New York: Harper & Row, Publishers, Harper Colophon Books, 1967.

Sullivan, Rosemary. *Theodore Roethke: The Garden Master.* Seattle: University of Washington Press, 1975.

Tanner, Tony. *The Reign of Wonder: Naivety and Reality in American Literature.* New York: Harper & Row, Perennial Library, 1967.

Teilhard de Chardin, Pierre. *Hymn of the Universe.* Translated by Simon Bartholomew. New York: Harper & Row, 1965.

———. *The Phenomenon of Man.* Introduced by Sir Julian Huxley. Translated by Bernard Wall. New York: Harper & Brothers, 1959.

Tillich, Paul. *The Courage To Be.* New Haven: Yale University Press, 1952.
———. *The Eternal Now.* New York: Charles Scribner's Sons, 1963.
———. *Systematic Theology.* 3 vols. Chicago: University of Chicago Press, 1951–63.
Truesdale, C. W. "Theodore Roethke and the Landscape of American Poetry." *Minnesota Review* 8, no. 4 (1968): 345–58.
Underhill, Evelyn. *Mysticism: A Study in the Nature and Development of Man's Spiritual Consciousness.* 12th ed. New York: Noonday Press, Meridian Book, 1955.
Vernon, John. *The Garden and the Map: Schizophrenia in Twentieth-Century Literature and Culture.* Urbana: University of Illinois Press, 1973.
Waggoner, Hyatt H. *American Poets: From the Puritans to the Present.* New York: Dell Publishing Co., Delta Book, 1970.
Whitehead, Alfred North. *Modes of Thought.* New York: Macmillan Co., 1938.
———. *Science and the Modern World.* New York: Free Press, 1967.
Wilbur, Richard. *The Poems of Richard Wilbur.* New York: Harcourt, Brace & World, Harvest Book, 1963.
———. *Walking to Sleep: New Poems and Translations.* New York: Harcourt, Brace & World, 1969.
Wilder, Amos N. *The New Voice: Religion, Literature, Hermeneutics.* New York: Herder & Herder, 1969.
Williams, Daniel Day. *God's Grace and Man's Hope.* New York: Harper & Bros. Publishers, 1949.
Williams, Harry. *"The Edge Is What I Have": Theodore Roethke and After.* Lewisburg: Bucknell University Press, 1977.

INDEX

INDEX OF WORKS BY THEODORE ROETHKE